CHAMBERS

CHILDREN'S ILLUSTRATED THESAURUS

CHAMBERS

CHILDREN'S ILLUSTRATED THESAURUS

George Marshall

Chambers

CHAMBERS
An imprint of Larousse plc
Elsley House, 24–30 Great Titchfield Street,
London W1P 7AD

First published by Chambers 1994

10 9 8 7 6 5 4 3 2 1

A CIP catalogue record for this book is available
from the British Library.

ISBN   0550 106537

Editor: John Grisewood

Illustrations: Gary Rees

Designer: Robert Wheeler

Printed and bound in Great Britain by
BPC Hazell Books Ltd
A member of
The British Printing Company Ltd

Introduction

THIS book is called a thesaurus, which is a Latin word of Greek origin, meaning 'a treasury or storehouse of information', particularly when it deals with words and collections of words. So, if you examine what this book contains, you will see that is exactly what it is: a collection of words. It is a kind of dictionary, with a list of words in alphabetical order.

Instead of simply giving the *meaning* of a word, it tells you of other words which have a *similar* meaning. Suppose you began a letter to a friend with the sentence *I hope you have a nice time on your holiday*. The word *nice* sounds dull in this case. If you look up the word *nice* in this thesaurus, you will find that it gives you a short list of words which you could use instead: *pleasant, agreeable, amiable, charming, delightful*. Such words are known as **synonyms**. The word *nice* also has another meaning, which is quite different: *precise, accurate, fine, subtle*.

To go back to our letter, you could now write *I hope you have a **pleasant** time on your holiday*. Your friends could write back to you and tell you that *We are having a **delightful** time on our holiday*! As you can see, the thesaurus helps you to write in a better style, and to use words other than the very ordinary, perhaps rather boring ones.

In addition to giving these alternative words, this thesaurus also shows you *opposite* words. In the case of *nice*, you will find the opposite word *nasty*. These opposite words are called **antonyms**. In many cases, there are cross-references to other words of similar meaning which are to be found elsewhere in the book. Below is a key to show you how to find the various words and their meaning.

Parts of speech: *adj.* = adjective; *adv.* = adverb; *conj.* = conjunction; *n.* = noun; *prep.* = preposition; *v.* = verb.

Opposite words: These are shown with an asterisk (★) and in ★**bold type**.

Cross-reference to other meanings: If a word is shown with an arrow ▷ and in *italics*, it means that you can look up that word to find further, similar, meanings. For example, if you look up the word *ruffian* you find, at the end of the list, the word ▷*rascal*. So, if you look under *rascal* you will find other, similar, words.

Homonyms: A homonym is a word which sounds the same as another, but which means something quite different. Such words are shown in small capitals, like this: GAMBOL

If a word has a number of quite different meanings, each different meaning is shown by a bold figure in a square: ⬛1, ⬛2, ⬛3.

George Marshall

5

A a

abandon *v.* forsake, give up, leave in the lurch, surrender, sacrifice, ▷*leave, quit*

abate *v.* lessen, slacken, dwindle, fade

abbey *n.* monastery, priory, cloister, church

abbreviate *v.* shorten, cut, contract, reduce, ▷*abridge* ★**expand**

abdicate *v.* resign, retire, renounce, ▷*quit*

ability *n.* aptitude, knack, flair, talent, gift, skill ★**inability**

able *adj.* skilful, competent, talented, strong, ▷*clever,* ★**incapable**

abnormal *adj.* unusual, exceptional, erratic ★**normal**

abode *n.* home, residence, haunt, dwelling, lodging

abolish *v.* destroy, cancel, do away with, exterminate ★**restore**

abominable *adj.* detestable, foul, hateful, horrible, loathsome, atrocious, ▷*awful* ★**desirable**

about *prep. & adv.* near, nearly, touching, concerning, around

above *prep. & adv.* over, beyond, exceeding, on high, aloft ★**below**

abridge *v.* condense, compact, ▷*abbreviate*

abroad *adv.* overseas, far, away, apart, adrift ★**home**

abrupt 1 *adj.* sudden, curt, blunt, brusque 2 steep, hilly ★**smooth**

absent *adj.* not present, away, elsewhere, missing ★**present**

absent-minded *adj.* distracted, heedless, forgetful ★**attentive**

absolute *adj.* perfect, complete, certain, positive, ▷*utter* ★**imperfect**

absorb *v.* take in, soak up, assimilate, devour, pull in, swallow, consume ★**emit**

absorbed *adj.* intent, rapt, engrossed, preoccupied

abstain *adj.* refuse, refrain, give up, keep from, avoid, forbear ★**indulge**

abstract 1 *adj.* theoretical, intangible 2 *v.* withdraw, steal, remove, take away

absurd *adj.* preposterous, nonsensical, foolish, ▷*silly* ★**sensible**

abundant *adj.* ample, profuse, rich, plentiful, overflowing ★**scarce**

abuse *v.* damage, injure, spoil, maltreat, misuse ★**protect**, *n.* mistreatment, attack

accelerate *v.* speed up, hasten, quicken, urge, ▷*hurry* ★**delay**

accent 1 *n.* stress, beat, rhythm, emphasis 2 brogue *Eileen speaks with an Irish brogue,* drawl, pronunciation

accept *v.* receive, take, admit, adopt, take on ★**refuse**

accident *n.* chance, casualty, disaster, calamity, mishap ★**purpose**

acclaim *v.* applaud, praise, approve ★**denounce**

accommodate *v.* oblige, lodge, receive, admit, adapt ★**deprive**

accompany *v.* be with, go with, escort, attend, convoy ★**abandon**

accomplice *n.* ally, confederate, helper, partner

accomplish *v.* perform, fulfil, finish, complete, ▷*achieve* ★**fail**

accord *v.* agree, consent, harmonize, allow ★**differ**, *n.* agreement, harmony

account 1 *n.* bill, invoice, record, score 2 tale, story *Mary told us the story of her trip to Australia,* narrative, history

accumulate *v.* collect, grow, gather, hoard, increase, amass ★**scatter**

accurate *adj.* careful, exact, faithful, precise, ▷*correct* ★**defective**

accuse *v.* charge, incriminate, taunt, denounce ★**defend**

accustom *v.* acclimatize, get used to, familiarize ★**estrange**

ache *n.* pain *v.* hurt, twinge, pain, sting, smart

achieve *v.* fulfil, accomplish, reach, ▷*attain* ★**fail**

achievement *n.* accomplishment, attainment, exploit, deed, completion ▷*feat*

acid *adj.* sharp, vinegarish, acrid, sour, tart ★**sweet, mellow**

acknowledge *v.* admit, avow, recognize, own, accept, yield ★**disclaim**

acquaint v. inform, tell, teach, notify, advise   ★**deceive**

acquaintance [1] n. friend, pal, associate [2] knowledge *You will need some knowledge of Spanish if you visit South America*, familiarity, experience

acquainted adj. aware, familiar, sensible

acquire v. gain, earn, obtain, get, capture   ★**forfeit, lose**

acquit v. discharge, release, exonerate, dismiss, liberate   ★**accuse**

acrid adj. bitter, harsh, sour, ▷*acid*   ★**mellow**

across adv. & prep. crosswise, athwart, slantingly, over against   ★**along**

act n. deed, performance, action, step, presentation, v. operate, work, function, perform *Our society is to perform a play by Ibsen*

action n. operation, movement, feat, deed, exercise   ★**rest**

actual adj. correct, true, positive, certain   ★**possible**

acute adj. sharp, pointed, keen, penetrating, severe, distressing   ★**blunt**

adapt v. fit, adjust, accommodate, suit, conform

adaptable adj. flexible, usable, adjustable

add [1] v. total, add up, tot up   ★**subtract** [2] affix, annex, connect   ★**detach**

address [1] n. residence, place, home, domicile, [2] v. talk to, speak to, accost, call

adept adj. expert, adroit, handy, skilful, ▷*clever*   ★**clumsy**

adequate [1] adj. sufficient, ample, plenty [2] equal, able, qualified *After three years at sea, she was well qualified as a sailor*

adjacent adj. near, neighbouring, next, bordering, touching   ★**separate**

adjoin v. border, touch, verge, annex

adjust [1] v. regulate, rectify, correct, amend, revise [2] get used to *Our puppy quickly got used to her new home*

administer [1] v. execute, perform, carry out, conduct, direct, manage [2] dole *The nurse doled out the pills each morning*, give

admirable adj. praiseworthy, commendable, excellent   ★**despicable**

admiration n. adoration, affection, approval, delight, respect   ★**contempt**

admire v. approve, esteem, approve, appreciate, ▷*respect*   ★**despise**

admit [1] v. pass, permit, grant, concede, allow, let in, acknowledge [2] confess, own up   ★**deny**

ado n. hubbub, commotion, fuss *Let's get on with the meeting without any fuss*, excitement

adopt v. assume, select, choose, employ, apply, take over

adore v. worship, idolize, admire, revere, venerate   ★**despise**

adorn v. beautify, decorate. embellish, deck, garnish   ★**deface**

adrift adv. loose, afloat, floating, distracted

adroit adj. handy, skilful, dexterous, expert ▷*adept*   ★**awkward**

adult adj. grown-up, mature, full-grown   ★**immature**

Adjust

Our puppy quickly got used to her new home.

advance [1] *v.* progress, increase, further, go, go on, proceed   *****retreat** [2] lend *Helen said she will lend me the money*, loan

advanced *adj.* beforehand, ahead, modern

advantage *n.* benefit, upper hand, opportunity, assistance, boon *****hindrance**

adventure *n.* experience, escapade, venture, undertaking

adversary *n.* foe, opponent, antagonist, rival, ▷*enemy* *****ally**

adverse *adj.* unfavourable, hard, hostile, unfortunate, ▷*unlucky* *****fortunate**

advice *n.* counsel, suggestion, guidance

advise *v.* urge, suggest, prompt, inform, persuade *****deter**

afar *adv.* far, far off, away, abroad *****near**

affable *adj.* courteous, gracious, easy, frank, open *****haughty**

affair *n.* matter, business, concern, duty

affect [1] *v.* assume, adopt, feign, sham, put on airs [2] sicken, upset *We were all upset to hear that Jo was ill*, afflict

affection *n.* desire, fondness, feeling, kindness, liking, ▷*love* *****indifference**

affectionate *adj.* warmhearted, fond, loving, ▷*tender* *****indifferent**

affirm *v.* assert, state, declare, endorse, maintain *****deny**

affix *v.* attach, fasten, unite, append *****detach**

afflict *v.* trouble, ail, distress, upset

afford [1] *v.* be wealthy, be rich [2] produce, provide *The stream provided good, clean water*, yield, bear *****deny**

afraid *adj.* timid, cautious, frightened, alarmed, ▷*fearful* *****fearless**

after *prep.* behind, later, following, succeeding *****before**

again *adv.* frequently, repeatedly, anew, afresh, further

against *prep.* opposite, over, opposing, resisting *****for**

age [1] *n.* period, date, time, date [2] old age, senility *****youth** [3] *v.* grow old, mature

aged *adj.* ancient, antiquated, ▷*old* *****youthful**

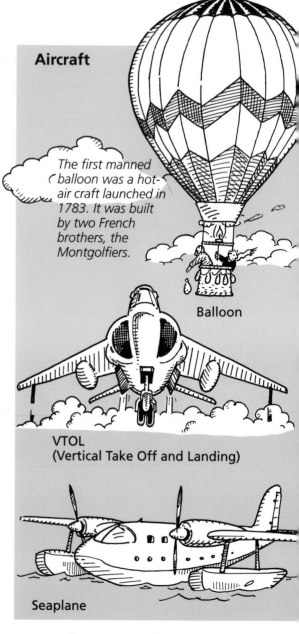

Aircraft

The first manned balloon was a hot-air craft launched in 1783. It was built by two French brothers, the Montgolfiers.

Balloon

VTOL (Vertical Take Off and Landing)

Seaplane

agent *n.* doer, actor, performer, operator, worker

aggravate *v.* exasperate, wound, provoke, increase, embitter, ▷*annoy* *****soothe**

aggressive *adj.* offensive, warlike, military, pushing *****peaceful**

aghast *adj.* astonished, dumbfounded, bewildered *****calm**

agile *adj.* nimble, active, fleet, brisk, alert, ▷*lithe* *****clumsy**

agitate *v.* disturb, trouble, excite, stir, fluster *****smoothe**

ago *adv.* past, gone, since *****hence**

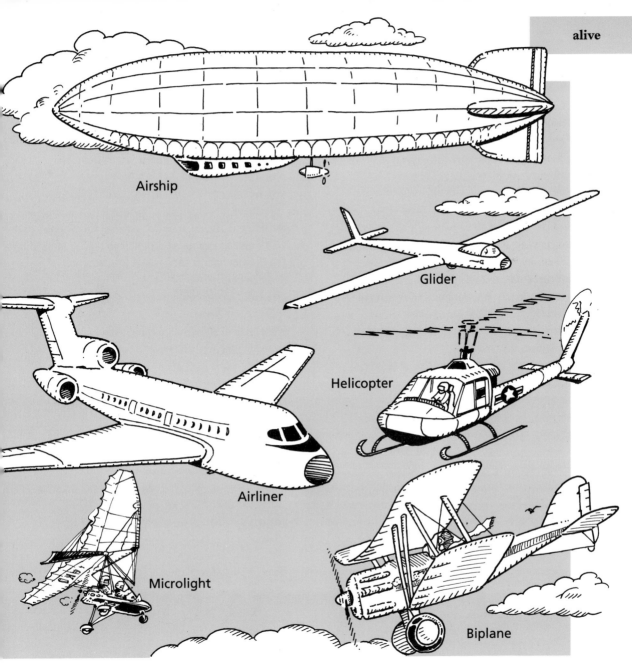

Airship

Glider

Helicopter

Airliner

Microlight

Biplane

agony *n.* torture, torment, distress, pangs, ▷*pain* ★**comfort**

agree *v.* accord, fit, harmonize, combine, tally, suit ★**differ**

agreeable *adj.* obliging, welcome, acceptable, grateful, ▷*pleasant* ★**disagreeable**

agreement *n.* contract, undertaking, obligation ★**difference**

ahead *adv.* forward, onwards, afore ★**behind**

aid *v.* assist, support, encourage, serve, ▷*help* ★**hinder**

aim *n.* object, goal, purpose, end, intention

aisle *n.* path, corridor, passage, way ISLE

akin *adj.* related, similar, allied, like ★**dissimilar**

alarm *v.* fear, frighten, terrify, startle, ▷*scare* ★**compose**

alert *adj.* active, ready, wakeful, watchful, ▷*agile* ★**drowsy**

alien *adj.* foreign, strange, remote ★**akin** *n.* foreigner, stranger

alike *adj.* similar, resembling, allied, like ★**unlike**

alive *adj.* living, breathing, warm, alert, brisk ★**dead**

all *adj.* whole, entire, complete, total
*some

allot *v.* apportion, give, deal, dispense, grant   ***retain**

allow *v.* grant, permit, concede, owe, tolerate, entitle   ***deny**

ally *n.* friend, companion, supporter, accomplice, colleague   ***foe**

almost *adj.* nearly, about, approximately, well-nigh

alone *adj.* lone, lonely, lonesome, forlorn
*together

aloud *adv.* loudly, noisily, clamorously, audibly   ***softly** ALLOWED

already *adv.* at this time, now, just now, previously

alter *v.* modify, vary, convert, transform, ▷*change*   ***retain** ALTAR

altogether *adv.* completely, wholly, outright, totally   ***partially**

always *adv.* ever, for ever, eternally   ***never**

amass *v.* collect, accumulate, heap, pile
*scatter

amaze *v.* astound, surprise, stun, dumbfound, ▷*astonish*

ambition *n.* aspiration, desire, longing, zeal, aim, ▷*goal*

amend *v.* revise, mend, correct, repair, improve, ▷*alter*   ***deteriorate**

amiable *adj.* affable, kindly, pleasant, amicable, ▷*agreeable*   ***churlish**

amount *n.* figure, volume, sum, number, total

ample *adj.* bountiful, liberal, sufficient, plentiful, ▷*abundant*   ***scanty**

amplify *v.* increase, raise, enlarge, elaborate *Our teacher explained the problem and went on to elaborate the details*, make louder
*abbreviate

amuse *v.* entertain, charm, beguile, please   ***bore**

ancestor *n.* forebear, parent, forefather, antecedent, predecessor

ancient *adj.* aged, antique, primeval, time-honoured, ▷*old*   ***modern**

anger *n.* wrath, ire, resentment, indignation, fury, ▷*rage*   ***patience**

angry *adj.* wrathful, irate, resentful, furious, infuriated, indignant   ***good-tempered**

angle 1 *n.* corner, bend, fork, branch 2 aspect, phase, point-of-view *We quarrelled at first, but then I saw my friend's point-of-view*

anguish *n.* torment, torture, pain, ▷*agony*
*ease

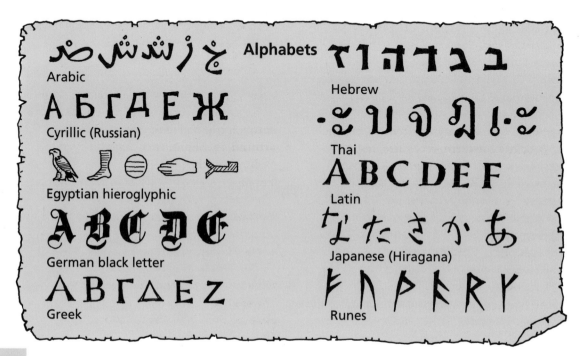

Alphabets

Arabic

Cyrillic (Russian)

Egyptian hieroglyphic

German black letter

Greek

Hebrew

Thai

Latin

Japanese (Hiragana)

Runes

announce v. broadcast, declare, propound, reveal, herald, ▷*proclaim* ★**conceal**

annoy v. tease, vex, irritate, disturb, harass, ▷*upset* ★**soothe**

answer n. reply, response, solution *It was quite a difficult puzzle, but Emma came up with the solution* ★**question**

anticipate v. expect, prepare, hope for, foresee, predict

anxious adj. fearful, afraid, apprehensive, worried ★**careless**

apart adv. away, separately, asunder, loosely ★**together**

aperture n. slit, hole, orifice, opening, cleft

apologize v. express regret, excuse, explain, plead, atone ★**insult**

apparel n. clothes, robes, vestments, raiment, trappings, attire

apparent adj. plain, conspicuous, unmistakable, clear, ▷*obvious* ★**dubious**

appeal v. address, request, urge, entreat, invite, ask ★**disclaim**

appear v. emerge, become visible, seem, look, come into view ★**disappear**

appearance n. aspect, look, shape, form, impression, likeness

appease v. pacify, moderate, satisfy, stay, soften ★**provoke**

appetite n. hunger, palate, relish, liking

applaud v. clap, cheer, praise, approve, encourage ★**denounce**

apply 1 v. use, appropriate, employ 2 devote, direct, dedicate *Sue was a real worker, dedicated to her job*

appoint v. name, assign, nominate, engage

appreciate v. esteem, recognize, respect, value, enjoy ★**misjudge**

appropriate 1 v. use, employ, adopt 2 adj. fitting, proper *If you do this job, you must use the proper tools*, timely

approve v. acclaim, admire, appreciate, favour, agree ★**disapprove**

approximate adj. near, close, rough

apt 1 adj. fit, clever, liable, likely ★**unfitted** 2 liable, prone, inclined *Jack and Meg are both inclined to be late, so we'll wait a while*

Apes

Chimpanzee

Gorilla

Orang-utan

Gibbon

ardent adj. passionate, warm, eager, fervent ★**indifferent**

arduous adj. hard, laborious, tough, strenuous, ▷*difficult* ★**easy**

area n. district, region, place, expanse, tract

argue 1 v. discuss, debate, talk over 2 quibble, quarrel, disagree

arid adj. parched, sterile, ▷*dry* ★**moist**

arise 1 v. awaken, get up 2 begin, come into existence, originate, crop up, take place

army n. troops, legion, force, soldiery

around adv. about, encircling, on every side ★**within**

arouse v. awaken, excite, disturb, alarm ★**pacify**

arrange v. sort, order, dispose, deal, classify ★**confuse**

arrest v. seize, take prisoner, hold, detain, stop ★**release**

arrive v. reach, attain, land, get to, appear ★**depart**

arrogant adj. supercilious, proud, haughty ★**modest**

art *n.* skill, artistry, cleverness, talent

artful *adj.* cunning, knowing, crafty, wily, sly   *innocent

article 1 *n.* thing, object, substance 2 essay, treatise, typescript

artificial *adj.* invented, fictitious, fabricated, synthetic   *real

ascend *v.* climb, rise, go up, get up, move up, scale, mount   *descend

ashamed *adj.* shamefaced, abashed, confused   *proud

ask *v.* demand, query, enquire, appeal, ▷request   *answer

aspect *n.* front, face, side, appearance, presentation, look, expression

aspire *v.* wish, long, desire, aim, hope, crave

ass 1 *n.* donkey, mule 2 fool, dunce, idiot, booby, dolt

assault *v.* attack, assail, set upon, charge, invade   *defend

assemble *v.* meet, gather, convene, come together, muster, collect   *disperse

assent *v.* agree, comply, accept, consent   *dissent

assert *v.* pronounce, maintain, state, aver, ▷declare   *deny

assess *v.* estimate, evaluate, appraise

assign *v.* appoint, name, apportion, entrust

assist *v.* aid, support, protect, maintain, sustain, ▷help   *obstruct

association *n.* union, connection, companionship, society, company, club

assortment *n.* variety, kind, sort, batch, parcel, collection

assume 1 *v.* believe, accept, suppose, admit 2 confiscate, take, possess oneself of

assure *v.* promise, guarantee, warrant, encourage   *deter

astonish *v.* startle, surprise, confound, alarm, scare, ▷amaze

astound *v.* stagger, stupefy, ▷astonish

astray *adj.* lost, gone, vanished, missing, loose   *safe

astute *adj.* shrewd, brainy, knowing, sharp, acute, cute, crafty   *simple

atrocious *adj.* monstrous, enormous, shameful, cruel, abominable, vile   *noble

attach *v.* fasten, append, unite, tie, ▷connect   *unfasten

attack *v.* assault, invade, set upon, pounce, descend upon   *defend

attain *v.* extend, master, obtain, acquire, grasp, ▷reach   *fail

attempt *v.* endeavour, strive, seek, tackle, ▷try   *abandon

attend 1 *v.* listen, heed, notice, observe, follow   *disregard 2 be present

attentive *adj.* mindful, particular, heedful, observant   *careless

attire *n.* costume, robes, clothes, garments, ▷apparel

attitude *n.* disposition, bearing, outlook, posture, position, aspect

attract 1 *v.* draw, influence, tempt, prompt, pull, drag 2 fascinate, enchant, captivate   *repel

attractive *adj.* agreeable, beautiful, handsome, pretty, tempting   *repellent

avail *v.* benefit, advantage, suffice, use, help, profit

available *adj.* convenient, handy, ready, attainable

avenge *v.* retaliate, revenge, pay back   *pardon

average *adj.* usual, medium, middling, ordinary   *extreme

avid *adj.* eager, greedy, grasping

avoid *v.* shun, desert, quit, keep clear of, evade, ▷dodge   *seek

awake *v.* rouse, arouse, awaken, stir   *lull

award *v.* reward, give, bestow, grant, donate   *withdraw

aware *adj.* conscious, sensible, informed, assured   *ignorant

away *adv.* absent, not present, afar, elsewhere   *near

awe *n.* fear, dread, shock, consternation, wonder

awful *adj.* fearful, terrible, alarming, dreadful   *commonplace OFFAL

awkward *adj.* ungainly, unwieldy, uncouth, clownish, gawky, ▷clumsy   *dexterous

awry *adj.* crooked, askew, twisted, wrong   *straight

B b

babble *v.* prattle, blab, cackle, chatter, gossip

baby *n.* babe, infant, child, bairn, toddler

back [1] *adj.* after, rear, hind, posterior ★**front** [2] *v.* uphold, support *The party will support Tina Johnson at the next election,* endorse, be loyal to

backer *n.* supporter, ally, champion

backward *adj.* slow, shy, reluctant, unwilling, retarded, ▷*dull* ★**forward**

bad [1] *adj.* imperfect, dreadful, unsound, awful, atrocious [2] naughty, wrong, wicked, ill-behaved [3] rotten *This barrel is full of rotten apples,* spoiled ★**good**

badge *n.* emblem, hall-mark, symbol, crest

badger *v.* bother, hector, nag, ▷*pester*

bad-mannered *adj.* impolite, boorish, uncivil, ▷*rude* ★**polite**

baffle *v.* puzzle, perplex, frustrate, bewilder, mystify, ▷*puzzle*

bag *n.* net, sack, holdall, pouch

bail *v.* scoop, ladle, dip

bait [1] *v.* tease, bother, rag, rib, needle, ▷*pester* [2] *n.* decoy, lure, snare BATE

bake *v.* cook, roast, harden

balance *v.* weigh, adjust, equalize, compare

bald *adj.* hairless, severe, stark, bare, unadorned

balk *v.* hinder, baffle, thwart, prevent, foil ★**aid**

ball [1] *n.* dance, masquerade [2] globe, orb, sphere

ballad *n.* ditty, song, serenade

ballot *n.* vote, election, franchise, poll

ban *v.* prohibit, forbid, deny, stop

band [1] *n.* stripe, strip, zone, belt [2] orchestra, ensemble, group BANNED

bandit *n.* outlaw, robber, highwayman, thief, crook

bang *v.* crash, slam, smash, collide

banish *v.* expel, eject, exclude, exile, deport, cast out, ▷*dismiss* ★**welcome**

bank [1] *n.* shore, ledge, terrace, coast, embankment [2] safe, vault, treasury

banner *n.* ensign, standard, streamer, ▷*flag*

banquet *n.* meal, feast, repast

banter *v.* chaff, tease, ridicule, joke

bar [1] *v.* obstruct, block, blockade, forbid, shut out [2] fasten, bolt, lock, latch

bare [1] *adj.* barren, empty, void [2] naked, unclothed [3] severe, blunt *We expected a polite reply, but got a blunt refusal,* bald BEAR

barely *adv.* hardly, scarcely *The barrel had run dry, and there was scarcely enough water for all of us,* only just, simply

bargain *n.* pact, deal, *adj.* low-priced, cheap

bark [1] *n.* rind, husk, peel [2] yelp, growl, cry

barrel *n.* cask, keg, drum, tub, cylinder

barren *adj.* bare, unfertile, empty, ▷*arid* ★**fertile** BARON

barrier *n.* obstruction, obstacle, block, fence, ▷*bar*

barter *v.* swap, exchange, trade

base [1] *adj.* low, sordid, cheap, corrupt [2] dishonourable, vile [3] humble, menial [4] *n.* bottom, foundation [5] *v.* found *Robinson Crusoe was founded on a true story* BASS

bashful *adj.* shy, timid, modest, coy ★**bold**

basin *n.* bowl, pot, vessel, tub

Band

Banned

13

batch *n.* lot, amount, assortment, collection

batter *v.* beat, strike, shatter, break, smash

battle *v.* clash, combat, fight, struggle, wrestle

bawl *v.* shout, yell, roar, bellow ★**whisper**

bay 1 *n.* inlet, gulf, basin, bight 2 *v.* bark, yelp BEY

be *v.* exist, live, breathe

beach *n.* shore, sands, seaside, strand BEECH

beacon *n.* signal, lamp, light, guide

beak *n.* snout, bill, nose

beam 1 *n.* ray, light, streak 2 plank, joist, girder

bear 1 *v.* tolerate, put up with, endure, suffer ★**protest** 2 bring, fetch, carry BARE

bearing *n.* manner, behaviour, appearance, attitude, posture *He was a tall man with a military bearing* BARING

bearings *n.* direction, whereabouts *In the storm we totally lost our whereabouts*, location

beat 1 *v.* strike, pound, thrash, ▷*batter* 2 throb, flutter, thump *My heart thumped when I heard the sound of shouting in the street* BEET

beautiful *adj.* handsome, lovely, graceful, delicate, gorgeous ▷*pretty* ★**ugly**

beauty *n.* elegance, charm, loveliness, grace ★**ugliness**

because 1 *conj.* for, owing to, by reason of, since *Since Tom and Jane are here, I will stay too*, as 2 *adv.* consequently

beckon *v.* signal, call, nod, summon

becoming *adj.* graceful, suitable, comely, fitting, attractive

before 1 *prep.* ahead, in front of, forward, preceding 2 *adv.* earlier *Here is a pie which I baked earlier*, previously ★**after**

beg *v.* ask, request, entreat, beseech, plead, pray ★**insist**

begin *v.* commence, initiate, found, launch, ▷*start* ★**end**

beginner *n.* novice, recruit, learner, pupil

beginning *n.* start, opening, origin, outset, foundation ★**end**

behaviour *n.* conduct, demeanour, manners, ▷*bearing* ★**misbehaviour**

behind 1 *prep.* after, following *Bill arrived to meet us, with his dog following* 2 *adv.* in the rear of, later, afterward ★**before**

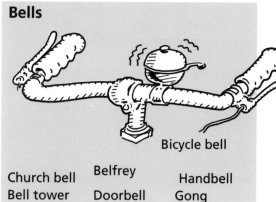

Bells

Bicycle bell
Church bell
Belfrey
Handbell
Bell tower
Doorbell
Gong

being *n.* creature, animal

belief *n.* faith, confidence, opinion, trust ★**disbelief**

believe *v.* trust, assent, have faith in, think, suspect ★**disbelieve**

bellow *v.* roar, shout, cry, ▷*bawl*

belong *v.* relate to, pertain, be owned by

below *adv.* under, beneath, underneath ★**above**

belt *n.* strap, sash, girdle, strip

bend *v.* curve, incline, turn, yield, relax ★**stiffen**

benefit *n.* boon, advantage, profit, favour, aid, blessing ★**disadvantage**

beside *adv.* alongside, side by side, next to, abreast, together ★**apart**

besides *adv.* in addition, furthermore, also, moreover

best *adj.* choice, prime, unequalled, finest ★**worst**

bestow *v.* award, donate, confer, present ★**deprive**

betray *v.* deceive, dupe, expose, unmask, play false ★**protect**

better *adj.* superior, finer, preferable *I think it would be preferable to visit the museum this afternoon rather than this morning* ★**inferior**

between *prep.* amidst, among, betwixt

beware *v.* be careful, refrain from, heed, avoid, mind ★**overlook**

bewilder *v.* confound, dazzle, mystify, confuse, ▷*astonish* ★**enlighten**

beyond *adv.* over, farther, past, more, after ★**near**

bicker v. quarrel, dispute, wrangle, argue *converse

bid v. proffer, present, tender, request, propose *forbid

big adj. large, great, wide, huge, bulky, fat, important *small

bill 1 n. statement *This is a statement of your investments with us*, account, invoice, chit, reckoning 2 beak, neb 3 poster, advertisement

bin n. box, tin, can, case, chest, crate, tub

bind v. tie, fasten, secure, lace, swathe *untie

birth n. origin, beginning, source, creation *death BERTH

bit n. morsel, piece, fragment, part, crumb *whole

bite v. gnaw, chew, rend, champ BIGHT

bitter 1 adj. harsh, sour, tart, ▷acid 2 severe, stern, ▷sarcastic *mellow

blame v. chide, rebuke, reproach, accuse, condemn *praise

bland adj. soft, mild, gentle, soothing *harsh

blank adj. empty, bare, void, bleak *full

blare v. blast, boom, clang, roar, sound

blast v. explode, split, discharge, burst

blaze v. burn, flare, glare, flicker

bleak adj. bare, open, exposed, dismal, stormy, chilly, raw, desolate *The moor was a cold and desolate place in winter* *sheltered

blemish n. spot, stain, mark, speck, flaw, blotch

blend v. mix, unite, harmonize, merge, fuse, combine *separate

bless v. hallow, praise, exalt, endow, enrich, consecrate *curse

blessing n. advantage, boon, approval, godsend *curse

blight n. pest, plague, disease

blind 1 adj. eyeless, sightless *These salamanders live in underground caves and are quite sightless*, unsighted, unseeing 2 ignorant, uninformed

blink v. wink, twinkle, glitter, gleam

bliss n. joy, ecstasy, rapture, blessedness, happiness *misery

block 1 n. lump, mass, chunk 2 v. obstruct, bar, arrest BLOC

bloom 1 n. flower, blossom, bud 2 v. blossom, flourish, flower, thrive *decay

blot n. stain, blotch, ▷blemish

blow 1 v. puff, gust, blast 2 n. shock, stroke, impact, bang

blue adj. azure, turquoise, indigo, ultramarine, cobalt BLEW

bluff 1 adj. frank, brusque, abrupt, plain-spoken *Freda Jones will never be elected mayor; she's too plain-spoken* 2 v. deceive, pretend *The lion closed its eyes, pretending it had not seen the antelope*, conceal

blunder 1 n. mistake, error, slip, fault *It was my fault that the plates were broken*, oversight 2 v. slip, err, bungle *correct

blunt 1 adj. plain, abrupt, curt, ▷bluff 2 dull, not sharp

blush v. redden, colour, crimson, flush

board 1 n. plank, table 2 committee, council 3 v. lodge *The new teacher is going to lodge at our house*, accommodate BORED

boast v. swagger, swell, bluster, ▷brag

boat n. ship, vessel, craft, bark, barge

body 1 n. corpse, trunk, carcase 2 corporation, company, society

The Body

Head
Hair
Eyes
Arm
Ears
Nails
Back
Hand
Elbow
Knee
Leg
Ankle
Foot

bog *n.* swamp, morass, marsh

bogus *adj.* fake, false, spurious, sham, counterfeit ★**genuine**

boil *v.* cook, steam, poach, seethe, foam

boisterous *adj.* tempestuous, stormy, uncontrolled, loud, noisy ★**serene**

bold *adj.* fearless, courageous, adventurous, valiant, daring, ▷*brave* ★**fearful** BOWLED

bolt [1] *v.* run away, take flight, flee *After the revolution, the queen had to flee the country* [2] devour, gorge, eat, ▷*gulp* [3] *n.* lock, latch, fastening

bond *n.* tie, link, joint, band, fastening

bonny *adj.* fair, handsome, healthy, shapely, buxom, ▷*pretty* ★**dull**

bonus *n.* premium, benefit, award, prize

booby *n.* blockhead, noodle, oaf, nincompoop, dunce, fool, numbskull ★**oracle**

boom [1] *n.* thunder, roar, rumble [2] prosperity *After the recession came years of prosperity*

boon *n.* blessing, windfall, advantage ▷*benefit* ★**drawback**

boorish *adj.* unrefined, loutish, bad-mannered, rude, clumsy ★**refined**

boost *v.* strengthen, upraise, heighten

border *n.* fringe, edge, margin, frontier

bore [1] *v.* tire, weary, annoy, vex *Mother is quite vexed if the cat sleeps on her bed* [2] drill, punch, perforate BOAR

bored *adj.* uninterested, tired, jaded, fed-up BOARD

borrow *v.* take, imitate, adopt, assume, raise money, hire ★**lend**

boss [1] *n.* stud, knob [2] chief, manager *Helen is manager of the new market garden*, employer

bossy *adj.* domineering, tyrannical, ▷*arrogant* ★**modest**

bother *v.* alarm, annoy, concern, distress, ▷*disturb* ★**calm**

bottom *adj.* undermost, deepest part, floor, ▷*base* ★**top**

bough *n.* branch, limb, shoot

boulder *n.* rock, slab, stone

bounce *v.* leap, spring, bound, bump, jump

bound *v.* rebound, prance, ▷*bounce*

boundary *n.* bounds, limits, border, frontier, ▷*barrier*

bounty *n.* donation, gift, grant, ▷*bonus*

bow *v.* bend, bob, nod, stoop, kneel, yield, submit BOUGH

bowl *n.* plate, basin, dish, vessel, casserole BOLE, BOLL

box [1] *n.* carton, case, chest, coffer *The town's coffers were empty, so they had to raise taxes*, pack [2] *v.* fight, spar, punch

boy *n.* lad, youth, fellow, youngster BUOY

brag *v.* crow, swagger, vaunt, ▷*boast*

braid *v.* entwine, weave, plait, ravel BRAYED

branch [1] *n.* shoot, limb, twig, ▷*bough* [2] department, office, division

brand [1] *n.* trade-mark, emblem, label *This label shows that the cloth is of high quality* [2] blot, stigma, stain

brandish *v.* flourish, parade, shake, swing, wave

brash *adj.* brazen, foolhardy, hasty, impetuous, impudent, ▷*rash*

brave [1] *adj.* audacious, fearless, daring, dauntless, gallant, heroic, ▷*bold* ★**cowardly** [2] *v.* dare, defy, endure

break *v.* batter, burst, crack, snap, fracture, shatter BRAKE

breathe *v.* draw in, gasp, inhale, sniff, gulp, wheeze, emit

breed *v.* reproduce, produce, cause, bear, rear

bribe *v.* corrupt, buy, grease the palm, fix

brief *adj.* short, little, concise, terse, crisp, curt ★**lengthy**

bright [1] *adj.* clear, cloudless, fair, airy [2] cheerful, genial *We were pleased to find so many genial members in the club* [3] clever, ingenious, acute ★**dull**

brilliant [1] *adj.* lustrous, shining, radiant, dazzling, luminous [2] clever, intelligent ★**dull**

brim *n.* edge, brink, rim, fringe

bring *v.* bear, fetch, deliver, carry, convey

bring about *v.* bring off, accomplish, achieve, cause, make happen

bring up *v.* breed, develop, raise, educate, foster

brink *n.* margin, border, boundary, limit

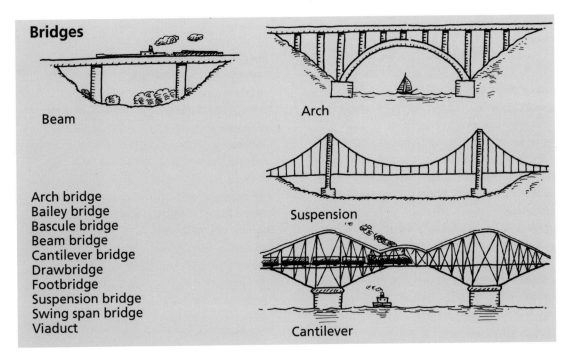

Bridges

Beam

Arch

Arch bridge
Bailey bridge
Bascule bridge
Beam bridge
Cantilever bridge
Drawbridge
Footbridge
Suspension bridge
Swing span bridge
Viaduct

Suspension

Cantilever

brisk *adj.* agile, alert, busy, energetic, active, nimble ★**sluggish**

brittle *adj.* breakable, fragile, delicate, ▷*frail*

broad *adj.* wide, expansive, roomy, open, vast, large ★**narrow**

brood *v.* sigh, agonize, dwell upon *You must try to forget your disappointment, and not dwell upon it*, languish BREWED

brook *n.* stream, beck, rivulet, watercourse

brow *n.* forehead, face, front, brink, edge, summit

bruise *v.* damage, discolour, blemish, injure, wound BREWS

brusque *adj.* abrupt, discourteous, gruff, ▷*blunt* ★**polite**

brutal *adj.* cruel, inhuman, savage, barbarous, bloodthirsty ★**humane**

bubble *n.* drop, droplet, blob, bead

buckle *n.* catch, clasp, clip, fastening

bud *n.* sprout, germ, shoot

budge *v.* propel, push, roll, shift, slide

build *v.* make, form, assemble, construct, erect, put up ★**demolish** BILLED

bulge *n.* bump, swelling, lump, billow

bulky *adj.* big, huge, unwieldy, massive, cumbersome *I never liked that chair; it's so big and cumbersome*

bully [1] *n.* ruffian, hector, bruiser, tyrant, browbeater [2] *v.* domineer, oppress, terrorize

bump *v.* collide, hit, knock, strike, jab, jolt

bunch *n.* batch, bundle, cluster, collection, lot

bundle *n.* group, mass, heap, pack, parcel

bungle *v.* bodge, blunder, mess up, ruin, fumble ★**succeed**

burden [1] *n.* load, weight [2] strain, hardship *We suffered great hardship during the war*

burly *adj.* beefy, big, hefty, brawny, muscular ★**frail**

burn *v.* blaze, flare, glow, singe, scorch, char, incinerate

burst *v.* break open, crack, explode, shatter, erupt

bury *v.* inter, conceal, cover up, hide, lay to rest BERRY

business [1] *n.* occupation, career, profession, [2] company, enterprise, firm [3] problem, duty, affair

busy *adj.* active, brisk, industrious, active, bustling ★**lazy**

buy *v.* acquire, get, purchase, procure *If I can procure a house, I'd like to settle here* ★**sell** BY, BYE

C c

cab *n.* taxi, taxicab, hackney carriage

cabin [1] *n.* hut, chalet, cottage, shack [2] berth, compartment

cabinet [1] *n.* cupboard, dresser, closet [2] council, committee

cackle *v.* chuckle, giggle, snigger

café *n.* restaurant, coffee bar, snack bar, tearoom

cage *v.* shut up, confine, imprison ★**free**

calamity *n.* catastrophe, disaster, misadventure, ▷*mishap* ★**blessing**

calculate *v.* reckon, figure, estimate, ▷*count*

call [1] *v.* cry out, shout, hail [2] name, address [3] visit *We shall visit you when we reach your town*, drop in

calling *n.* occupation, job, profession

callous *adj.* unfeeling, harsh, hard-bitten ★**sympathetic**

calm [1] *v.* soothe, ease, pacify, comfort [2] *adj.* easy, composed, mild, ▷*peaceful* ★**excited**

can *n.* tin, container, canister

cancel *v.* abolish, erase, put off, obliterate ★**confirm**

candid *adj.* fair, honest, open, sincere, truthful, ▷*frank* ★**devious**

capable *adj.* talented, able, competent, ▷*clever* ★**incompetent**

capacity [1] *n.* space, volume, extent [2] ability, aptitude *Jenny has an aptitude for learning languages*, intelligence

caper [1] *v.* dance, gambol, frolic [2] *n.* jape, jest, lark

capital [1] *n.* cash, assets, funds, finance [2] *adj.* chief, excellent, important

captain *n.* chief, head, commander, master, skipper

capture *v.* seize, arrest, trap, ▷*catch* ★**release**

car *n.* automobile, vehicle, motor-car, conveyance, carriage, coach

carcase *n.* body, corpse, skeleton

care [1] *v.* take care, beware, heed, mind [2] *n.* attention, protection ★**carelessness**

careful *adj.* heedful, prudent, watchful, ▷*cautious* ★**careless**

careless *adj.* neglectful, slack, casual, thoughtless ★**careful**

carelessness *n.* inaccuracy, negligence, slackness ★**care**

caress *v.* hug, stroke, cuddle, embrace ★**tease**

carriage *n.* car, coach, cab, chariot

carry *v.* bring, convey, lift, support, ▷*bear*

carry on *v.* continue, maintain, persist

carry out *v.* perform, achieve, fulfill, do

cart *n.* wagon, truck, van, buggy, barrow

carton *n.* bin, case, casket, crate, ▷*box*

carve *v.* sculpt, cut, chisel, fashion, whittle, ▷*shape*

case *n.* casket, bin, cover, ▷*box*

cash *n.* money, coins, banknotes, coinage CACHE

cask *n.* barrel, keg, drum

cast [1] *v.* mould, form, shape [2] fling, heave, sprinkle, ▷*throw* CASTE

casual *adj.* accidental, chance, random, ▷*occasional* ★**regular**

catch *v.* grasp, seize, arrest, ▷*capture* ★**lose**

catching *adj.* infectious, contagious

cause [1] *v.* bring about, create, provoke [2] *n.* reason, source, origin CAWS

caution *n.* watchfulness, heed, vigilance, wisdom, ▷*care* ★**rashness**

cautious *adj.* careful, discreet, prudent, ▷*watchful* ★**heedless**

cavity *n.* dent, hole, gap, hollow

cease *v.* stop, conclude, end, refrain, terminate ★**begin**

celebrate *v.* commemorate, observe, honour, glorify, rejoice, praise

cell *n.* chamber, cavity, cubicle, compartment SELL

cellar *n.* vault, basement, crypt, cave SELLER

cement [1] *v.* stick, bind, glue, gum, unite [2] *n.* plaster, mortar, adhesive

censor *v.* cut, examine, take out CENSER

censure *v.* blame, rebuke, reprimand, chide, ▷*scold* ★**praise**

centre *n.* middle, core, heart, nucleus

ceremony *n.* ritual, custom, performance

certain [1] *adj.* decided, definite, undoubted, ▷*sure* ★**dubious** [2] particular *I had a particular reason for inviting you*, special

certainty *n.* confidence, assurance, trust, sureness ★**doubt**

certificate *n.* document, permit, deed, diploma, testimonial

chafe *v.* rub, rasp, grate, irritate

chain *v.* bind, fetter, shackle, tether, bond

challenge *v.* dare, demand, dispute, defy, object to

chamber *n.* apartment, bedroom, compartment, hollow, room

champion *n.* defender, victor, master, winner ★**loser**

chance [1] *n.* fortune, hazard, luck, gamble, lottery, wager [2] opportunity, occasion, risk ★**certainty**

change *v.* alter, vary, turn, shift, reform, transform ★**conserve**

chant *v.* intone, drone, croon, recite, ▷*sing*

chaos *n.* turmoil, confusion, disorder, pandemonium ★**order**

chapter *n.* clause, division, part, period *It was a period in my life which I shall never forget*, phase

character [1] *n.* letter, mark, emblem, device [2] reputation *She had the reputation of being very generous*, temperament, qualities

charge [1] *n.* attack, stampede, advance [2] cost, amount, price [3] accusation, blame *The men were all guilty, but it was Harry Smith who took the blame*, indictment

charm *v.* please, delight, enchant, bewitch, ▷*attract* ★**irritate**

charming *adj.* delightful, appealing, lovely, pleasant, ▷*attractive* ★**ugly**

chart *n.* map, sketch, diagram, plan

chase *v.* hunt, pursue, follow, run after, hurry

chaste *adj.* virgin, pure, virtuous, innocent ★**immodest** CHASED

chastise *v.* punish, whip, flog, beat, scold, tell off

chat *v.* converse, gossip, ▷*talk*

chatter *v.* babble, gossip, ▷*talk*

cheap *adj.* inexpensive, low-priced, bargain, reasonable, inferior ★**dear**

Chews

Choose

cheat *v.* swindle, bilk, defraud, fleece, ▷*trick*

check [1] *v.* inspect, compare, examine *The customs officer examined our luggage*, make sure [2] *n.* bill, invoice, reckoning

cheek *n.* audacity, boldness, impertinence, insolence

cheer [1] *v.* comfort, console, elate, buck up, [2] applaud *The audience applauded the leading soprano*, clap, hail

cheerful *adj.* lively, bright, happy, merry, joyful, ▷*happy* ★**sad**

cheery *adj.* blithe, breezy, bright, merry ★**downcast**

cherish *v.* caress, hold close, care for, shelter, treasure

chest [1] *n.* case, coffer, ▷*box* [2] bosom, torso

chew *v.* bite, gnaw, grind, munch, ▷*eat*

chide *v.* scold, criticize, blame, tell off

chief *adj.* main, principal, leading, foremost ★**minor**

child *n.* baby, infant, bairn, juvenile

chilly *adj.* cool, crisp, brisk, cold, unfriendly ★**warm**

chip *v. & n.* crack, splinter, dent, flake

chirp *v.* warble, trill, cheep, chirrup, twitter

choice [1] *n.* option *I had no option but to take the job*, preference, alternative [2] *adj.* select, dainty, precious, cherished, special

choke *v.* throttle, suffocate, gag, stifle, strangle, ▷*stifle*

choose *v.* pick, elect, decide, fancy, ▷*select* CHEWS

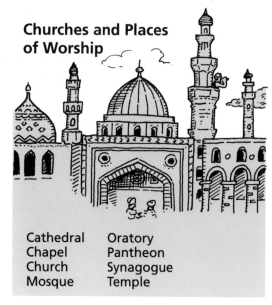

Churches and Places of Worship

Cathedral   Oratory
Chapel   Pantheon
Church   Synagogue
Mosque   Temple

chop *v.* cut, hack, clip, cleave, sever, lop

chubby *adj.* plump, buxom, portly, round, stout **★slim**

chum *n.* comrade, pal, friend, mate, companion

chuck *v.* throw, toss, fling, heave, sling

chuckle *v.* cackle, chortle, snicker, giggle, **★laugh**

chunk *n.* piece, lump, mass, portion, slab

churlish *adj.* brusque, harsh, impolite, morose *Dad had a headache and was in rather a morose mood*, ▷surly **★polite**

circle 1 *n.* ring, band 2 company, group, class

circular 1 *adj.* round, disk-like 2 *n.* handbill, notice *The notice on the board announced the new play at the theatre*, poster

circulate *v.* broadcast, distribute, publicize

cistern *n.* tank, sink, basin, reservoir

cite *v.* mention, specify, name, quote SIGHT, SITE

civil *adj.* polite, courteous, polished, ▷affable **★churlish**

claim *v.* demand, ask, require, insist, call for

clamour *n.* babel, blare, din, row, hubbub, racket, ▷noise **★silence**

clamp *v.* fasten, fix, hold, grasp

clap *v.* applaud, acclaim, cheer

clarify 1 *v.* make clear, explain, simplify 2 cleanse, purify

clash 1 *v.* battle, conflict, quarrel 2 bang, crash, clang, clatter

clasp 1 *v.* grasp, grip, seize, hold, fasten 2 *n.* buckle, catch, pin

class *n.* category, type, sort, grade, group, species

classical *adj.* pure, refined, scholarly, elegant, polished, well-proportioned

classify *v.* grade, sort, arrange, catalogue

clean 1 *adj.* pure, fresh, spotless, unsoiled 2 *v.* cleanse, scrub, ▷wash **★dirty**

cleanse, purify, scour, ▷ clean **★defile**

clear 1 *adj.* bright, fair, fine, light **★dim** 2 distinct, audible, lucid **★vague** 3 free, open, empty

cleft *n.* crack, cranny, slit, split, aperture

clever *adj.* able, astute, apt, brainy, skilful, talented, ▷expert **★foolish**

cliff *n.* precipice, height, bluff, crag, overhang

climax *n.* crisis, head, summit, turning point

climb *v.* mount, scale, ascend, soar, go up

cling *v.* adhere, attach, embrace, grasp, hold

clip 1 *n.* fastener, clasp 2 *v.* trim, prune, snip, cut

clog *v.* block, dam up, hinder, jam, impede

close 1 *v.* shut, bolt, bar, obstruct *The curtains were thick and obstructed a lot of light*, end 2 *adj.* near, neighbouring, adjacent **★far** 3 heavy, stuffy, uncomfortable

closet *n.* wardrobe, cabinet

clothing *n.* garments, dress, attire, raiment

cloud *n.* vapour, fog, billow, haze

clown *n.* buffoon, comedian, jester, joker

club 1 *n.* cudgel, stick, truncheon 2 company, group, society

clue *n.* evidence, inkling, lead, sign CLEW

clump *n.* cluster, group, bunch

clumsy *adj.* awkward, gawky, ungainly, blundering **★graceful**

clutch *v.* snatch, clasp, grasp, seize, grip

clutter *n.* litter, muddle, mess

coach 1 *n.* bus, car, carriage, vehicle 2 trainer, tutor

coarse 1 *adj.* rough, unrefined, unpolished 2 brutish, rude, uncivil **★refined** COURSE

coat 1 *n.* jacket, jumper 2 fleece, fur, skin, hide

Clothing

Coats and jackets
anorak
blazer
cloak
dinner jacket
macintosh
poncho
suit

Tops
blouse
blouson
cardigan
pullover
shirt
T shirt
vest

Dresses and trousers
Bermuda shorts
cocktail dress
dress

evening gown
hula skirt
jeans
jodhpurs
kilt
miniskirt
petticoat
sari
sarong
trousers

Foot and legwear
boot
clog
galoshes
moccasin
socks
stockings
tights
trainers

Headwear *see page 56*

---

coax *v.* cajole, wheedle, urge, persuade, beguile *We sat for hours as Aunt Anna beguiled us with stories* ★**dissuade** COKES

coddle *v.* pamper, spoil, indulge, baby, mollycoddle

coffer *n.* casket, case, chest, treasury COUGHER

cog *n.* tooth, prong, fang, tusk

coil *v.* twist, wind, loop

coincide *v.* match, agree, accord, synchronize, tally

cold *adj.* cool, chilly, frigid, freezing, frosty, frozen ★ **hot**

collapse *v.* founder, topple, break down, crumple, fall down

collect *v.* accumulate, amass, assemble, save, ▷ *gather* ★**scatter**

collide *v.* crash, smash, hit, strike, meet

colossal *adj.* enormous, gigantic, immense, massive, ▷*huge* ★**tiny**

column [1] *n.* pillar, post, shaft [2] file *The file of soldiers marched onto the parade*, line, procession, line

combat *v.* battle, contend, contest, oppose, defy ★**submit**

combine *v.* unite, join, link, fuse, merge, mix ★**separate**

come *v.* arrive, appear, enter, reach, advance ★**go**

come by *v.* get, procure, acquire *I acquired a new TV set in the sale*

comfort *v.* cheer, hearten, calm, soothe, console ★**torment**

comfortable *adj.* restful, convenient, cosy, agreeable ★**uncomfortable**

comforting *adj.* cheering, encouraging, consoling

command [1] *v.* order, dictate, direct [2] rule, dominate

commence *v.* start, begin, initiate, originate ★**finish**

comment *v.* mention, remark, observe, point out

commiserate *v.* sympathize, show pity, be sorry for ★**congratulate**

commit *v.* carry out, do, enact, perform, promise, entrust

common [1] *adj.* ordinary, vulgar, habitual, customary [2] public, social, communal

commonplace *adj.* everyday, humdrum, ordinary, obvious ★**rare**

commotion *n.* excitement, flurry, stir, uproar, ▷*fuss*

communicate *v.* tell, disclose, impart, reveal

community *n.* society, partnership, association, ▷*group*

compact *adj.* dense, close, tight, firm, condensed, concise

companion *n.* comrade, friend, chum, mate, colleague, comrade ★**rival**

company *n.* association, league, alliance, business, firm

compare *v.* match, liken, equal, parallel

compartment *n.* cubicle, alcove, bay, cell, carriage

compassion *n.* kindness, mercy, sympathy, charity, understanding, ▷*pity* ★**indifference**

compel *v.* make, coerce, drive, force, urge ★**coax**

compensate *v.* make good, refund, reimburse, repay, reward ★**injure**

compete *v.* contest, contend, rival, strive, oppose

competent *adj.* able, adapted, capable, ▷*clever* ★**incompetent**

Compel

competition *n.* match, contest, game, contest, rivalry

compile *v.* amass, put together, unite, ▷*collect*

complacent *adj.* self-satisfied, contented, ▷*smug* ★**diffident**

complain *v.* protest, gripe *They're a miserable couple; always griping about something,* grumble, grouse, ▷*nag* ★**rejoice**

complement *v.* complete, round off, add to, supplement COMPLIMENT

complete [1] *v.* finish, accomplish, achieve [2] *adj.* finished, full, entire

complex *adj.* complicated, intricate, mixed, tangled ★**simple**

complicated *adj.* entangled, involved, ▷*complex*

compliment *v.* flatter, admire, congratulate, ▷*praise* COMPLEMENT

comply *v.* agree to, assent to, abide by, perform, yield ★**refuse**

compose [1] *v.* make up, put together, form, construct, write [2] calm, quieten, quell

composure *n.* assurance, calm, confidence ★**consternation**

compound *n.* mixture, alloy, blend, combination

comprehend *v.* grasp, discern, take in, ▷*understand* ★**misunderstand**

compress *v.* condense, contract, abbreviate, ▷*squeeze* ★**expand**

comprise *v.* contain, consist of, include, make up

compromise [1] *v.* meet halfway, strike a balance, adjust, agree [2] imperil, weaken, jeopardize

compulsory *adj.* forced, obligatory *Everyone in the school has to go to the meeting; it's obligatory,* required ★**voluntary**

compute *v.* calculate, figure, reckon, estimate

computer *n.* calculator, word processor

comrade *n.* companion, pal, chum, mate, ▷*friend* *enemy

conceal *v.* bury, camouflage, cover, ▷*hide* *reveal

concede *v.* allow, admit, yield, acknowledge, surrender *dispute

conceit *n.* vanity, self-importance, arrogance, ▷*pride* *modesty

conceited *adj.* proud, vain, arrogant *modest

conceive *v.* create, design, devise *We devised a way of sharpening the scissors*, form, think up

concentrate *v.* focus on, centralize, heed, pay attention

concept *n.* idea, thought, theory, idea, view

concern 1 *v.* affect, touch 2 *n.* affair, matter, interest, business

concerning *prep.* as regards, respecting, about

concise *adj.* brief, condensed, short, ▷*compact* *expansive

conclude 1 *v.* finish, terminate, ▷*end* 2 deduce, judge, reckon, presume

conclusion *n.* result, termination, end

concoct *v.* contrive, hatch, plan, devise, invent

concord *n.* agreement, understanding, good will, harmony *discord

concrete 1 *adj.* actual, definite, real 2 *n.* cement, mortar

concur *v.* approve, agree, coincide, consent *disagree

condemn *v.* blame, denounce, reprove, sentence, disapprove *approve

condense *v.* compress, concentrate, abridge, thicken *expand

condition *n.* shape, way, state, position, plight, situation, ▷*predicament*

condone *v.* overlook, disregard, forgive, excuse *censure

conduct 1 *n.* attitude, bearing, behaviour 2 *v.* guide, direct, lead

confederate *n.* accomplice, ally, associate, partner

confer *v.* bestow, grant, award, give, present

conference *n.* convention, meeting, forum, council

confess *v.* admit, acknowledge, own up, divulge *deny

confide *v.* tell, divulge, reveal, whisper, entrust

confidence *n.* assurance, belief, boldness, firmness *doubt

confident *adj.* certain, assured, poised, fearless *diffident

confine *v.* restrict, limit, detain, imprison, limit *free

confirm *v.* verify, assure, approve, endorse, attest *deny

confiscate *v.* seize, impound, commandeer *The old house was commandeered by the army*

conform *v.* agree with, comply with, yield, adjust

confound *v.* perplex, mystify, puzzle, baffle, fluster, ▷*bewilder* *enlighten

confront *v.* challenge, defy, face, oppose, menace

confuse *v.* baffle, bemuse, mystify, ▷*bewilder* *clarify

congenial *adj.* companionable, natural, sympathetic, agreeable, ▷*friendly* *disagreeable

congested *adj.* jammed, crowded, clogged, packed, teeming *clear

congratulate *v.* rejoice, compliment, praise, wish one joy *commiserate

congregate *v.* assemble, meet, come together, converge *disperse

congress *n.* meeting, assembly, council, convention

conjecture *v.* guess, surmise, suspect, imagine, assume

connect *v.* unite, join, combine, fasten, link *disconnect

conquer *v.* beat, crush, overcome, overpower, triumph, ▷*defeat* *surrender

conscientious *adj.* moral, scrupulous, careful, diligent, ▷*honest* *careless

conscious *adj.* alert, alive, aware, sensible, responsible *unconscious

consecutive *adj.* chronological, in sequence, successive, continuous

consent *v.* assent, permit, concur, approve, comply, ▷*agree* *oppose

conserve *v.* keep, preserve, protect, save, store up, safeguard *squander

consider *v.* discuss, examine, ponder, reflect *Alone on the island, I reflected on all that had happened*, take account of ★**ignore**

considerable *adj.* abundant, ample, great, large, noteworthy, important ★**insignificant**

consist of *v.* comprise, be composed of, contain, include

consistent *adj.* uniform, constant, regular, steady ★**inconsistent**

console *v.* comfort, cheer, sympathize, soothe, solace ★**upset**

conspicuous *adj.* noticeable, marked, apparent, obvious, prominent ★**inconspicuous**

conspire *v.* plot, intrigue, scheme *He was thrown into a dungeon for treason*

constant 1 *adj.* regular, stable, uniform, ▷*consistent* 2 loyal, faithful, staunch, true ★**fickle**

consternation *n.* dismay, horror, fear, awe, stupefaction, ▷*alarm* ★**composure**

constitute *v.* compose, set up, fix, form, establish ★**destroy**

constrict *v.* tighten, strain, tauten, draw together, choke, pinch ★**expand**

construct *v.* erect, compose, compound, assemble, ▷*build* ★**demolish**

consult *v.* ask, ask advice, discuss, confer, debate

consume *v.* use up, absorb, eat up, devour

contact *n.* touch, connection, communication

contagious *adj.* catching, infectious

contain *v.* comprise, consist of, hold, accommodate, enclose

contaminate *v.* pollute, soil, stain, sully, taint, infect

contemplate *v.* think, reflect, deliberate, consider, ponder

contempt *v.* disdain, scorn, disregard, derision ★**admiration**

contend *v.* compete, contest, conflict, strive, struggle ★**concede**

content 1 *adj.* (con-*tent*) satisfied, contented, smug 2 *v.* satisfy, delight, gratify 3 (*con*-tent) *n.* matter, text, subject

contest 1 *n.* (*con*-test) competition, match, tournament 2 (con-*test*) *v.* dispute, argue

continue *v.* go on, keep up, endure, last, persist ★**stop**

contract 1 (con-*tract*) *v.* condense, lessen, shrink 2 (*con*-tract) *n.* agreement, pact, understanding

contradict *v.* deny, dispute, challenge, oppose

contrary *adj.* opposed, adverse, counter, opposite ★**agreeable**

contrast 1 *n.* (*con*-trast) difference, disparity, comparison 2 *v.* (con-*trast*) compare, differ, oppose, distinguish

contribute *v.* donate, present, bestow, provide ★**withhold**

contrive *v.* form, fashion, construct, create, design, invent

control *v.* command, direct, dominate, lead, supervise

convene *v.* call together, rally, meet, muster *We mustered on the quayside before boarding the ship*, assemble ★**dismiss**

convenient *adj.* handy, fit, helpful, suitable, accessible ★**awkward**

conversation *n.* chat, talk, communication, discussion

convert *v.* alter, change, transform, adapt

convey *v.* carry, transport, conduct, bear, transmit

convict 1 *n.* (*con*-vict) prisoner, captive, criminal 2 *v.* (con-*vict*) find guilty, condemn

convince *v.* assure, persuade, prove to, win over

cook *v.* boil, broil, heat, warm, steam, fry, stew, bake

cool 1 *adj.* chilly, frigid, ▷*cold* 2 self-composed, calm, relaxed

co-operate *v.* collaborate, combine, aid, assist, join forces

cope (with) *v.* deal, handle, struggle, grapple, manage

copy *v.* duplicate, reproduce, imitate, mimic, simulate

cord *n.* string, rope, twine, line CHORD

cordial *adj.* hearty, sincere, congenial, jovial, affable ★**hostile**

core *n.* heart, kernel, pith, crux *Now we're getting to the crux of the problem!*, centre CORPS

corner *n.* angle, bend, crook, cavity, cranny, niche, compartment

corpse *n.* body, carcass, remains

correct *adj.* true, actual, accurate, exact, precise ★**wrong**

correspond [1] *v.* fit, harmonize, agree, coincide [2] write letters

corridor *n.* hallway, passage, aisle

corroborate *v.* confirm, certify, endorse, establish ★**contradict**

corrode *v.* erode, waste, eat away, rust

corrupt *adj.* dishonest, fraudulent, rotten [2] *v.* bribe, deprave, entice

cost *n.* charge, amount, price, outlay [2] penalty, forfeit, sacrifice

costly *adj.* expensive, dear, valuable, precious

costume *n.* suit, outfit, ensemble, attire, dress

cot *n.* bed, bunk, berth

cottage *n.* bungalow, cabin, chalet, shack, lodge

couch *n.* bed, sofa, chaise longue

council *n.* assembly, committee, congress, convention COUNSEL

counsel [1] *n.* lawyer, attorney, advocate [2] *v.* advise, instruct, recommend COUNCIL

count *v.* add up, calculate, check, compute, reckon, tally

counter [1] *n.* token, coin, disc [2] table, bench, board [3] *adj.* against, opposed

counterfeit *adj.* forged, fraudulent, fake, bogus *She entered the country on a bogus passport*, false

country [1] *n.* nation, people, realm, state [2] *adj.* rural, backwoods, farmland

couple [1] *n.* pair, brace, two [2] *v.* link, yoke, unite, join, connect

courage *n.* bravery, valour, boldness, gallantry, daring, pluck ★**cowardice**

Cooking utensils

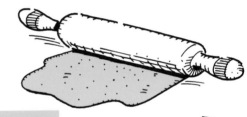
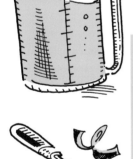

Beaker	Grill	Rolling
Blender	Jar	Pin
Bottle	Kettle	Saucepan
Bowl	Ladle	Saucer
Casserole	Lemon squeezer	Sieve
Colander	Masher	Skillet
Cup	Pan	Spoon
Dish	Peeler	Tureen
Frying pan	Plate	Wok
Grater	Pot	
Gridiron	Ramekin	

courageous *adj.* brave, bold, fearless, valiant, ▷*plucky* **★cowardly**

course [1] *n.* route, channel, path, road, track, trail [2] policy, plan, manner COARSE

court [1] *n.* yard, alley, lane, quad, cloister [2] bar, bench, tribunal [3] make love, woo, flatter

courteous *adj.* considerate, polite, refined, elegant **★discourteous**

courtesy *n.* politeness, civility, manners, gentility

cove *n.* inlet, bay, creek, firth

cover [1] *v.* conceal, hide, secrete [2] include, embody, incorporate [3] *n.* cap, case, lid, canopy

covet *v.* want, desire, envy, hanker after, long for

cow [1] *v.* frighten, bully, terrorize [2] *n.* female ox

coward *n.* weakling, craven, funk, sneak **★hero** COWERED

cowardice *n.* fear, funk, faint-heartedness **★courage**

cowardly *adj.* fearful, weak, scared, spineless **★courageous**

cower *v.* cringe, grovel, flinch, crouch

coy *adj.* demure, skittish, blushing, bashful, shy **★forward**

crack [1] *n.* slit, split, cleft, cranny, crevice, breach [2] *v.* snap, split, splinter

craft [1] *n.* cunning, deceit [2] ability, cleverness, expertise [3] occupation, business [4] boat, ship, plane

crafty *adj.* cunning, artful, wily, shrewd

cram *v.* ram, stuff, squeeze, press

cramp *v.* restrict, obstruct, hinder, confine

crash *v.* bang, clash, clatter, break, fall, topple

crass *adj.* stupid, oafish, boorish, obtuse **★sensitive**

crave *v.* long for, hanker after, need, yearn for, beg, plead

crawl *v.* creep, drag, slither, grovel

crazy *adj.* insane, mad, beserk, deranged, idiotic **★sane**

creak *v.* grate, grind, rasp, groan CREEK

crease *n.* fold, pucker, ridge, fold, tuck

create *v.* bring into being, compose, concoct, make, invent

creation invention, handiwork, foundation, production **★destruction**

creature *n.* animal, beast, being, brute *It was a huge brute, the biggest crocodile I ever saw,* person

credible *adj.* believable, likely, plausible **★incredible**

credit [1] *n.* acclaim, kudos, merit [2] belief, faith, confidence

creek *n.* bay, bight, cove CREAK

creep *v.* crawl, slither, squirm, wriggle

crest *n.* top, crown, pinnacle

crestfallen *adj.* downcast, dejected, discouraged **★elated**

crevice *n.* cleft, chink, crack, cranny, gap

crew *n.* team, company, party, gang

crime *n.* misdeed, offence, fault, felony

criminal [1] *n.* culprit, convict, felon, crook [2] *adj.* unlawful, wicked

cringe *v.* cower, flinch, duck, shrink, grovel

cripple *v.* disable, mutilate, paralyse, weaken, damage

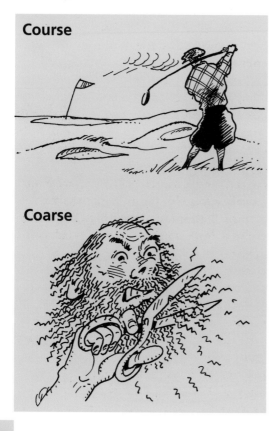

Course

Coarse

Creek

Creak

CREAK!

crisis *n.* climax, turning point, catastrophe, disaster

crisp *adj.* brittle, crumbly, crunchy, firm, crusty

critical *adj.* crucial, all-important, acute, grave

criticize *v.* find fault with, disapprove of, condemn **★praise**

crony *n.* accomplice, ally, confederate, comrade, chum, ▷*friend*

crooked 1 *adj.* bent, bowed, distorted, twisted 2 dishonest, criminal

crop 1 *n.* harvest, gathering, yield 2 *v.* graze, shorten, browse

cross 1 *adj.* angry, annoyed, crusty 2 *v.* bridge, pass over 3 *n.* crucifix

crouch *v.* stoop, squat, bow, cringe

crow 1 *v.* gloat, shout, brag, bluster 2 *n.* jackdaw, raven

crowd *n.* mob, multitude, flock, assembly, swarm, throng

crowded *adj.* jammed, packed, congested, cramped

crucial *adj.* decisive, critical, acute

crude *adj.* raw, unrefined, rustic, unpolished, ▷*coarse* **★refined**

cruel *adj.* unkind, brutal, inhuman, ruthless, ▷*savage* **★kind**

cruise *n.* voyage, sail, crossing CREWS

crumb *n.* bit, morsel, seed, grain, scrap, shred

crumble *v.* decay, grind, powder, crunch

crumple *v.* crinkle, crush, wrinkle, pucker

crunch *v.* chew, grind, masticate, munch ▷*crush*

crush *v.* squash, mash, pound, compress

cry 1 *v.* exclaim, call, shout, shriek 2 weep, bawl, blubber, sob

cuddle *v.* hug, embrace, fondle, cosset, pet, snuggle

cue *n.* hint, key, nod, sign, signal QUEUE

cull *v.* choose, pick, thin out, amass, collect

culprit *n.* criminal, convict, felon, offender, malefactor

cultivated *adj.* refined, civilized, cultured, educated, trained **★neglected**

cumbersome *adj.* bulky, awkward, clumsy, hefty **★convenient**

cunning *adj.* artful, astute, crafty **★gullible**

curb *v.* check, tame, restrain

cure 1 *n.* remedy, medicine, drug 2 *v.* heal, remedy, treat, attend

curious 1 *adj.* odd, peculiar, singular 2 inquisitive, prying, nosy

curl *v.* coil, twist, curve, crimp

current 1 *adj.* present, contemporary, topical, fashionable 2 *n.* stream, course, flow, electrical flow CURRANT

curse 1 *v.* swear, condemn, damn 2 *n.* oath, denunciation

curt *adj.* brusque, blunt, churlish, crusty, gruff, ▷*terse* **★polite**

curtail *v.* trim, shorten, clip, truncate *It was usually a long film, but we saw a truncated version,* ▷*abbreviate* **★lengthen**

curve *n.* loop, hook, curl, twist, wind, coil, ▷*bend*

cushion *n.* pillow, bolster, pad, support

custom *n.* habit, usage, convention, rite, ▷*fashion*

customer *n.* purchaser, buyer, client, patron

cut *v.* carve, whittle, chisel, cleave, sever, gash, slice

cut off *v.* disconnect, interrupt

cute *adj.* charming, attractive, pretty

cutting *adj.* sharp, biting, bitter, sarcastic

D d

dab *v.* blot, swab, touch, pat

dabble *v.* toy, trifle, meddle, tinker, potter

daft *adj.* silly, innocent, idiotic, cracked, soppy, dopey **★bright**

dagger *n.* dirk, bayonet, stiletto

daily 1 *adj.* everyday, normal, common *It is quite common to see squirrels in the wood* 2 *n.* newspaper

dainty *adj.* delicate, charming, exquisite, choice, tasty

dally *v.* play, trifle, dawdle, linger, loiter

damage *n.* mischief, sabotage, vandalism, injury, hurt

damn *v.* curse, swear, condemn, criticize **★bless**

damp *adj.* humid, clammy, dank, ▷*moist* **★dry**

damsel *n.* girl, maid, maiden, miss

dance *v.* hop, skip, jump, prance, frolic, gambol

danger *n.* peril, hazard, risk, jeopardy, menace **★safety**

dangerous *adj.* perilous, precarious, unsafe, risky, hazardous **★safe**

dangle *v.* hang, swing, sway

dank *adj.* sticky, muggy, moist, soggy, ▷*damp*

dapper *adj.* spruce, natty, neat, stylish, ▷*smart* **★scruffy**

dare *v.* brave, face, risk, defy, challenge, venture

daring *adj.* adventurous, dashing, bold, fearless, ▷*brave* **★timid**

dark *adj.* dusky, swarthy, shady, dim, dingy, shadowy **★light**

darling *n.* pet, love, dear, favourite, beloved, precious

darn *v.* mend, sew, patch, repair

dart 1 *n.* arrow, missile 2 *v.* dash, hurtle *The express train hurtled through the tunnel,* charge, gallop

dash *v.* rush, gallop, run, career, fly, hasten

date 1 *n.* time, point 2 appointment *I have an appointment to see the doctor,* engagement 3 *v.* become old, become dated

Dances

Bolero	Samba
Bop	Square dance
Cha-cha	Tango
Charleston	Tarantella
Conga	Two-step
Country dance	Twist
Fandango	Waltz
Flamenco	
Fox trot	
Gavotte	
Highland fling	
Jitterbug	
Jive	
Mazurka	
Minuet	
Morris dance	
Paso doble	
Polka	
Polonaise	
Quadrille	
Quickstep	
Rumba	

daub v. plaster, spread, smear, coat, paint

daunt v. intimidate, terrify, scare, confront

dauntless adj. fearless, gallant, courageous, ▷*brave* ★**discouraged**

dawdle v. linger, loiter, lag, waste time, ▷*dally* ★**hurry**

dawn n. beginning, daybreak, daylight, morning, sunrise ★**dusk**

daze v. deaden, muddle, blind, dazzle, ▷*bewilder* DAYS

dazzle v. blind, glare, confuse, ▷*daze*

dead adj. deceased, departed, gone, lifeless, dull ★**live**

deaden v. paralyze, blunt, muffle, drown

deadly adj. fatal, lethal, mortal, baleful, venomous

deaf adj. hard of hearing, unhearing, heedless

deal v. bargain, trade, market, communicate, traffic, give out

dealer n. merchant, trader, tradesman

dear [1] adj. expensive, high-priced, costly *She wore a costly gown of pure silk* ★**cheap** [2] darling, beloved, loved DEER

death n. decease, end of life, mortality ★**life**

debate v. argue, discuss, dispute, question, contend

debris n. trash, junk, ▷*rubbish*

debt n. obligation, debit, dues, liability ★**credit**

decay [1] v. decompose, rot *The potatoes had been left too long and had rotted*, spoil [2] decline, sink, dwindle, waste

deceive v. dupe, hoax, trick, cheat, mislead, ▷*betray* ★**enlighten**

decent adj. respectable, chaste, proper, fair, modest ★**indecent**

decide v. determine, rule, judge, resolve

declare v. avow, state, profess, proclaim, announce

decline [1] v. descend, dwindle *The profits of the business had dwindled*, drop, fall [2] refuse, say no ★**assent** [3] n. descent, slope, slant, dip, pitch

decorate v. embellish, adorn, ornament

decoy [1] v. entice *We were enticed into the café by the smell of roasting coffee*, ensnare, mislead, tempt [2] n. lure, bait

decrease v. diminish, lessen, wane, decline, reduce ★**increase**

decree n. law, edict, manifesto, rule, decision

decrepit adj. senile, infirm, crippled, feeble, frail ★**robust**

dedicate v. devote, apportion, assign, surrender, pledge

deduce v. draw, infer, conclude, glean, surmise, reason

deduct v. subtract, take from, remove, withdraw ★**add**

deed [1] n. act, feat, stunt [2] document, paper, contract *Greta Garbo was under contract to the film studio*

deep [1] adj. profound *Mary and John have a profound love of nature*, bottomless, low [2] learned, wise, sagacious

deface v. disfigure, deform, injure, mar, blemish ★**adorn**

defeat v. beat, conquer, overcome, triumph, vanquish ★**triumph**

defect n. flaw, fault, weak point, blemish, error

defective adj. imperfect, faulty, deficient, insufficient ★**perfect**

defend v. protect, guard, fortify, support, sustain, uphold ★**attack**

defer v. postpone, put off, adjourn, waive, yield ★**hasten**

defiant adj. mutinous, rebellious, resistant, aggressive ★**submissive**

deficient adj. wanting, imperfect, defective, faulty ★**superfluous**

defile v. taint, infect, pollute, sully, disgrace ★**cleanse**

define v. explain, interpret, designate, mark out, specify ★**obscure**

definite adj. clear, certain, clear-cut, distinct, ▷*sure* ★**vague**

deform adj. misshape, distort, contort, twist, warp

defraud v. fleece, swindle, embezzle, diddle, ▷*cheat*

defy v. resist, withstand, disregard, challenge, disobey ★**obey**

degrade v. humble, debase, corrupt, downgrade, cheapen ★**improve**

degree *n.* grade, step, measure, rate, scale *The rebellion turned into a full-scale war,* class

dejected *adj.* depressed, downcast, crestfallen, disheartened, ▷*gloomy* ★**elated**

delay *v.* postpone, put off, detain, halt, hinder, impede ★**hurry**

deliberate 1 *adj.* wilful, calculated, intentional, planned ★**unintentional** 2 *v.* reflect, contemplate, discuss

delicate *adj.* dainty, refined, soft, luxurious, modest, fragile, tender ★**harsh**

delicious *adj.* palatable, luscious, mellow, savoury, choice, ▷*scrumptious* ★**unpleasant**

delight *n.* enjoyment, pleasure, rapture, bliss, ▷*happiness* ★**displease**

delightful *adj.* enjoyable, cheery, enchanting, lovely, ▷*agreeable* ★**horrible**

deliver 1 *v.* transfer, hand over, bear *I bear good news of your family,* carry, convey 2 free, liberate, release

delude *v.* cheat, hoax, hoodwink, mislead, ▷*deceive* ★**guide**

deluge *n.* inundation, swamp, spate, ▷*flood*

demand 1 *v.* request, ask, appeal, entreat 2 badger, pester, nag *The children have been nagging me to take them to the park*

demeanour *n.* bearing, manner, conduct, air

demented *adj.* distracted, foolish, insane, ▷*mad* ★**sane**

demolish *v.* destroy, wreck, ruin, smash, overthrow, knock down ★**build up**

demon *n.* fiend, imp, devil, evil spirit

demonstrate *v.* prove, exhibit, illustrate, ▷*show*

demote *v.* degrade, downgrade, relegate ★**promote**

demur *v.* hestitate, object, protest, doubt, waver ★**consent**

demure *adj.* coy, sedate, staid, sober, prudish, discreet ★**indiscreet**

den 1 *n.* nest, cave, haunt, lair 2 hideaway, retreat *This little room is my retreat, where I can sit and think,* study

denote *v.* designate, indicate, mean, show, point out

denounce *v.* decry, defame, attack, brand, ▷*accuse* ★**praise**

dense 1 *adj.* thick, solid, stout, compact ★**sparse** 2 stupid, thick, stolid, obtuse ★**clever** DENTS

dent *n.* notch, cavity, chip, dimple, hollow

deny 1 *v.* refuse, reject, repudiate 2 disagree with *I am afraid that I disagree with what you say,* oppose, contradict ★**admit**

depart *v.* quit, go, retire, withdraw, vanish, ▷*leave* ★**arrive**

department *n.* section, division, office, branch, province

depend on *v.* lean on, rely upon, trust in

depict *v.* decribe, sketch, portray, outline, draw

deplorable *adj.* distressing, disastrous, shameful, scandalous ★**excellent**

deplore *v.* regret, lament, mourn ★**praise**

deport *v.* banish, exile, expel, oust

deposit *v.* drop, lay, place, put, bank, entrust, save ★**withdraw**

depot 1 *n.* warehouse, storehouse 2 terminus, station

depraved *adj.* corrupted, immoral, evil, sinful, vile *After calling me vile names, he left* ★**upright**

depreciate 1 *v.* devalue, lessen, lose value *From the moment it was bought the car began losing value,* reduce 2 belittle, disparage, deride ★**appreciate**

depress 1 *v.* dishearten, dispirit, cast down ★**cheer** 2 flatten, push down

depressed *adj.* dispirited, disheartened, despondent, fed up

deprive *v.* take away, rob, starve, divest *The traitor had been divested of all her honours* ★**bestow**

depth *n.* pit, shaft, well, chasm, gulf, abyss

deputy *n.* agent, delegate, lieutenant, assistant, councillor

derelict *adj.* abandoned, deserted *The **Mary Celeste** sailing ship was found deserted in the Atlantic,* forlorn

deride *v.* laugh at, jeer, ridicule, ▷*mock* ★**praise**

derive *v.* develop *Many English words developed from Norman-French,* obtain, arise from, originate

descend v. fall, drop, lower, decline, collapse, ▷sink **★ascend**

describe v. depict, portray, detail, define, tell

desert ①(*dez*-ert) n. wasteland, wilderness ② adj. desolate, arid, barren ③ v. (dez-*ert*) forsake, leave, ▷abandon DESSERT

deserve v. be worthy of, merit, warrant, be entitled to **★forfeit**

design n. drawing, painting, plan, pattern, scheme

desirable ① adj. agreeable, pleasing, good ② attractive, alluring, adorable

desire ① v. wish, require, need ② long for, yearn after, pine for *My sister lived abroad, but always pined for the old country* **★detest**

desist v. abstain, avoid, break off, cease, end

desolate adj. lonely, forlorn, miserable, wretched, alone **★cheerful**

despair n. depression, misery, hopelessness, sorrow, ▷gloom **★hope**

desperate adj. drastic, reckless, frantic, rash, wild **★hopeful**

despicable adj. contemptible, low, detestable, degrading **★noble**

despise v. abhor, detest, loathe, look down upon, ▷hate **★prize**

despite prep. in spite of, notwithstanding

despondent adj. depressed, dispirited, broken-hearted, ▷miserable **★hopeful**

dessert n. sweet, sweets, pudding DESERT

destination n. goal, terminus, end, objective, journey's end

destiny n. fate, lot, fortune, future, prospect, doom

destitute adj. poor, needy, bankrupt, penniless, wanting **★wealthy**

destroy v. ruin, demolish, spoil, smash, exterminate, ▷wreck **★create**

destruction n. desolation, downfall, ruin, defeat, havoc **★creation**

detach v. separate, part, divide, loosen, undo **★attach**

detail n. item, fact, circumstance, point

detain v. delay, retard, restrain, arrest, hold up **★release**

detect v. notice, discover, observe, scent, track down **★hide**

Desert

Dessert

deter v. prevent, hold back, check, stop, ▷detain **★encourage**

deteriorate v. become worse, worsen, corrode, decline, decompose **★improve**

determine v. find out, decide, identify, choose, regulate

detest v. abhor *Lucy was a peaceful woman, and abhorred violence,* loathe, despise, ▷hate **★adore**

devastate v. lay waste, ravage, overwhelm, ▷destroy

develop v. mature, ripen, grow up, evolve, extend **★restrict**

deviate v. diverge, differ, vary, contrast, wander **★continue**

device n. apparatus, contrivance, instrument, appliance

devil n. imp, evil spirit, demon, fiend, Satan

devious adj. tricky, sly, subtle, cunning, roundabout **★straightforward**

devise v. contrive, fashion, form, plan, conceive

devoid adj. barren, empty, free, without, lacking **★endowed**

devote v. allocate, allot, give, assign, dedicate

devoted adj. dedicated, devout, loyal, caring, ardent **★indifferent**

devour *v.* swallow, gulp, gorge, consume, ▷*eat*

devout *adj.* pious, devoted, religious, faithful, passionate ★**insincere**

dexterous *adj.* able, active, deft, nimble, ▷*skilful* ★**clumsy**

diagram *n.* outline, plan, sketch, draft, chart, drawing

dictate *v.* speak, utter, say, instruct, ordain, command

die *v.* expire, finish, end, pass away, perish, cease ★**live** DYE

differ [1] *v.* vary, contrast, diverge *In this case, my views diverge strongly from yours* [2] argue, conflict, clash

difference *n.* variance, distinctness, divergence, subtlety ★**agreement**

different *adj.* contrary, variant, distinct, original, unusual ★**same**

difficult *adj.* hard, puzzling, baffling, complex, laborious ★**easy**

difficulty *n.* trouble, bother, predicament, ★**plight**

diffident *adj.* bashful, reserved, retiring, timid, unsure, ▷*shy* ★**confident**

dig *v.* burrow, excavate, grub, delve, scoop

digest [1] *v.* (di-*gest*) absorb, assimilate, dissolve [2] *n.* (*di*-gest) *n.* abridgement, condensation, précis

digit [1] *n.* cipher, number, figure [2] finger, toe, thumb

dignified *adj.* grand, grave, majestic, noble, lofty ★**undignified**

dignity *n.* grandeur, merit, fame, gravity, nobility

dilapidated *adj.* neglected, unkempt, crumbling, decayed

dilemma *n.* quandary, plight, difficulty, predicament

dilute *v.* water down, weaken, reduce, thin

dim *adj.* dark, faint, pale, gloomy, ▷*obscure* ★**distinct**

diminish *v.* reduce, lessen, decrease, become smaller ★**enhance**

din *n.* uproar, racket, babel, ▷*noise* ★**quiet**

dingy *adj.* murky, dark, dreary, sombre, gloomy, ▷*dismal* ★**bright**

dip *v.* sink, subside, immerse, plunge

dire *adj.* alarming, appalling, awful, horrible, ▷*terrible* DYER

direct [1] *adj.* straight, even, blunt, candid [2] *v.* aim, level, train, point

direction *n.* course, trend, way, track, route

dirt *n.* impurity, filth, grime, muck, soil

dirty *adj.* unclean, impure, filthy, sordid, squalid, nasty ★**clean**

disable *v.* cripple, lame, maim, disarm

disadvantage *n.* inconvenience, burden, damage, loss, obstacle ★**advantage**

disagree *v.* differ, revolt, decline, refuse, dissent, argue ★**agree**

disagreeable *adj.* unpleasant, obnoxious, unwelcome, offensive ★**agreeable**

Dogs

Afghan Hound
Airedale
Alsatian
Basenji
Bassett Hound
Beagle
Bloodhound
Borzoi
Boxer
Bulldog

disappear *v.* vanish, dissolve, fade, melt, depart, expire ★**appear**

disappoint *v.* frustrate, disillusion, let down, dismay, dissatisfy ★**please**

disapprove *v.* condemn, denounce, criticize, reproach ★**approve**

disaster *n.* calamity, catastrophe, accident, misfortune ★**triumph**

disbelief *n.* incredulity, distrust, doubt, suspicion ★**belief**

discard *v.* eliminate, get rid of, reject, scrap
Once we got a new car, I scrapped the old one, throw away ★**adopt**

discern *v.* note, discover, distinguish

discharge ① *v.* dismiss, give notice to, expel
② detonate, emit, fire

disciple *n.* follower, learner, pupil, attendant

discipline *n.* correction, training, self-control, obedience

disclaim *v.* repudiate, disown, renounce, deny, reject ★**acknowledge**

disclose *v.* discover, show, reveal, expose, betray, ▷*divulge* ★**conceal**

disconcert *v.* abash, confuse, confound, upset, baffle ★**encourage**

disconnect *v.* separate, detach, cut off, sever, uncouple ★**connect**

disconsolate *adj.* distressed, sad, forlorn, melancholy, desolate, ▷*unhappy* ★**cheerful**

discontented *adj.* displeased, disgruntled, unsatisfied, reluctant ★**content**

discord *n.* disagreement, strife ★**concord**

Chihuahua	Golden Retriever	Pug
Chow	Great Dane	Red Setter
Cocker Spaniel	Greyhound	Retriever
Collie	Labrador	St Bernard
Corgi	Mastiff	Setter
Dachshund	Old English Sheepdog	Saluki
Dalmatian	Pekingese	Spaniel
Dobermann	Pointer	Terrier
Foxhound	Poodle	Whippet

discourage v. depress, dishearten, dismay, dispirit *Today everything went wrong, and I am quite dispirited*, put off ★**encourage**

discouraged adj. crestfallen, daunted, depressed, downcast ★**encouraged**

discourteous adj. blunt, crude, churlish, outspoken, abrupt ★**courteous**

discover v. locate, surprise, unearth, uncover, ▷*find* ★**conceal**

discreet adj. prudent, cautious, careful, tactful, sensible ★**indiscreet** DISCRETE

discriminate v. distinguish, penetrate, favour, judge, assess ★**confound**

discuss v. confer, consider, talk over, debate, argue

disdain n. ridicule, scorn, contempt, derision ★**admiration**

disease n. infection, contagion, illness, plague, ailment, sickness

disfigure v. blemish, deface, deform, mar, scar, spoil ★**adorn**

disgrace n. scandal, dishonour, shame, infamy, stigma ★**honour**

disguise v. conceal, mask, falsify, cloak, deceive, fake

disgust 1 n. revulsion, loathing, distaste *The room was messy, and I viewed it with distaste* 2 v. repel, revolt, nauseate ★**admire**

dish n. plate, platter, bowl

dishearten v. depress, cast down, deter, deject, ▷*discourage* ★**encourage**

dishonest adj. deceitful, unscrupulous, shady, crooked ★**honest**

disintegrate v. crumble, moulder, decompose, rot, fall apart ★**unite**

dislike v. hate, loathe, detest, abhor, abominate, ▷*despise* ★**like**

dismal adj. dreary, ominous, cheerless, depressing, ▷*hopeless* ★**cheerful**

dismiss v. banish, discard, abandon, dispel, repudiate, release ★**appoint**

disobey v. rebel, transgress, resist, defy, ignore ★**obey**

disorder n. confusion, disarray, commotion, chaos ★**order**

dispel v. diperse, drive away, dismiss, allay, scatter ★**collect**

dispense v. distribute, arrange, allocate, supply, measure out ★**accept**

disperse v. scatter, separate, break up, spread abroad, distribute ★**gather**

display v. show, exhibit, unfold, expose, flaunt *He wears expensive clothes, which he flaunts to his companions*, flourish, ▷*reveal* ★**hide**

displease v. annoy, anger, irritate, upset, vex ★**please**

dispose v. arrange, place, position, regulate, order

dispose of v. discard, dump, destroy, eliminate, throw away ★**keep**

dispute 1 n. (dis-*pute*) conflict, quarrel, argument 2 v. (*dis*-pute) argue, refute, contend

disregard v. overlook, misjudge, despise, ignore, snub ★**heed**

disreputable adj. discreditable, dishonourable, disgraceful, ▷*shameful* ★**honourable**

dissect v. examine, scrutinize, analyze, dismember

dissent n. disagreement, difference, repudiation, opposition ★**assent**

dissimilar adj. different, diverse, unlike, various ★**similar**

dissolve v. melt, thaw, break up, fade

dissuade v. deter, discourage, warn, put off ★**persuade**

distance n. extent, remoteness, range, reach, span, stretch

distinct 1 adj. separate, independent, detached 2 clear, conspicuous, lucid ★**hazy**

distinguish v. discern, discover, differentiate

distinguished adj. important, notable, great, famed, celebrated ★**ordinary**

distort v. deform, misshape, twist, bend, buckle

distract 1 v. beguile, bewilder, disturb, confuse 2 entertain

distress v. harass, embarrass, trouble, grieve, ▷*worry* ★**soothe**

distribute v. give out, deliver, disperse, circulate, ▷*dispense* ★**collect**

Domesticated animals

Budgerigar   Horse
Camel   Parrot
Canary   Pig
Cat   Pigeon
Cattle   Sheep
Chicken
Dog
Donkey
Duck
Elephant
Goat
Goose

district *n.* area, community, locality *Pat and Mike have moved to a new locality*, neighbourhood, region

distrust *v.* suspect, discredit, doubt, disbelieve ★**trust**

disturb *v.* annoy, bother, disquiet, unsettle, upset, confuse ★**calm**

dither *v.* waver, hesitate, falter, oscillate

dive *v.* plunge, pitch, swoop, descend, drop

diverse *adj.* different, various, dissimilar, numerous, separate ★**identical**

divert 1 *v.* alter, change, deflect 2 entertain, gratify

divest *v.* disrobe, undress, strip

divide *v.* separate, dissect, part, divorce, distribute, apportion, split ★**join**

division *n.* portion, fragment, section, compartment, department

divorce *v.* annul, cancel, separate, divide, part, split up

divulge *v.* betray, disclose, tell, announce, broadcast, uncover

dizzy *adj.* giddy, confused, shaky, wobbling, muddled, staggering

do 1 *v.* carry out, perform, act 2 be adequate, suffice

do away with *v.* destroy, abolish, eliminate, kill

do up, *v.* fasten, tie, fix

docile *adj.* amenable, tame, meek, orderly, manageable ★**unco-operative**

doctrine *n.* article, belief, creed, dogma, teaching

document *n.* paper, deed, certificate, form

dodge *v.* avoid, parry, duck, elude, fend off

dogged *adj.* obstinate, morose, sullen, persistent, steadfast ★**docile**

doleful *adj.* dismal, woebegone, depressing, rueful, sad, ▷*gloomy* ★**merry**

domestic 1 *adj.* homely, household *The children always help with the household jobs*, family, internal 2 domesticated, tame

dominant *adj.* masterful, superior, supreme, prevalent ★**subordinate**

dominate *v.* rule, control, direct, tyrannize, overbear ★**yield**

donation *n.* gift, present, contribution

doom *n.* judgment, fate, verdict, destiny, destruction

door *n.* entrance, doorway, gate, gateway, portal

dose *n.* draught, potion, quantity, amount

doubt *v.* hesitate, waver, demur, suspect, mistrust, be dubious ★**trust**

doubtful *adj.* suspicious, dubious, indefinite, uncertain, unclear ★**certain**

dour *adj.* austere, dreary, grim, hard, severe ★**cheery**

dowdy *adj.* dull, plain, dingy, frumpish, ▷*shabby* ★**smart**

downcast *adj.* crestfallen, downhearted, dejected, ▷*miserable* ★**happy**

downfall *n.* ruin, overthrow, misfortune, disgrace, failure

downright *adj.* blunt, candid, absolute, forthright, straightforward

doze *v.* snooze, slumber, sleep, nod off, drowse DOES

drab *adj.* colourless, cheerless, dull, gloomy, grey, ▷*dreary* ★**bright**

draft *v.* sketch, outline, draw, design, plan

drag *v.* draw, pull, haul, tug, tow, lug

drain 1 *v.* draw, strain, drip, percolate, empty, dry, drink up 2 conduit, sewer, pipe

dramatic *adj.* theatrical, exciting, surprising, sensational ★**ordinary**

drape *v.* hang, suspend, droop, cover

drastic *adj.* extreme, dire, desperate, harsh, radical ★**mild**

draw 1 *v.* pull, tug, drag, haul 2 sketch, design, depict, portray

drawback *n.* weakness, shortcoming, failing, defect, handicap ★**advantage**

dread *n.* fear, terror, horror, alarm, awe, dismay, ▷*fright* ★**confidence**

dreadful *adj.* fearful, terrible, horrible, alarming, ▷*awful* ★**comforting**

dream *n.* trance, vision, fancy, reverie, fantasy, illusion

dreary *adj.* dingy, gloomy, sombre, cheerless, ▷*dismal* ★**bright**

drench *v.* saturate, soak, steep, flood

dress *n.* clothing, vestments, costume, garb, apparel, attire

dress up *v.* play-act, don fancy-dress

drift *v.* float, flow, wander, stray, meander *The little stream meandered through lush countryside*

drill 1 *v.* teach, exercise, train, discipline 2 bore, penetrate, pierce

drink *v.* imbibe, swallow, absorb, quaff, sip

drip *v.* drop, ooze, percolate, drizzle, trickle

drive 1 *v.* make, compel, force, oblige, prod, goad 2 propel, direct, operate, actuate

drivel *n.* nonsense, babble, twaddle, bunkum, gibberish

drizzle *v.* dribble, mizzle, shower, spit, ▷*rain*

droll *adj.* whimsical, comical, comic, ▷*funny*

droop *v.* flag, sink, decline, languish, drop, bend, wilt

drop 1 *v.* fall, sink, dip, plunge, plummet 2 droplet, globule, drip

drown *v.* sink, immerse, swamp, submerge, extinguish

drowsy *adj.* sleepy, somnolent, dazed, tired

drudge *v.* toil, labour, struggle, plod, slave

drug *v.* dope, deaden, sedate, stupefy, poison

dry 1 *adj.* arid, parched, moistureless, dried up ★**wet** 2 uninteresting, boring, tedious

dubious *adj.* suspicious, fishy, suspect, untrustworthy, ▷*doubtful* ★**trustworthy**

duck 1 *n.* water fowl 2 *v.* plunge, submerge, dip, dodge, lurch

due 1 *adj.* owing, unpaid, payable 2 just, fair, proper 3 scheduled, expected DEW

duel *n.* contest, battle, swordplay

duffer *n.* blunderer, bungler, booby, clot

dull 1 *adj.* stupid, stolid, obtuse, dimwitted 2 blunt, not sharp 3 boring, uninteresting, tedious

dumb 1 *adj.* silent, speechless, mute 2 foolish, ▷*dull* ★**intelligent**

dummy 1 *n.* mannikin, puppet, doll 2 blockhead, dimwit 3 *adj.* artificial, fake, false

dump *v.* deposit, ditch, empty, throw away

dunce *n.* dimwit, dolt, blockhead, duffer, ignoramus ★**genius**

dungeon *n.* cell, prison, lock-up, vault

dupe *v.* cheat, defraud, deceive, outwit

duplicate *n.* copy, facsimile, replica, reproduction

durable *adj.* lasting, enduring, permanent, stable, reliable ★**fragile**

dusk *n.* twilight, nightfall, evening, gloaming ★**dawn**

dusty *adj.* grimy, dirty, filthy, grubby ★**polished**

duty 1 *n.* obligation, responsibility, allegiance, trust, task 2 impost, tax, excise

dwarf *n.* pygmy, gnome, mannikin, goblin

dwell *v.* stop, stay, rest, linger, tarry, live, reside

dwell on *v.* emphasize, linger over, harp on

dwindle *v.* diminish, decrease, decline, waste, shrink, become smaller ★**increase**

dye *n.* pigment, colouring matter, colour, stain, tint DIE

E e

eager *adj.* avid, ambitious, ardent, zealous, enthusiastic, ▷*keen* ★**indifferent**

early *adj.* advanced, forward, soon ★**late**

earn *v.* make money, deserve, merit, rate, win, acquire ★**spend** URN

earnest *adj.* serious, sedate, staid, passionate, determined ★**flippant**

earth 1 *n.* soil, dust, dry land 2 world, globe, sphere

ease *n.* calm, repose, quiet, peace, dexterity ★**difficulty**

easy *adj.* effortless, smooth, simple, practicable ★**difficult**

eat *v.* consume, dine, chew, swallow, gorge

ebb *v.* flow back, fall back, recede, decline, wane ★**flow**

eccentric *adj.* queer, strange, odd, erratic, whimsical, ▷*peculiar* ★**normal**

echo *v.* vibrate, reverberate, imitate

economical *adj.* moderate, reasonable, frugal, ▷*thrifty* ★**expensive**

ecstasy *n.* joy, happiness, delight, elation, ▷*bliss* ★**torment**

edge *n.* border, rim, brink, fringe, margin, tip, ▷*end*

edible *adj.* eatable, comestible, safe, wholesome ★**inedible**

edit *v.* revise, correct, adapt, censor, publish

educate *v.* instruct, teach, tutor, coach, train

educated *adj.* learned, cultured, erudite, literate, well-bred ★**illiterate**

eerie *adj.* weird, unearthly, uncanny, awesome

effect 1 *n.* outcome *What was the outcome of your interview?*, end, result 2 *v.* cause, make, bring about, accomplish

effective *adj.* operative, serviceable, competent ★**useless**

efficient *adj.* competent, proficient, able, ▷*effective* ★**inefficient**

effort *n.* exertion, toil, labour, accomplishment, ▷*feat*

eject *v.* drive out, force out, expel, evict, oust, discharge

elaborate *adj.* complex, elegant, ornate, intricate ★**simple**

elated *adj.* excited, gleeful, joyous, overjoyed, ▷*pleased* ★**downcast**

Eating verbs

bolt breakfast
chew chomp consume
devour dig in dine drink
eat eat up
feast feed finish off
gobble gorge gulp guzzle
imbibe
lap up lunch
masticate munch
nibble nosh
partake peck at pick at
quaff
relish
sample savour set to sip slurp
snack swallow sup swig swill
taste tuck in
wash down wine and dine wolf
down

elderly *adj.* old, aged, ancient ★**youthful**

elect *v.* choose, determine, vote, select, pick

elegant *adj.* refined, luxurious, polished, classical, ▷*graceful* ★**inelegant**

elementary *adj.* easy, effortless, basic, clear, ▷*simple* ★**complex**

elevate *v.* raise, erect, hoist, upraise, ▷*lift* ★**lower**

eligible *adj.* qualified, suitable, acceptable, proper, ▷*fit* ★**unfit**

eliminate *v.* do away with, abolish *The government has abolished many old laws*, exterminate, erase, delete ★**accept**

elude *v.* evade, avoid, depart, dodge, escape

embarrass *v.* abash, confuse, disconcert, fluster, shame

emblem *n.* badge, mark, brand, sign, crest, device

embrace 1 *v.* hug, squeeze, cuddle, caress, hold 2 include *The census figures include new arrivals this year*, encompass, enclose

emerge *v.* come out, exit, appear, arise, turn up ★**disappear**

emergency *n.* crisis, danger, extremity, predicament, ▷*plight*

eminent *adj.* famous, noted, renowned, well-known, esteemed, ▷*important* ★**unknown**

emit *v.* give off, belch, radiate, discharge, eject, vent ★**absorb**

emotion *n.* sentiment, feeling, fervour, passion

emotional *adj.* affected, sensitive, responsive, temperamental ★**cold**

emphasize *v.* accentuate, accent, intensify, ▷*stress* ★**understate**

employ *v.* engage, hire, retain, apply, adopt, ▷*use*

employee *n.* worker, workman, staff-member, job-holder

empty 1 *adj.* bare, barren, vacant *That house has been vacant for months*, hollow, unoccupied ★**full** 2 *v.* discharge, drain, unload, pour out ★**fill**

enchant *v.* enthral, bewitch, delight, gratify, ▷*charm* ★**bore**

enclose *v.* surround, encircle, encompass, contain, include ★**open**

encounter *v.* come upon, meet, experience, face

encourage *v.* cheer, hearten, console, comfort, support, ▷*urge* ★**dissuade**

encroach *v.* intrude, transgress, overstep, trespass, infringe

end 1 *n.* conclusion, finish, limit, boundary *This river marks the boundary of the county* 2 *v.* complete, close, terminate, ▷*finish* ★**start**

endanger *v.* hazard, imperil, jeopardize, ▷*risk* ★**protect**

endeavour *v.* aspire, aim, strive, struggle, try, ▷*aim*

endless *adj.* ceaseless, continuous, everlasting, limitless

endorse *v.* undersign, uphold, support, guarantee, vouch for ★**disapprove**

endow *v.* settle upon, invest, award, bequeath, provide, ▷*bestow* ★**divest**

endowed *adj.* talented, gifted, enhanced

endure *v.* bear, tolerate, suffer, go through, experience, cope with

enemy *n.* foe, adversary, rival, antagonist, opponent ★**friend**

energetic *adj.* dynamic, lively, vigorous, brisk, ▷*active* ★**sluggish**

energy *n.* vigour, endurance, stamina, vitality, force, power

enforce *v.* apply, administer, carry out, compel

engage 1 *v.* employ, hire, charter, rent 2 occupy *That new book has occupied my mind for weeks*, oblige, operate 3 pledge, betroth

engine *n.* machine, device, motor, turbine, appliance

engrave *v.* etch, stipple, incise, sculpture, carve, chisel

engrossed *adj.* absorbed, fascinated, enthralled ★**bored**

enhance *v.* intensify, strengthen, amplify, improve ★**decrease**

enigma *n.* riddle, puzzle, cryptogram, mystery, problem

enjoy *v.* like, be fond of, delight in, appreciate, savour, ▷*relish* ★**detest**

enjoyable *adj.* likeable, amusing, delicious, ▷*agreeable* ★**disagreeable**

Engines
Diesel engine
Internal combustion engine
Jet engine
Piston engine
Steam engine
Turbojet engine
Turboprop
Wankel engine

enlarge *v.* amplify, make bigger, expand, extend, magnify, ▷*swell* ★**shrink**

enlighten *v.* inform, teach, explain to, educate, instruct ★**confuse**

enlist *v.* conscript, employ, engage, muster, sign up, volunteer

enmity *n.* animosity, acrimony, bitterness, hostility, ▷*hate* ★**friendship**

enormous *adj.* immense, vast, tremendous, massive, ▷*huge* ★**tiny**

enough *adj.* sufficient, adequate, ample, plenty ★**insufficient**

enquire or **inquire** *v.* ask, examine, inspect, check, question

enrage *v.* aggravate, incite, incense, infuriate, ▷*anger* ★**soothe**

enrich *v.* decorate, embellish, adorn, improve, adorn ★**impoverish**

enrol *v.* sign up, enlist, subscribe, accept, admit ★**reject**

enslave *v.* bind, conquer, dominate, overpower, yoke ★**free**

ensue *v.* develop, follow, result, arise, ▷*happen* ★**precede**

ensure *v.* confirm, guarantee, insure, protect, secure

entangle *v.* tangle, snarl, ensnare, complicate, ▷*bewilder* ★**extricate**

enter *v.* go in, arrive, enrol, invade, commence, penetrate ★**leave**

enterprise *n.* endeavour, adventure, undertaking, concern, establishment

entertain *v.* amuse, charm, cheer, please, divert, beguile ★**bore**

enthral *v.* captive, charm, entrance, fascinate ★**bore**

enthusiasm *n.* fervour, ardour, interest, hobby, passion, eagerness

entice *v.* attract, beguile, coax, lead on, wheedle

entire *adj.* complete, intact, total, whole, full ★**partial**

entirely *adj.* absolutely, wholly, utterly *Our old dog came home, utterly tired and exhausted,* altogether ★**partially**

entitle [1] *v.* allow, authorize, empower *As president, I am empowered to sign this document,* enable [2] call, christen, term

entrance [1] *n.* way in, access *There is an access to the garden on the far side,* doorway, gate, opening [2] *v.* bewitch, captivate, charm ★**repel**

entreat *v.* beg, beseech, implore, ask

entry *n.* access, admission, ▷*entrance* ★**exit**

envelop *v.* wrap, wind, roll, cloak, conceal, enfold

envious *adj.* jealous, grudging, covetous, resentful ★**content**

environment *n.* surroundings, neighbourhood, vicinity, background

envy *v.* covet, grudge, desire, crave, resent

episode *n.* occasion, affair, circumstance, happening, instalment

equal [1] *adj.* matching, like, alike, same ★**different** [2] fit *Is Joe really fit for this job?,* adequate

equip *v.* furnish, provide, supply, fit out, rig

equipment *n.* stores, supplies, outfit, tackle, gear

equivalent *adj.* equal, comparable, alike, similar, interchangeable ★**unlike**

era *n.* epoch, age, generation, period, time, stage

eradicate *v.* uproot, weed out, remove, stamp out, ▷*abolish*

erase *v.* cancel, rub out, obliterate, eliminate, ▷*delete* ★**mark**

erect [1] *adj.* upright, upstanding, rigid *The tent had a rigid metal frame* ★**relaxed** [2] *v.* build, construct, put up ★**demolish**

err *v.* be mistaken, blunder, go astray, mistake, misjudge, sin ★**correct**

errand *n.* mission, assignment, duty, job, ▷*task*

erratic *adj.* eccentric, irregular, unstable, unreliable ★**stable**

erroneous *adj.* untrue, false, faulty, inaccurate, ▷*wrong* ★**correct**

error *n.* mistake, fault, flaw, fallacy, untruth, ▷*blunder* ★**truth**

erupt *v.* blow up, explode, burst, vent, ▷*discharge* ★**absorb**

escape *v.* break free, get away, dodge, elude, evade, ▷*flee* ★**capture**

escort [1] *n.* guard, conductor, aide, attendant, procession [2] *v.* accompany, conduct

especially *adv.* chiefly, principally, notably

essay [1] *n.* effort, trial [2] theme, manuscript, composition *Whoever writes the best composition gets a prize*

essence [1] *n.* extract, juice, perfume [2] substance *He spoke well, but there was no substance in his speech*, core, pith, character

essential *adj.* necessary, needed, vital, requisite ★**superfluous**

establish *v.* situate, place, station, found, organize, set up ★**upset**

estate *n.* property, land, fortune, inheritance

esteem *v.* honour, respect, admire, ▷*like* ★**dislike**

estimate *v.* consider, calculate, figure, assess, reckon

estrange *v.* alienate, antagonize, separate ★**unite**

eternal *adj.* endless, ceaseless, for ever, immortal, undying ★**temporary**

evacuate *v.* leave, desert, quit, ▷*abandon* ★**occupy**

evade *v.* elude, avoid, get away from, escape from ★**face**

evaporate *v.* vanish, dissolve, disappear, condense, dry up

even [1] *adj.* smooth, plane, flat, flush [2] balanced, equal ★**uneven** [3] yet, still

evening *n.* eve, eventide, sunset, ▷*dusk* ★**morning**

event *n.* occurrence, incident, happening

ever *adv.* always, evermore, perpetually, for ever ★**never**

everlasting *adj.* continual, endless, permanent, lasting ★**temporary**

everyday *adj.* common, frequent, daily, familiar ★**occasional**

everything *n.* all, the whole, the lot

evict *v.* expel, eject, cast out, remove, kick out

evidence *n.* appearance, proof, sign, token, testimony

evident *adj.* obvious, apparent, plain, visible, conspicuous ★**uncertain**

evil *v.* wicked, sinister, wrong, bad, hurtful, sinful ★**good**

exact *adj.* accurate, precise, definite, correct, ▷*right* ★**inexact**

exaggerate *v.* magnify, overstate, overestimate, amplify ★**modify**

examine *v.* check, inspect, scrutinize, test, quiz, question

example *n.* case, sample, specimen, pattern, model, illustration

exasperate *v.* provoke, anger, annoy, aggravate ★**soothe**

excavate *v.* mine, quarry, shovel, dig up, discover, unearth ★**bury**

exceed *v.* excel, surpass, better, beat, outstrip

excel *v.* outdo, ▷*exceed*

excellent *adj.* admirable, good, superb, exquisite, ▷*splendid* ★**inferior**

except *prep.* with the exception of, barring, save, saving, omitting

exceptional *adj.* unique, unusual, rare *Margaret has a rare gift for the piano*, uncommon ★**common**

excess *n.* too much, extreme, glut, extravagance, extreme, ▷*surplus* ★**scarcity**

exchange *v.* trade, barter, swap, convert, change

excite *v.* inflame, inspire, provoke, rouse, thrill ★**quell**

excited *adj.* ablaze, wild, ecstatic, frantic, thrilled ★**bored**

exclaim *v.* state, say, utter, ejaculate, declare, cry out

exclude *v.* bar, shut out, prevent, boycott, forbid, leave out ★**include**

exclusive *adj.* only, personal, choice, particular, special ★**inclusive**

excuse *v.* forgive, pardon, absolve, exempt, release ★**accuse**

execute *v.* accomplish, do, carry out *The work was carried out just as I had expected*, achieve [2] put to death, hang

exempt *v.* excuse, release, discharge, relieve, exonerate

exercise [1] *n.* performance, lesson, lecture, training [2] *v.* apply, train, practise *We have been practising our tennis for months*

exert *v.* apply, exercise, strain, struggle, toil

exhale *v.* breathe out, expel, expire ★**inhale**

exhaust [1] *v.* use up *We have used up all our butter*, consume, deplete, empty [2] overtire, fatigue, weaken

exhibition *n.* spectacle, show, fair, pageant, display

exhilarate *v.* invigorate, animate, stimulate, thrill ★**discourage**

exile *v.* deport, banish, relegate, transport, dismiss

exist *v.* be, live, breathe, subsist, stand

exit *n.* way out, outlet, egress, door

expand *v.* inflate, spread, dilate, extend, amplify, ▷*swell* ★**contract**

expansive *adj.* affable, genial, friendly, open, comprehensive

expect *v.* look out for, anticipate, assume, foresee, contemplate

expedition [1] *n.* outing, excursion, exploration, quest *As a child I spent long hours in the library in the quest for knowledge* [2] speed, dispatch, alacrity

expel *v.* evict, eject, discharge, throw out ★**admit**

expend *v.* spend, lay out, waste, consume, use up, ▷*exhaust* ★**save**

expensive *adj.* costly, dear, high-priced, valuable, rich ★**cheap**

experience [1] *n.* training, practice, wisdom, knowledge [2] *v.* encounter, try, undergo, endure

experiment *n.* trial, test, check, venture

expert *n.* specialist, master, authority, professional ★**novice**

expire [1] *v.* breathe out, exhale [2] die, lapse *The lease on this house will lapse at the end of the year*, run out ★**begin**

explain *v.* elucidate, spell out, define, expound, teach ★**mystify**

explanation *n.* definition, outline, answer, meaning

explode *v.* detonate, blow up, go off, burst, discharge

exploit [1] *n.* deed, feat, act, stunt [2] *v.* take advantage of, profit by

export *v.* ship, sent out, send abroad

expose *v.* show, reveal, exhibit, present, lay bare, betray ★**cover**

express [1] *v.* phrase, voice, put into words, utter [2] squeeze out [3] *adj.* speedy, fast

expression [1] *n.* phrase, idiom, sentence, statement [2] look, countenance, appearance

exquisite *adj.* dainty, subtle, fine, refined, ▷*beautiful* ★**coarse**

extend *v.* stretch, reach, lengthen, ▷*expand* ★**shorten**

extent *n.* breadth, expanse, width, bulk, mass, reach, duration

exterior [1] *n.* outside, surface [2] *adj.* external, outer, outdoor ★**interior**

extinct *adj.* defunct, dead, exterminated ★**living**

extinguish *v.* put out, blow out, abolish, destroy, quench ★**establish**

extract *v.* take out, select, remove, withdraw ★**insert**

extraordinary *adj.* unusual, incredible, strange, uncommon, marvellous ★**common**

extravagant *adj.* wasteful, reckless, prodigal, lavish ★**rational**

extreme [1] *adj.* excessive, outrageous, intense ★**moderate** [2] farthest, final, remote

extricate *v.* loose, loosen, remove, retrieve, pull out

exultant *adj.* rejoicing, jubilant, joyous, triumphant, ▷*elated* ★**depressed**

F f

fable n. myth, legend, story, fantasy ★**fact**

fabric n. cloth, textile, material

fabulous adj. imaginary, legendary *Robin Hood was a legendary figure, for he never existed,* mythical, marvellous, ▷*wonderful*

face [1] n. countenance, visage [2] front, frontage, façade *Although it was a new building, the old façade remained* [3] v. confront, be opposite

facetious adj. frivolous, jocular, humorous, witty, comical, ▷*funny* ★**serious**

facility n. ease, readiness, quickness, adroitness, knack

facsimile n. replica, copy, repro, photocopy

fact n. truth, deed, occurrence, event, reality, actuality ★**fiction**

factory n. plant, mill, works, shop

factual adj. true, actual, accurate, correct, ▷*real* ★**false**

fad n. craze, fashion, passion, desire, mania *My sister has a mania for cuddly toys,* vogue

fade v. discolour, bleach, dwindle, dim

fail v. collapse, fall, miss, trip, lose, flop ★**succeed**

failing n. frailty, weakness, fault, flaw, ▷*defect* ★**advantage**

failure n. collapse, crash, fiasco, downfall ★**success**

faint [1] adj. indistinct *The writing was so indistinct that we could hardly read it,* soft, low, dim, feeble [2] v. swoon, pass out, collapse
FEINT

fair [1] adj. just, equal, reasonable ★**unfair** [2] mediocre *He was not a good piano player, just mediocre,* middling, moderate [3] blonde, light-skinned, beautiful

faith n. trust, confidence, belief, fidelity, creed

faithful [1] adj. loyal, constant, staunch, true ★**faithless** [2] accurate, dependable *My watch is very dependable; it keeps accurate time* ★**inaccurate**

faithless adj. false, unfaithful, untrue ★**faithful**

fake adj. false, fictitious, pretended, ▷*bogus* ★**genuine**

fall [1] v. fall down, stumble, drop [2] decline, dwindle *My mother's shares had dwindled and were worth much less,* lower ★**rise**

fall down v. stumble, lose one's balance

fall through v. collapse, fail, founder *The family business had foundered during the recession*

fallacy n. flaw, fault, mistake, illusion, deception

false [1] adj. untrue, counterfeit, fake, inaccurate [2] dishonest, disloyal ★**reliable**

falsehood n. lie, fiction, fable, fabrication, untruth, fib ★**truth**

falter v. reel, totter, stumble, waver, tremble

fame n. glory, distinction, honour, eminence, renown

familiar [1] adj. common, frequent, well-known [2] intimate *Joe and Mary are intimate friends of mine,* close, dear

famine n. scarcity, hunger, shortage, starvation

famished adj. hungry, starving, ravenous

famous adj. famed, well-known, celebrated, legendary *My grandmother was very attractive: her beauty was legendary* ★**unknown**

fan v. ventilate, cool, blow, stimulate

fanatic n. enthusiast, zealot, follower, fan

fanciful adj. romantic, fantastic, imaginary, unreal ★**ordinary**

fancy [1] adj. decorative, beautiful, ornamental [2] v. desire, hanker after *I had been hankering after a sea trip all year,* yearn

fantastic adj. strange, bizarre, unfamiliar, romantic, ▷*fanciful* ★**ordinary**

far adj. distant, faraway, remote ★**near**

fare [1] v. manage *I managed quite well while my parents were abroad,* get along, happen [2] n. charge, cost, fee [3] food, meals, menu

farewell n. goodbye, parting, adieu

farm [1] v. cultivate, raise, grow [2] n. farmstead, homestead, holding *We owned a small holding of land in the west*

fascinate v. bewitch, beguile, enthall, engross ★**bore**

fashion [1] *n.* style, fad, mode, manner [2] *v.* form, carve, sculpt, devise

fast [1] *adj.* rapid, quick, speedy, brisk [2] *v.* starve, famish, go hungry

fasten *v.* fix, tie, attach, bind, hitch, truss **★unfasten**

fat *adj.* stout, corpulent *Uncle Harry was a corpulent old man,* ▷plump **★thin** [2] *n.* grease, oil, tallow

fatal *adj.* deadly, lethal, destructive, mortal **★harmless**

fate *n.* lot, portion, fortune, destiny, future FETE

fathom *v.* unravel, understand, follow, comprehend

fatigue [1] *n.* tiredness, weariness [2] *v.* tire, fag, exhaust, languish *The passengers from the shipwreck languished in an open boat*

fault [1] *n.* defect, flaw, imperfection [2] blame, responsibility, error

faulty *adj.* imperfect, defective, unreliable, unsound **★perfect**

favour [1] *n.* boon, courtesy, benefit [2] *v.* indulge, prefer, approve **★disapprove**

favourite [1] *n.* choice, darling, preference [2] *v.* best-liked, chosen, preferred

fawn *v.* crouch, crawl, grovel FAUN

fear [1] *n.* fright, alarm, terror, panic, shock **★courage** [2] *v.* dread, be afraid, doubt

fearful *adj.* timid, anxious, alarmed, worried, ▷afraid **★courageous**

fearless *adj.* gallant, courageous, daring, valiant *Despite her illness, my mother made a valiant effort to recover,* ▷brave **★timid**

feast *n.* banquet, repast, dinner

feat *n.* deed, exploit, achievement, performance, stunt FEET

feature *n.* mark, peculiarity, distinction, characteristic

fee *n.* charge, commission, cost

feeble *adj.* frail, faint, flimsy, puny, ▷weak **★strong**

feed *v.* nourish, sustain, foster, nurture *These plants must be nurtured if they are to survive*

feel *v.* touch, handle, perceive, comprehend, know, suffer

Feat

Feet

feign *v.* fake, pretend, act, sham FAIN

feint *n.* bluff, pretence, dodge, deception FAINT

fellow *n.* companion, mate, associate, colleague

female *adj.* feminine, womanly, girlish, maidenly **★male**

fence [1] *n.* barrier, paling, barricade [2] *v.* dodge, evade, parry *The morning attack was parried by the defenders,* duel

ferocious *adj.* fierce, savage, brutal, grim, vicious **★gentle**

fertile *adj.* fruitful, productive, rich, abundant **★barren**

fervent *adj.* warm, passionate, enthusiastic, zealous ▷ardent

festival *n.* celebration, carnival, fête, jubilee

festive *adj.* convivial, jovial, sociable, gleeful, cordial ★**sombre**

fetch *v.* bear, bring, carry, deliver, convey

fête *n.* bazaar, carnival, fair, festival FATE

fetter *v.* manacle, handcuff, shackle, restrain

feud *n.* dispute, grudge, conflict, discord ★**harmony**

fever *n.* illness, infection, passion, excitement

few *adj.* scant, scanty, meagre, paltry, not many

fiasco *n.* washout, calamity, disaster, failure

fib *n.* lie, falsehood, untruth

fickle *adj.* unstable, changeable, faithless, disloyal ★**constant**

fiction *n.* stories, fable, myth, legend, invention ★**fact**

fidelity *n.* faithfulness, loyalty, allegiance *I owe allegiance to my family and my country* ★**treachery**

fidget *v.* be nervous, fret, fuss, jiggle, squirm

field *n.* farmland, grassland, green, verdure, meadow

fiend *n.* devil, demon, imp, beast, brute

fiendish *adj.* atrocious, cruel, devilish, diabolical

fierce *adj.* barbarous, cruel, brutal, merciless, ▷*savage* ★**gentle**

fiery *adj.* passionate, inflamed, excitable, flaming ★**impassive**

fight *n. & v.* conflict, encounter, combat, contest, battle

figure 1 *n.* symbol, character, numeral 2 form, shape, model 3 *v.* calculate, reckon *Bella has reckoned the amount correctly*

filch *v.* steal, thieve, sneak, purloin *Someone has purloined the letters from our mailbox*

file 1 *v.* scrape, grind, grate, rasp 2 *n.* binder, case, folder

fill *v.* load, pack, cram, replenish, occupy ★**empty**

filter *v.* sieve, sift, refine, clarify, screen, percolate PHILTRE

filth *n.* impurity, dirt, soil, slime, smut ★**purity**

filthy *adj.* unclean, impure, nasty, foul, ▷*dirty* ★**pure**

final *adj.* terminal, closing, ultimate, conclusive, ▷*last*

find *v.* discover, achieve, locate, obtain, perceive, meet with *Our plans met with the approval of the committee* ★**lose** FINED

fine 1 *adj.* thin, minute, smooth, slender 2 excellent, sharp, keen, acute 3 *n.* forfeit penalty

finesse *n.* skill, competence, deftness

finger 1 *v.* feel, grope, handle, touch 2 *n.* digit, thumb

finish *v.* accomplish, complete, close, conclude, ▷*end* ★**begin**

fire 1 *n.* blaze, conflagration, heat 2 *v.* ignite, light, discharge

firm 1 *adj.* stable, steady, solid, substantial 2 *n.* company, business

first *adj.* beginning, earliest, initial, chief, principal

fishy *adj.* suspicious, dubious, doubtful ★**honest**

fissure *n.* breach, cleft, crack, cranny FISHER

fit *adj.* suitable, fitting, able, trim, hale, healthy

fitting *adj.* proper, suitable, appropriate, correct ★**unsuitable**

fix 1 *v.* repair, mend, attach, fasten 2 *n.* predicament, jam, pickle, plight *After the earthquake, the town was in a desperate plight*

flabby *adj.* baggy, drooping, feeble, sagging, slack

flag 1 *v.* droop, languish, dwindle, fail 2 banner, ensign, colours *The regimental colours were flying at half-mast*

flagrant *adj.* arrant, blatant, bold, brazen ★**secret**

flair *n.* knack, talent, faculty, ability, gift FLARE

flame *n.* fire, blaze, radiance

flap *v.* agitate, flutter, wave, swing, dangle

flare 1 *v.* blaze, burn, glare, flash, glow 2 *n.* signal, beacon FLAIR

flash *v.* gleam, glimmer, sparkle, twinkle, scintillate

flat 1 *adj.* level, smooth, even, horizontal 2 *n.* apartment, chambers

flatter *v.* blandish, toady, soft-soap, butter up, curry favour *He gives me presents, but only to curry favour with me* ★**criticize**

Flags

Signalling flags

Jack

Banner

Burgee

Streamer

Standard

Pennant

Ensign

Jolly Roger

Bunting

flavour *n.* taste, savour, tang, aroma, quality

flaw *n.* fault, defect, blemish, mark, weakness

flawless *adj.* perfect, immaculate, faultless, sound ⋆**imperfect**

flee *v.* escape, abscond, run away, bolt, vanish ⋆**stay** FLEA

fleet 1 *adj.* rapid, speedy, quick, nimble, ▷*swift* ⋆**slow** 2 navy, armada, flotilla *A flotilla of gunboats sailed up the river*

fleeting *adj.* passing, brief, momentary, temporary ⋆**lasting**

flexible *adj.* pliant, pliable, supple, elastic

flicker *v.* blaze, glitter, flare, burn, sparkle

flimsy *adj.* slight, meagre, fragile, trivial ⋆**sturdy**

flinch *v.* cower, cringe, shrink, wince *I had twisted my ankle, and winced with pain as I climbed from the hill*

fling *v.* pitch, throw, cast, heave, ▷*hurl*

flippant *adj.* saucy, pert, brash, cheeky, glib ⋆**earnest**

float *v.* drift, glide, hover, sail, swim

flock *n.* herd, drove, crush, group

flog *v.* beat, chastize, flay, lash, spank

flood *v.* deluge, engulf, inundate *The town was inundated after the river overflowed*, drown

floor *n.* deck, base, bottom, platform, level, storey

flop *v.* flap, fall, drop, droop, fall flat

florid *adj.* ruddy, flushed, red, ornate ⋆**pale**

flounce *v.* bounce, fling, jerk, spring, bob

flounder 1 *v.* bungle, fail, falter, fumble 2 *n.* flatfish

flour *n.* meal, bran, farina FLOWER

flourish 1 *v.* shake, brandish, flaunt 2 blossom, bloom, prosper, ▷*thrive*

flow *v.* run, stream, glide, sweep, swirl, ▷*gush* FLOE

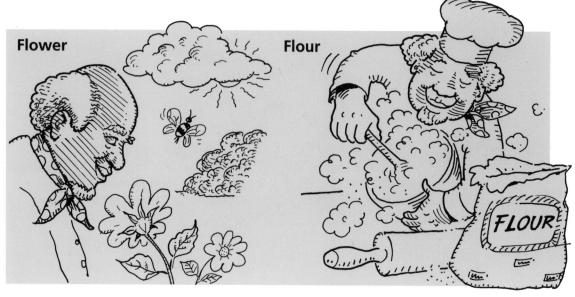

Flower **Flour**

flower *n. & v.* blossom, bloom, bud FLOUR

fluent *adj.* vocal, facile, articulate *Sally is very articulate, and has a great command of language,* flowing, fluid

fluid *adj.* watery, flowing, liquid, runny **★solid**

flummox *v.* baffle, confuse, fluster, confound, ▷*bewilder* **★explain**

flush 1 *v.* glow, bloom, blush 2 douche, drench, rinse 3 *adj.* level, even

fluster *v.* bother, confuse, perturb, ▷*fuss* **★calm**

flutter *v.* wave, flap, flop, flitter, hover, flit

fly 1 *v.* take flight, glide, soar, float 2 escape, hasten 3 *n.* winged insect

foam *n.* froth, scum, lather, suds, surf

foe *n.* enemy, opponent, rival, adversary **★friend**

fog *n.* mist, vapour, haze, cloud

foil 1 *v.* defeat, overcome, elude 2 *n.* sheet metal, film, flake

fold *n. & v.* crease, hem, seam, crimp, pleat FOALED

follow 1 *v.* pursue, succeed, come after 2 understand, catch on to

folly *n.* silliness, foolishness, absurdity, craziness, ▷*nonsense* **★wisdom**

fond *adj.* tender, loving, caring, ▷*affectionate* **★hostile**

fondle *v.* pet, stroke, cuddle, caress, coddle **★tease**

food *n.* nourishment, nutriment, provender, provisions, fare

fool 1 *n.* idiot, dunce, clown, blockhead, simpleton 2 *v.* deceive, trick, swindle

foolhardy *adj.* reckless, impetuous, madcap, ▷*rash* **★cautious**

foolish *adj.* absurd, daft, ridiculous, ▷*silly* **★wise**

for *prep.* on behalf of, towards, because of **★against** FORE, FOUR

forbid *v.* bar, ban, prohibit, deter, hinder, prevent **★allow**

force 1 *n.* energy, strength, might, power 2 *v.* make, compel, coerce *It's no use, you can't coerce me into flying home,* push

fore *adj.* first, front, leading FOR, FOUR

forecast *v.* foresee, predict, foretell, prophesy

foreign *adj.* alien, strange, remote, outlandish **★domestic**

foremost *adj.* chief, leading, principal, uppermost

forfeit *v.* abandon, give up, lose, relinquish, sacrifice **★reward**

forge 1 *v.* counterfeit, falsify, copy, imitate 2 construct, form, make, fashion

forgery *n.* fake, dud, counterfeit, imitation, phoney

forget *v.* overlook, neglect, lose sight of **★remember**

forgive *v.* pardon, absolve, reprieve, let off, overlook **★blame**

forlorn *adj.* lonely, desolate, miserable, wretched ★**hopeful**

form 1 *v.* make, fabricate, fashion, contrive, create 2 *n.* manner, fashion, style 3 shape, figure *Models need to have an excellent figure*

formal *adj.* stiff, solemn, ceremonial, ritual, aloof ★**informal**

former *adj.* earlier, previous, prior, ★**later**

formidable *adj.* awful, terrible, alarming, terrifying, serious ★**trivial**

forsake *v.* abandon, give up, desert, discard, leave, ▷*quit* ★**resume**

forth *adv.* ahead, forward, onward, outward

forthright *adj.* frank, candid, direct, bald, blunt ★**devious**

forthwith *adv.* immediately, directly, at once, instantly ★**soon**

fortify 1 *v.* strengthen, confirm, corroborate, hearten 2 garrison, protect, buttress *The old house was crumbling, and the walls needed to be buttressed* ★**weaken**

fortitude *n.* courage, endurance, braveness, composure, ▷*strength* ★**cowardice**

fortunate *adj.* happy, felicitous, auspicious, rosy, ▷*lucky* ★**unfortunate**

fortune 1 *n.* affluence, wealth, treasure 2 chance, destiny, fate

forward 1 *adv.* onward, forth, ahead, before 2 *adj.* progressive, bold, audacious ★**modest** 3 advance, send, transmit

foster 1 *v.* help, promote, aid 2 care for, cherish, nurse

foul *adj.* mucky, nasty, filthy, dirty, murky ★**fair** FOWL

found *v.* create, build, erect, establish

foundation *n.* establishment, base, basis, groundwork *You will soon pick up Spanish, for you already know the groundwork*

fountain *n.* spring, well, reservoir, source

fowl *n.* bird, chicken, poultry FOUL

foxy *adj.* crafty, slick, cunning, tricky, ▷*artful* ★**naïve**

fraction *n.* portion, part, division, ▷*fragment*

fracture *n.* break, cleft, crack, fissure, opening, ▷*split*

fragile *adj.* brittle, frail, delicate, dainty, ▷*flimsy* ★**robust**

fragment *n.* portion, bit, chip, morsel, piece, ▷*fracture*

fragrance *n.* aroma, smell, odour, ▷*scent*

frail *adj.* weak, feeble, infirm, ▷*fragile*

frame *n.* framework, casing, shape, mount, chassis

frank *adj.* sincere, candid, open, honest, blunt, ▷*truthful* ★**insincere**

frantic *adj.* excited, furious, distracted, wild, mad, ▷*frenzied* ★**calm**

fraud *n.* deceit, fake, extortion, swindle, ▷*forgery*

fraudulent *adj.* sham, fake, counterfeit, ▷*bogus* ★**genuine**

fray *n.* combat, contest, battle, brawl, ▷*rumpus*

freak *adj.* abnormal, bizarre *I felt so strange in that bizarre world*, queer, odd, unusual ★**common**

free 1 *adj.* unhindered, at liberty, liberated, unrestricted 2 gratuitous, gratis, without cost 3 *v.* let loose, unleash, release

freeze *n.* glaciate, ice, frost, refrigerate FREES, FRIEZE

frenzied *adj.* agitated, excited, furious, hysterical, ▷*frantic* ★**placid**

frequent *adj.* repeated, numerous, recurrent, common, ▷*regular* ★**rare**

frequently *adv.* often, many times, commonly ★**rarely**

fresh *adj.* new, young, vigorous, blooming, recent, wholesome ★**stale**

fret *v.* worry, harass, irritate, torment, ▷*vex* ★**calm**

friction 1 *n.* rubbing, grating, contact, abrasion 2 ill-feeling, discord, dispute

friend *n.* companion, associate, ally, crony *On Saturdays, my father plays cards with some of his cronies*, pal, ▷*chum*

friendly *adj.* affable, amicable, kindly, cordial, ▷*genial* ★**hostile**

friendship *n.* affection, fellowship, fondness, harmony, ▷*concord* ★**enmity**

fright *n.* alarm, dread, dismay, terror, ▷*fear* ★**calm**

frighten *v.* daunt, dismay, scare, alarm, ▷*terrify* ★**reassure**

frightful *adj.* alarming, shocking, ghastly, ▷*horrible* ★**pleasant**

frigid *adj.* cool, chilly, icy, frozen, wintry ★**warm**

fringe *n.* edge, border, limits, outskirts

frisky *adj.* lively, spirited, playful, active ★**quiet**

frivolous *adj.* frothy, facetious, flippant, foolish, ▷*trivial* ★**serious**

frock *n.* robe, dress, gown, smock

frolic *v.* gambol, caper, frisk, sport

front *n.* fore, brow, forehead, face, façade, beginning ★**back**

frontier *n.* border, boundary, edge, limit

frosty *adj.* chilly, frigid, frozen, freezing, ▷*cold* ★**warm**

froth *n.* scum, bubbles, ▷*foam*

frown *v.* glower, grimace, glare, ▷*scowl* ★**smile**

frugal *adj.* thrifty, economical, careful, sparing *We were poor in the old days, and needed to be sparing with our money,* ▷*meagre* ★**wasteful**

Futile

I shall go in for the race but it's a forlorn hope I shall win!

fruitful *adj.* fertile, productive, flourishing ★**barren**

fruitless *adj.* unprofitable, sterile, barren, pointless ★**fruitful**

frustrate *v.* thwart, balk, foil, hinder, defeat ★**fulfil**

fugitive *n.* escaper, runaway, deserter

fulfil *v.* perform, render, please, accomplish, achieve ★**frustrate**

full *adj.* loaded, packed, laden, charged, abundant, complete ★**empty**

fumble *v.* grope, spoil, mismanage, flail, ▷*bungle*

fun *n.* sport, frolic, gaiety, jollity, entertainment, amusement

function ①　*n.* service, purpose, activity ② affair, party, gathering ③　*v.* act, operate, work

fund *n.* stock, supply, pool, store, treasury *The city treasury has a good surplus this year*

fundamental *adj.* basic, essential, primary, essential ★**unimportant**

funny *adj.* comical, droll, amusing, ridiculous, ▷*humorous* ★**solemn**

furious *adj.* agitated, angry, fierce, intense, ▷*frantic* ★**calm**

furnish ①　*v.* supply, provide, offer ② equip, fit out

furrow *n.* groove, channel, hollow, seam, rib

further *adj.* extra, more, other, supplementary, *v.* advanced, aid, hasten

furtive *adj.* secretive, sly, hidden, ▷*stealthy* ★**open**

fury *n.* anger, frenzy, ferocity, passion, ▷*rage* ★**calm**

fuse *v.* melt, smelt, combine, merge, solder, ▷*join*

fuss *n.* stir, excitement, tumult, bustle, ▷*ado* ★**calm**

fussy *adj.* busy, faddish, fastidious, finicky, exacting ★**plain**

futile *adj.* useless, in vain, hopeless, barren, forlorn *I shall go in for the race, but it's a forlorn hope that I could win,* ineffective ★**effective**

future *adj.* forthcoming, coming, impending, eventual

fuzzy *adj.* murky, foggy, misty, unclear

G g

gain *v.* get, win, acquire, attain, profit

gale *n.* storm, wind, hurricane

gallant *adj.* courageous, noble, chivalrous, ▷*brave*

gallop *v.* dash, run, career, rush

gamble *v.* bet, risk, wager, chance GAMBOL

gambol *v.* prance, romp, frisk, frolic, ▷*jump* GAMBLE

game [1] *n.* sport, pastime, contest, competition *★work [2] *n.* quarry, prey

gammon *n.* ham, bacon

gang *n.* crew, team, troop, crowd, cluster, party

gap *n.* space, blank, hole, break, cranny, chink, opening, crack, interval

gape *v.* yawn, stare, gaze, gawk, ▷*look*

garbage, *n.* trash, rubbish, refuse, waste, slops

garden *n.* yard, patio, park

garment *n.* clothes, dress, attire, robe, costume, ▷*clothing*

garret *n.* attic, loft, back room

gas *n.* vapour, fume, mist, smoke

gasp *v.* gulp, pant, choke, ▷*breathe*

gate *n.* door, portal, gateway GAIT

gather [1] *v.* collect, pick up, pick, draw, amass, assemble, flock, hoard, acquire *★disperse [2] *v.* understand *I understand that you have been elected chair*, presume, judge

gathering *n.* meeting, assembly, function, affair, company, collection

gaudy *adj.* flashy, cheap, tawdry, loud, showy

gaunt, *adj.* thin, lean, skinny, spare, ▷*haggard ★robust*

gauge [1] *n.* measure, meter, rule [2] *v.* judge, measure, estimate *We must estimate what the weather conditions will be*, probe GAGE

gaze *v.* stare, look, regard, contemplate

gear *n.* tackle, array, accessories, machinery, harness, equipment

gem *n.* jewel, stone, treasure

general *adj.* normal, usual, habitual, customary, total, whole *★local*

generous *adj.* free, liberal, kind *★selfish*

genial *adj.* cheerful, cheery, sunny, hearty, cordial, ▷*jolly ★cold*

genius *n.* brilliance, prowess, talent, power, skill, cleverness, brains *★stupidity*

genteel *adj.* refined, polished, civil, courteous, well-bred, polite, elegant *★boorish*

gentle [1] *adj.* easy, mild, soft, kind, moderate, tender, humane [2] *adj.* gradual, faint, feeble, slight *The field had a slight slope as it came down to the river*

genuine [1] *adj.* real, authentic, true, sound [2] *adj.* sincere, honest, candid, frank *★false*

germ *n.* microbe, seed, embryo, nucleus

gesture *n.* sign, signal, motion, nod, shrug, movement

get [1] *v.* acquire, obtain, gain, win, receive, secure, achieve, inherit *★forfeit [2] *v.* understand, catch on *It took little Johnny some time to catch on to what I meant*, fathom, figure out, learn

get up *v.* arise, awake, awaken

get rid of *v.* discard, reject, throw away, scrap

ghastly *adj.* shocking, frightful, hideous, horrible, fearful, terrible

ghost *n.* spook, spirit, spectre, banshee, phantom

ghostly *v.* uncanny, haunted, eerie, weird

giant *adj.* mammoth, huge, colossal, enormous, tremendous, immense, ▷*big, gigantic ★tiny*

gibber *v.* gabble, prattle, jabber

gibberish *n.* nonsense, drivel, rubbish

gibe *v.* jeer, sneer, scoff, deride, ▷*taunt*

giddy *adj.* dizzy, whirling, reeling, unsteady, wild, reckless

gift [1] *n.* present, donation, bounty, boon [2] *n.* talent, skill *Her skill was so great, that I knew she must have been born with it*, ability, power

gigantic *adj.* stupendous, titanic, colossal, ▷*giant ★minute*

giggle *v.* chuckle, chortle, cackle, snigger, ▷*laugh*

gingerly *adv.* carefully, daintily, warily, cautiously

girder *n.* rafter, joist, beam

girl *n.* maid, maiden, miss, damsel, young woman, lass, wench

girlish *adj.* maidenly, dainty, feminine

girth *n.* circumference, perimeter, fatness, breadth

gist *n.* essence, substance, kernel, nub, pith

give 1 *v.* donate, grant, distribute, bestow 2 *v.* bend, yield *The wooden footbridge soon yielded under his weight and crashed into the stream*, relax, recede 3 *v.* produce, yield 4 *v.* pronounce, utter, emit, ★**take**

give back *v.* return, restore

give forth *v.* emit, send out, radiate

give in *v.* surrender, quit, yield

give off *v.* belch, emit, exude

give up *v.* surrender, give in, relinquish, hand over

giver *n.* donor, bestower, presenter

glad *adj.* joyful, joyous, delighted, pleased, ▷*happy* ★**sorry**

gladden *v.* make happy, gratify, delight, elate, ▷*please* ★**grieve**

gladly *adv.* freely, readily, cheerfully, willingly

glamour *n.* romance, interest, fascination, attraction, enchantment

glance 1 *n.* look, glimpse, peep 2 *v.* peer, notice 3 *v.* brush, graze, shave *The bullet merely grazed his head*

glare 1 *v.* blaze, glow, flare, sparkle, dazzle 2 frown, glower, stare

glaring 1 *adj.* sparkling, dazzling 2 *adj.* blatant, notorious, conspicuous

glass *n.* tumbler, goblet, beaker, mirror, looking-glass

glaze *v.* polish, gloss, burnish, varnish

gleam *v.* sparkle, glitter, flash, glisten, twinkle

glee *n.* jollity, gaiety, elation, triumph, ▷*happiness*

glib *adj.* fluent, slick, smooth, facile, talkative

glide *v.* slide, slither, slip, soar, sail, skate, skim

glimmer *v.* sparkle, scintillate, flicker, glow, gleam

glimpse *v.* spy, spot, glance, view

glisten *v.* shine, glitter, glow, gleam

glitter *v.* gleam, sparkle, flash, glint, glisten, scintillate

gloat *v.* whoop, exult, crow, revel, triumph

globe *n.* ball, sphere, planet, earth, world

gloom *n.* darkness, gloaming, dusk, shadow, dimness, bleakness ★**light**

gloomy *adj.* cheerless, black, dark, bleak, cloudy, overcast, dismal, dour, glum, melancholy, ▷*dreary* ★**happy**

glorious *adj.* brilliant, lustrous, noble, exalted, renowned, ▷*splendid* ★**dull**

glory *n.* brilliance, radiance, pride, ▷*splendour*

gloss *n.* lustre, sheen, shimmer, polish, ▷*glaze*

glossy *adj.* shiny, burnished, sleek, slick, polished

glow *n. & v.* glare, glitter, bloom, blush, flush, shine, gleam, twinkle

glower *v.* frown, stare, scowl, glare

glue 1 *n.* gum, paste, cement, plaster, adhesive, mucilage 2 *v.* stick, fasten

glum *adj.* sullen, sulky, morose, miserable, dejected, downcast, ▷*gloomy*

glut *n.* abundance, plenty, too much, surplus

glutton *n.* gorger, stuffer, crammer, pig, gormandizer, gourmand

gnash *v.* grind, champ, bite, crunch

gnaw *v.* chew, nibble, bite, champ, consume

go 1 *v.* walk, pass, move, travel, depart, proceed 2 *v.* stretch, reach, extend *The prairie extended as far as the mountain range*

go after *v.* pursue, chase, follow

go ahead *v.* progress, proceed, continue

go away *v.* leave, depart, vanish, disappear

go back *v.* return, resume, withdraw

go by *v.* pass, elapse, vanish

go in *v.* enter, advance, invade, penetrate

go in for *v.* enter, take part, participate, compete

go off *v.* explode, blow up, depart

go on *v.* continue, advance, proceed, move ahead, keep up

go up *v.* climb, mount, rise, ▷*ascend*

goad *v.* prod, incite, impel, drive, urge, sting, worry

goal *n.* target, ambition, aim, object, destination

gobble *v.* devour, gorge, swallow, gulp, bolt

goblin *n.* sprite, demon, gnome, elf

God *n*. the Creator, the Father, the Almighty, Jehovah, the Divinity, the Holy Spirit, King of Kings, the Supreme Being

godless *adj*. unholy, unclean, wicked, savage, profane **★righteous**

golden *adj*. excellent, precious, brilliant, bright

good [1] *adj*. excellent, admirable, fine [2] favourable, *Spring is a favourable time to clean the house* advantageous, profitable, [3] righteous, moral, true *My neighbours are nice people, honest and true* [4] clever, skilful, expert [5] fit, proper, suited **★bad**

goodness *n*. excellence, merit, worth, honesty, kindness, ▷*virtue* **★evil**

goods *n*. wares, commodities, cargo, load, material, belongings

gorge [1] *v*. swallow, gulp, devour, ▷*eat* [2] *n*. canyon, glen, valley

gorgeous *adj*. beautiful, ravishing, stunning, superb, magnificent

gossip *v*. chat, chatter, talk, tittle-tattle

gouge *v*. excavate, groove, dig out

govern *v*. rule, reign, manage, direct, guide, control, conduct, command

government *n*. rule, administration, supervision, parliament, council, command, authority

governor *n*. director, manager, leader, chief, overseer, head of state

gown *n*. robe, dress, frock

grace *n*. elegance, refinement, polish, symmetry, ▷*beauty*

graceful *adj*. beautiful, lovely, shapely, refined, ▷*elegant*

gracious *adj*. amiable, kind, suave, urbane, affable, elegant **★churlish**

grade [1] *n*. class, rank, degree [2] *n*. slope, gradient, incline, slant

gradual *adj*. by degrees, step by step, continuous, little by little **★sudden**

graft [1] *v*. splice, insert, bud, plant [2] *n*. bribery, corruption

grain *n*. fibre, crumb, seed, particle, atom, bit, drop

grand *adj*. splendid, impressive, stately, magnificent, wonderful, superb

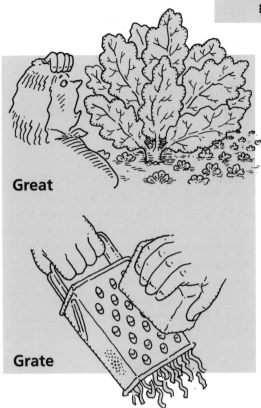

Great

Grate

grandeur *n*. magnificence, splendour, majesty, lordliness

grant [1] *n*. bounty, award, subsidy [2] *v*. bestow, donate *We all donated some money to help the earthquake victims*, confer, give

grapple *v*. struggle, tussle, wrestle, seize, grasp, clutch

grasp [1] *v*. grip, seize, take, grab, hold [2] *v*. understand, comprehend

grasping *adj*. greedy, avaricious, covetous, miserly **★generous**

grate [1] *v*. rasp, file, jar, clash, rub, grind [2] *v*. annoy, irritate, vex [3] *n*. fireplace GREAT

grateful *adj*. thankful, appreciative, obliged, indebted

gratify *v*. delight, satisfy, please, content, enchant, indulge, favour **★displease**

gratitude *n*. thankfulness, appreciation, obligation

grave [1] *adj*. solemn, sober, momentous, dignified, majestic [2] *adj*. essential, important *I have important news to reveal* [3] *n*. tomb, vault, shrine

gravity [1] *n*. seriousness, solemnity, importance, significance [2] *n*. force, gravitation, weight

graze 1 *v.* scrape, brush, shave, glance 2 browse, crop, bite GREYS

grease *n.* fat, suet, tallow, oil

great 1 *adj.* large, considerable, bulky, huge, ample 2 important, elevated, noted *Here is a list of noted citizens of this town* 3 main, chief, principal GRATE

greedy *adj.* gluttonish, voracious, grasping, selfish, acquisitive ★**unselfish**

green 1 *adj.* emerald, jade, turquoise 2 *adj.* ungrown, immature, raw *During the war, many recruits to the army were raw country lads*, untrained ★**expert**

greet *v.* welcome, accost, hail, salute, salaam, address

grief *n.* woe, sadness, regret, distress, anguish, ▷*sorrow* ★**joy**

grievance *n.* injury, hardship, complaint, wrong, trial ★**boon**

grieve *v.* lament, deplore, mourn, sorrow, be sad, afflict, hurt ★**rejoice**

grievous *adj.* lamentable, deplorable, grave, critical, severe, mortal

grill 1 *v.* fry, broil, griddle 2 *n.* grating, grid

grim 1 *adj.* serious, stern, harsh, solemn, dour, forbidding 2 *adj.* horrid, dreadful, terrible, ▷*sombre* ★**mild**

grime *n.* smut, soil, dust, soot, ▷*dirt*

grin *n.* & *v.* smile, beam, smirk, simper

grind 1 *v.* scrape, file, crush, powder 2 *v.* sharpen, whet, grate

grip *v.* grasp, grab, snatch, clasp, seize, ▷*hold* ★**loosen**

grisly *adj.* horrid, horrible, dreadful, ghastly, ▷*grim*

grit 1 *n.* powder, dust, sand, gravel 2 nerve, mettle, pluck, ▷*courage*

groan *v.* moan, complain, grumble, creak GROWN

groom 1 *n.* husband, bridegroom 2 *n.* stable-boy, servant, ostler 3 *v.* spruce, prim, tidy, preen

groove *n.* furrow, ridge, corrugation, channel, rut, score

grope *v.* feel, handle, finger, manipulate, touch, pick

Groups of Animals

a chatter of budgerigars
a drey of squirrels
a drove of cattle
a flock of birds
a herd of elephants
a mob of kangaroos
a pack of wolves
a pride of lions
a school of porpoises
a sloth of bears
a swarm of bees
a troop of monkeys
a colony of seals
a cete of badgers
a skulk of foxes
a litter of cats

gross 1 *adj.* large, bulky, unwieldy, massive 2 coarse, vulgar, crude 3 outrageous, glaring, flagrant *The car driver was arrested for a flagrant disregard of the safety rules*

grotesque *adj.* deformed, malformed, misshapen, freakish, abnormal, bizarre, odd, fantastic

ground 1 *n.* dry land, soil, earth, dust 2 bottom, base, foundation

grounds 1 *n.* foundation, cause, basis, excuse 2 dregs, sediment, silt 3 garden, parkland, estate

Growls, grunts, and other animal noises

Bees buzz	Horses neigh
Cats meow	Lions roar
Cockerels crow	Mice squeak
Cows moo	Owls hoot
Dogs bark	Pigs grunt
Dogs also growl	Snakes hiss
Ducks quack	Wolves howl

group 1 *n.* division, section, branch 2 gang, throng, cluster, bunch, class, set

grovel *v.* fawn, crouch, crawl, toady, cringe, wallow, cower

grow 1 *v.* increase, advance, expand, extend, develop, raise 2 *v.* sprout, germinate, shoot

growl *v.* snarl, snap, threaten, thunder

growth *n.* expansion, development, advance, ▷*increase*

grow up *v.* mature, develop, ripen

grubby *adj.* messy, dirty, mucky

grudge *n. & v.* hate, envy, dislike, spite

gruesome *adj.* frightful, hideous, ghastly, ▷*grisly*

gruff *adj.* husky, throaty, croaky, blunt, churlish, crusty, curt ★**affable**

grumble *v.* complain, snivel, murmur, growl, protest

grumpy *adj.* disgruntled, dissatisfied, surly, sour, irritable, sullen ★**affable**

grunt *n. & v.* snort, groan ★**growl**

guarantee *n.* warranty, assurance, security, pledge

guard 1 *n.* protector, sentry, guardian, watchman 2 *v.* protect, defend, watch over, shelter, shield

guess *v.* surmise, conjecture, judge, think, suspect, suppose

guest *n.* visitor, caller GUESSED

guide 1 *n.* pilot, director, leader, controller 2 *v.* steer, navigate, lead, direct, manage, conduct *Our teacher conducted us to the bus, and we all climbed aboard*

guild *n.* club, trade union, association, federation, fellowship, band, society

guile *n.* knavery, foul play, trickery, deceit, cunning, fraud ★**honesty**

guilty *adj.* blameworthy, sinful, wicked, wrong ★**innocent**

guise *n.* garb, pose, posture, role, aspect, appearance GUYS

gulch *n.* valley, gully, ravine

gulf 1 *n.* bay, basin, inlet 2 *n.* chasm, opening, abyss, depths

gullible *adj.* credulous, innocent, naïve, trusting

gully *n.* trench, ditch, channel, ravine

gulp *v.* swallow, consume, guzzle, devour

gum *n.* paste, cement, ▷*glue*

gun *n.* rifle, cannon, revolver, pistol, automatic, shotgun

gurgle *v.* ripple, murmur, purl, babble

gush *v.* stream, spurt, spout, flow, run, pour out

gust *n.* blast, blow, squall, wind

gusto *n.* relish, zest, eagerness, zeal, pleasure

gutter *n.* moat, ditch, dike, drain, gully, channel, groove

guzzle *v.* gulp, imbibe, drink, swill, quaff

H h

habit [1] *n.* routine, way, custom, practice, rule [2] mannerism *Jim had a mannerism of holding his ear as he thought*, addiction, trait

hack *v.* chop, mangle, gash, slash

hackneyed *adj.* stale, trite, commonplace, tired ***new**

hag *n.* crone, harridan, witch, virago *I know I have a temper, but Julia is a real virago*

haggard *adj.* drawn, wan, pinched, thin, ▷*gaunt* ***hale**

haggle *v.* bargain, barter, bicker, dispute ***yield**

hail [1] *v.* salute, call to, accost, welcome, greet [2] *n.* shower, storm, torrent *Last summer it rained in torrents* HALE

hair *n.* locks, mane, tresses, strand

hale *adj.* hearty, robust, sound, fit, ▷*healthy* ***ill** HAIL

half *n.* division, fraction, segment

hall *n.* entrance, saloon, corridor, lobby, vestibule *Tom was waiting for us in the hotel vestibule* HAUL

hallow *v.* sanctify, consecrate, bless, dedicate, make holy

hallucination *n.* illusion, fantasy, delusion, mirage, dream ***reality**

halt *v.* end, pause, rest, cease, *stop* ***start**

halting *adj.* faltering, hestitating, wavering, awkward ***fluent**

hammer [1] *v.* beat, pound, bang [2] *n.* mallet, gavel *The leader banged his gavel on the desk and called for order*

hamper [1] *v.* hinder, interfere, impede, curb ***aid** [2] *n.* basket, creel *We watched the fishermen carrying creels of herring*, crate

hand [1] *v.* give, pass, present, yield [2] *n.* fist, palm

handicap *n.* defect, disability, drawback, restriction ***advantage**

handicraft *n.* skill, hobby, art, workmanship, craft, occupation

handle [1] *n.* shaft, holder, grip [2] *v.* feel, touch, finger, work, wield

Habitations

Apartment
Bungalow
Cabin
Castle
Chalet
Chateau
Cottage
Flat
Hacienda
Igloo
Lodge
Mansion
Palace
Ranch-house
Shack
Shanty
Villa

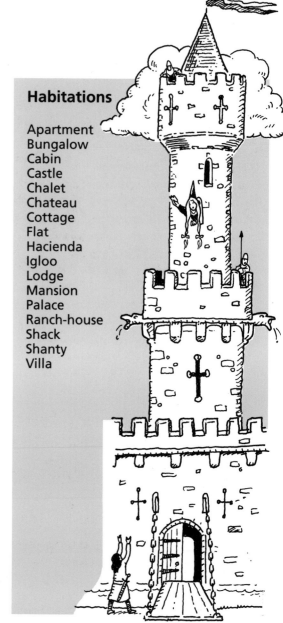

handsome [1] *adj.* good-looking, graceful, attractive [2] generous, lavish *Aunt Betsy is always so lavish with presents for the children.* HANSOM

handy *adj.* ready, convenient, deft, skilled ***clumsy**

hang *v.* dangle, suspend, sag, droop, swing

hanker for *v.* long for, yearn for, crave, desire ***dislike**

haphazard *adj.* accidental, random, aimless, casual, ▷*chance* ***deliberate**

hapless *adj.* ill-fated, luckless, unlucky, ▷*miserable* ***lucky**

happen *v.* occur, take place, come about, result

happening n. event, incident, occurrence, occasion

happiness n. delight, ecstasy, gaiety, joy, enjoyment, ▷bliss ***unhappiness**

happy adj. cheerful, blithe, content, joyous, jubilant, ▷merry ***unhappy**

harass v. beset, annoy, upset, bother, ▷distress ***assist**

harbour 1 n. port, anchorage, mooring 2 refuge, shelter, safety *At last we were back in the safety of our home,* 3 v. give shelter to

hard 1 adj. firm, stony, rocky, solid ***soft** 2 difficult, tough *I had a very tough problem to solve,* perplexing ***easy** 3 stern, severe

hardly adv. seldom, rarely, scarcely, slightly

hardship n. trouble, suffering, want, ▷difficulty ***ease**

hardy adj. rugged, sturdy, tough, healthy, rugged, ▷robust ***weak**

hark v. listen, hear, ▷listen

harm 1 n. damage, mischief, ruin, wrong, abuse, sin 2 v. abuse, blemish, hurt *I'm sorry, I didn't mean to hurt you,* injure ***benefit**

harmful adj. injurious, evil, wicked, damaging ***harmless**

harmless adj. safe, gentle, innocuous, innocent ***harmful**

harmony n. agreement, conformity, accord, unity, goodwill ***discord**

harp 1 n. lyre, stringed instrument 2 v. (on) dwell upon *I tried to forget our quarrel, but Celia continued to dwell upon it,* allude to

harrow v. agonize, taunt, distress, torture, harry, ▷harass ***hearten**

harsh 1 adj. jarring, coarse, rough 2 severe, strict, ruthless ***mild**

harvest v. plough, harrow, reap, pluck

hash 1 n. mess, confusion, muddle 2 hotpot, stew, goulash

hassle n. argument, bother, difficulty, squabble, struggle ***peace**

haste n. rush, bustle, dispatch, urgency, swiftness, ▷hurry ***delay**

hasten v. hurry, hustle, quicken, accelerate, speed up ***dawdle**

hasty adj. hurried, rushed, abrupt, indiscreet ***deliberate**

hate v. abhor, detest, loathe, ▷despise ***like**

hateful adj. abominable, loathsome, odious, despicable ***pleasing**

haughty adj. arrogant, disdainful, scornful, snobbish ***humble**

haul v. pull, draw, tug, drag, heave HALL

have v. possess, occupy, own, receive, take in

haven n. harbour, port, refuge, retreat, sanctum *This is my inner sanctum, the room where I relax alone,* shelter

havoc n. wreckage, ruin, destruction, disorder, mayhem

hay n. pasture, soilage, grass, straw HEY

haze n. cloud, vapour, fog, mist, vagueness HAYS

hazy adj. foggy, misty, murky, vague, uncertain ***clear**

head 1 n. visage, skull, cranium, pate 2 adj. chief, main, principal

heading n. caption, headline, title, inscription

headlong adj. rough, dangerous, reckless, ▷rash

heal v. soothe, treat, cure, mend, restore HEEL, HE'LL

healthy adj. fine, fit, hearty, sound, vigorous, ▷hale ***sick**

heap n. pile, mass, mound, collection

hear v. listen to, hearken, overhear HERE

hearten v. assure, encourage, embolden, inspire ***dishearten**

heartless adj. brutal, callous, cold, ▷unkind ***kind**

hearty adj. cordial, sincere, earnest, honest, jovial ***cold**

heat 1 n. warmth, temperature 2 passion, ardour, fervour *She spoke with great fervour about what she believed*

heave v. fling, cast, hurl, hoist, pull, tug

heavenly adj. beautiful, blessed, divine, lovely ***hellish**

heavy adj. weighty, hefty, ponderous, loaded ***light**

hectic adj. excited, fast, frenzied, wild, ▷frantic ***leisurely**

heed v. listen, pay attention, follow, respect ***ignore**

Headgear

Beret
Boater
Bonnet
Cap
Fedora
Fez

Glengarry
Homburg
Hood
Kepi
Mortarboard
Panama
Porkpie
Shako
Skullcap
Sombrero
Sou'wester

Stetson
Strawhat
Tam o'shanter
Three-cornered hat
Top hat
Toque
Trilby
Turban
Tyrolean hat
Yarmulke

heedful *adj.* attentive, cautious, prudent, watchful ★**heedless**

heedless *adj.* thoughtless, reckless, unwary, ▷*careless* ★**heedful**

height *n.* altitude, stature, top, apex, peak ★**depth**

hellish *adj.* abominable, awful, inhuman, fiendish ★**heavenly**

help 1 *n.* aid, support, assistance 2 *v.* lend a hand *We all lent a hand in building the hut*, aid, assist ★**hinder**

helpful *adj.* caring, considerate, ▷*useful* ★**useless**

helping *n.* ration, portion, piece, serving *Mike would like a second helping. He's still hungry*, share

helpless *adj.* incapable, powerless, unfit, forlorn, ▷*weak* ★**strong**

hem *n.* edge, border, fringe, margin

hence *adv.* accordingly, thus, therefore

herd *n.* crowd, crush, flock, group, mass, mob, horde HEARD

here *adv.* present, attending, hereabouts, in this place HEAR

heritage *n.* inheritance, legacy, birthright, tradition

hermit *n.* recluse, solitary, monk

hero *n.* champion, daredevil, star, idol, conqueror ★**villain**

heroic *adj.* bold, fearless, lion-hearted, gallant, ▷*brave* ★**cowardly**

heroine *n.* celebrity, goddess *Mary Pickford was a goddess of the silent screen*, idol, star, lead

hesitate *v.* falter, dither, doubt, be uncertain, wait

hew *v.* chop, cut, fashion, carve, sculpt HUE

hidden *adj.* concealed, covered, veiled, unseen ★**open**

hide *v.* conceal, cover, obscure, bury, cloak ★**reveal** HIED

hideous *adj.* repulsive, unsightly, gruesome, horrible, ▷*ugly* ★**beautiful**

hiding *n.* beating, thrashing, caning

high 1 *adj.* tall, towering, lofty, elevated 2 shrill *The referee blew his whistle which had a shrill tone*, treble, strident 3 expensive, dear, costly ★**low**

highbrow *adj.* brainy, educated, intellectual

hijack *v.* raid, kidnap, seize, snatch, steal

hike *v.* walk, ramble, tramp

hilarious *adj.* amusing, gleeful, jocular, entertaining, ▷*funny* ★**serious**

hill *n.* hummock, rise, climb, height, elevation, slope

hinder *v.* hamper, impede, obstruct, retard, frustrate, ▷*handicap* ★**help**

hindrance *n.* impediment, obstruction, check, barrier ★**aid**

hint *n.* clue, inkling *We had just an inkling of what was in store*, whisper, tip, suggestion

hire *v.* book, charter, rent, lease, retain, engage ★**dismiss** HIGHER

hiss *v.* boo, hoot, jeer, deride, whistle, ▷*ridicule* ★**applaud**

history *n.* narration, account, saga, story, chronicle *The new book was a chronicle of the last war*

hit 1 *v.* strike, slap, beat, batter, whack 2 collide, strike, clash ★**miss** 3 *n.* stroke, collision, blow 4 success, triumph

hitch 1 *v.* attach, connect, fasten 2 *n.* delay, hold-up, problem, snag *The work went smoothly for hours, until we hit a snag*

hoard *v.* accumulate, save, collect, treasure ★**squander** HORDE

hoarse *adj.* raucous, croaky, husky, throaty ★**mellow** HORSE

hoax *n.* trick, deception, fraud, leg-pull, joke, spoof

hobble *v.* dodder, falter, shuffle, stagger

hobby *n.* pastime, amusement, recreation, interest

hoist *v.* lift, raise, erect, heave

hold 1 *v.* have, possess, own, retain, keep, grasp 2 contain, accommodate *This cabin can accommodate four people* 3 stop, arrest 4 *n.* fortress, keep, storeplace HOLED

hole *n.* aperture, slot, perforation, opening, cavity WHOLE

hollow 1 *adj.* concave, empty, vacant 2 insincere, artificial 3 *n.* basin, depression *Water had accumulated in a small depression*, crater, channel

holy *adj.* sacred, pure, consecrated, blessed, hallowed ★**wicked** WHOLLY

home *n.* homestead, house, dwelling

homely 1 *adj.* humble, unpretentious, comfortable, modest 2 ordinary, plain, simple 3 unattractive, plain

honest *adj.* upright, straightforward, fair, sincere, honourable ★**devious**

honesty *n.* integrity, honour, sincerity, morality ★**treachery**

honour *n.* morality, honesty, reputation, integrity, uprightness ★**disgrace**

honourable *adj.* honest, respectable, high-minded, virtuous ★**dishonest**

hook *n.* clasp, link, catch, fastener, barb *The fishing line ended in a number of small barbs*

hoop *n.* loop, ring, band, circle WHOOP

hoot *v.* call, cry, howl, shout, shriek, yell

hop *v.* jump, leap, skip, spring, vault, caper

hope *v.* anticipate, envisage, desire, expect, foresee ★**despair**

hopeful *adj.* expectant, confident, optimistic ★**pessimistic**

hopeless *adj.* despairing, desperate, downhearted, unattainable ★**hopeful**

horde *n.* crowd, gang, band, throng, swarm *We were suddenly attacked by a swarm of hornets*

horrible *adj.* awful, atrocious, frightful, ghastly, ▷*horrid* ★**agreeable**

horrid *adj.* beastly, bloodcurdling, dreadful, frightening, ▷*horrible* ★**pleasant**

horror *n.* dread, fear, fright, outrage, panic, loathing ★**attraction**

horse *n.* mount, charger, hack, stallion, mare, filly, colt, foal HOARSE

hose 1 *n.* tubing, pipe 2 socks, stockings HOES

hospitable *adj.* sociable, neighbourly, charitable, welcoming ★**hostile**

host 1 *n.* landlord, innkeeper, presenter 2 army, band, legion, horde

hostile *adj.* unfriendly, antagonistic, alien, malevolent ★**friendly**

hot 1 *adj.* warm, fiery, scalding, roasting, heated ★**cold** 2 pungent, peppery, sharp

hotel *n.* inn, hostelry *The stage coach pulled in to a local hostelry for refreshment*, tavern, public-house

house *n.* home, residence, dwelling, abode

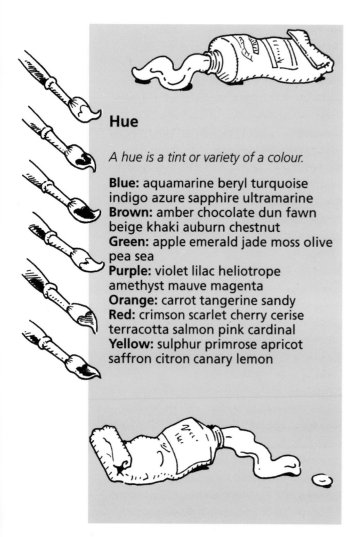

Hue

A hue is a tint or variety of a colour.

Blue: aquamarine beryl turquoise indigo azure sapphire ultramarine
Brown: amber chocolate dun fawn beige khaki auburn chestnut
Green: apple emerald jade moss olive pea sea
Purple: violet lilac heliotrope amethyst mauve magenta
Orange: carrot tangerine sandy
Red: crimson scarlet cherry cerise terracotta salmon pink cardinal
Yellow: sulphur primrose apricot saffron citron canary lemon

hovel *n.* cabin, shed, den, shack, shanty

hover *v.* fly, float, hang, dither, dally, linger

howl *v.* hoot, cry, bellow, shriek, ▷*scream*

hub *n.* centre, axis, focal point, pivot

hubbub *n.* babel, bedlam, chaos, clamour, uproar, ▷*row* ★**calm**

huddle *v.* cluster, flock, gather, herd, nestle ★**separate**

hue *n.* colour, dye, shade, tinge, tint HEW

huff *n.* anger, passion, mood, pique *My cousin stormed off in a fit of pique,* ▷*sulk*

hug *v.* clasp, embrace, enfold, ▷*cuddle*

huge *adj.* enormous, monstrous, colossal, immense, ▷*vast* ★**tiny**

hum *v.* drone, croon, buzz, pulsate, throb

human *adj.* reasonable, understandable, mortal, ▷*humane* ★**inhuman**

humane *adj.* benign, forgiving, gentle, lenient, kind ★**inhumane**

humble *adj.* low, lowly, meek, unassuming, ▷*modest* ★**arrogant**

humbug *n.* bluff, bunkum, claptrap *The salesman's goods were rubbish, and he talked a lot of claptrap about them,* quackery, trickery

humdrum *adj.* monotonous, commonplace, everyday, boring, ▷*dreary* ★**exceptional**

humid *adj.* clammy, damp, moist, wet, vaporous ★**dry**

humiliate *v.* embarrass, humble, abash, degrade, deflate ★**boost**

humorous *adj.* amusing, droll, comical, whimsical, ▷*funny* ★**serious** HUMERUS

humour 1 *n.* comedy, fun, banter, whimsy 2 *v.* flatter, coax, pamper, spoil

hunch 1 *n.* feeling, guess, idea, inkling 2 *v.* crouch, curl up, squat *We squatted in the long grass where we were out of sight*

hunger 1 *n.* craving, desire, starvation 2 *v.* crave, desire, hanker

hungry *adj.* famished, starving, voracious

hunt *v.* chase, seek, scour, search, stalk, trail

hurdle *n.* barrier, fence, hedge, obstruction

hurl *v.* cast, fling, heave, pitch, throw, propel, toss

hurry *v.* dash, hustle, quicken, accelerate, ▷*hasten* ★**dally**

hurt 1 *v.* harm, wound, pain, sting, suffer 2 upset, annoy, distress 3 *adj.* rueful, sad, offended

hurtful *adj.* cutting, cruel, distressing, wounding ★**kind**

hurtle *v.* chase, charge, dash, rush, speed, tear

hush *v.* calm, quieten, soothe ★**disturb**

husky *adj.* croaking, gruff, harsh, ▷*hoarse*

hustle *v.* bustle, speed, hasten, ▷*hurry*

hut *n.* cabin, shelter, shanty, shack

hymn *n.* anthem, chant, carol, psalm HIM

hypnotize *v.* mesmerize, fascinate, spellbind *We stood spellbound as we watched the trapeze artiste,* bewitch

hypocrite *n.* fraud, deceiver, impostor, mountebank

hysterical 1 *adj.* neurotic, distraught, mad 2 comical, hilarious, farcical ★**calm**

I i

icy *adj.* freezing, frozen, cold, frigid, frosty

idea *n.* notion, thought, belief, fancy, impression, image

ideal *adj.* perfect, absolute, supreme, best, model, complete

identical *adj.* same, alike, twin, duplicate, equal ★**different**

identify *v.* detect, recognise, know, distinguish, spot

identity *n.* existence, self, singularity, individuality

idiot *n.* imbecile, moron, fool, dimwit, dolt

idiotic *adj.* crazy, stupid, simple, fatuous, ▷*foolish* ★**sane**

idle 1 *adj.* unoccupied, unemployed, unused 2 lazy, frivolous, sluggish ★**active** IDOL

idol 1 *n.* image, icon, god, fetish 2 hero, favourite, star *Buster Keaton was a star of the silent movies* IDLE

ignite *v.* kindle, set light to, spark off, catch fire

ignorant *adj.* unknowing, ill-informed, unread, stupid, thick ★**wise**

ignore *v.* disregard, neglect, omit, overlook, pass over ★**note**

ill 1 *adj.* ailing, diseased, frail, infirm, sick, poorly ★**well** 2 cross, malicious *Cinderella's sisters were cruel and malicious*, evil, harmful ★**fortunate**

ill-mannered *adj.* coarse, crude, boorish, uncivil, ▷*rude* ★**polite**

ill-tempered *adj.* bad-tempered, curt, irritable ★**good-tempered**

ill-treat *v.* abuse, harm, injure, neglect, oppress ★**care for**

ill-will *n.* animosity, hard feelings, dislike, hatred, hostility, ▷*malice* ★**good-will**

illegal *adj.* unlawful, wrong, villainous, illicit, contraband ★**legal**

illegible *adj.* unreadable, indecipherable, obscure, indistinct ★**legible**

illegitimate *adj.* illegal, unlawful, improper, wrong ★**legitimate**

illiterate *adj.* uneducated, unlearned, unread, untaught ★**literate**

illness *n.* ailment, attack, complaint, disease, disorder

illuminate *v.* brighten, clarify, enlighten, light up ★**darken**

illusion *n.* apparition, fancy, fantasy, mirage, deception ★**reality**

illustration *n.* picture, drawing, explanation, sketch

image *n.* likeness, effigy, portrait, replica, reflection, double

imaginary *adj.* unreal, fanciful, fantastic, visionary ★**real**

imagination *n.* idea, notion, thought, illusion, conception, fancy, vision, impression ★**reality**

imagine *v.* assume, believe, invent, pretend, think up, ▷*visualize*

imbecile *n.* blockhead, fool, idiot, bungler, dolt

imitate *v.* emulate, follow, reproduce, simulate, mock, ▷*copy*

immaculate *adj.* clean, spotless, faultless, stainless, ▷*pure* ★**spoiled**

immature *adj.* callow, raw, crude, childish, unripe ★**mature**

immediate 1 *adj.* instant, instantaneous, prompt 2 nearest, next, neighbouring *As children, my mother and father lived in neighbouring houses* ★**distant**

immediately *adv.* at once, directly, without delay, forthwith

immense *adj.* tremendous, enormous, vast, ▷*huge* ★**tiny**

immerse *v.* plunge, dip, douse, submerge, ▷*sink*

imminent *adj.* impending, approaching, looming, close

immobile *adj.* at rest, at a standstill, motionless ★**moving**

immodest *adj.* shameless, barefaced, indelicate, improper ★**modest**

immoral *adj.* evil, unscrupulous, vicious, vile, depraved, ▷*wicked* ★**moral**

immortal *adj.* undying, eternal, everlasting, constant ★**mortal**

immune *adj.* privileged, exempt, resistant, safe *★susceptible*

imp *n.* rogue, villain, scamp, demon, evil spirit, elf

impact *n.* blow, shock, stroke, collision, crash, knock

impair *v.* destroy, spoil, devalue, cheapen, harm, ▷*hinder* ★**enhance**

impart *v.* communicate, render, bestow, disclose *I am unable to disclose where I heard that story,* ▷*tell*

impartial *adj.* unbiased, candid, fair-minded, impersonal ★**prejudiced**

impatient *adj.* intolerant, irritable, hasty, curt ★**patient**

impede *v.* hamper, interfere with, obstruct, ▷*hinder* ★**aid**

impel *v.* goad, incite, urge, actuate, push, ▷*drive* ★**dissuade**

impending *adj.* approaching, coming, forthcoming, looming ★**remote**

imperfect *adj.* defective, unsound, blemished, flawed, ▷*faulty* ★**perfect**

imperial *adj.* superior, august, majestic, lofty, regal

imperious *adj.* arrogant, domineering, overbearing ★**humble**

impersonal *adj.* aloof, detached, remote, neutral ★**friendly**

impersonate *v.* ape, imitate, mimic, masquerade as, pose as

impertinent *adj.* insolent, impudent, discourteous, ▷*cheeky* ★**polite**

impetuous *adj.* sudden, unexpected, impulsive, spontaneous, ▷*hasty* ★**careful**

implement [1] *v.* accomplish, bring about, fulfil *To visit Japan was a dream which I was able to fulfil* [2] *n.* instrument, tool, gadget

implicate *v.* connect, entangle, involve, throw suspicion on ★**absolve**

implicit *adj.* involved, indicated, understood, tacit

implore *v.* beseech, entreat, beg, crave, plead

imply *v.* hint at, intimate, insinuate, ▷*suggest* ★**declare**

impolite *adj.* discourteous, ill-mannered, ▷*rude* ★**polite**

import [1] *v.* bring in, carry in [2] *n.* meaning, purport *When I grew old enough I realized the purport of my mother's advice,* sense

important *adj.* notable, outstanding, serious, substantial, ▷*great* ★**trivial**

imposing *adj.* impressive, massive, magnificent, ▷*stately* ★**modest**

impossible *adj.* hopeless, not possible, unworkable, unacceptable ★**possible**

impostor *n.* impersonator, masquerader, deceiver, bluffer, pretender

impoverish *v.* bankrupt, diminish, weaken, ruin, beggar ★**enrich**

impractical *adj.* impossible, unworkable, idealistic, unusable ★**practical**

impress [1] *v.* influence, affect, sway, inspire [2] emboss *She wore a crown of gold embossed with diamonds,* engrave, indent

impression [1] *n.* belief, concept, fancy, effect [2] dent, imprint, stamp, printing *The book had sold 5,000 copies, and a new printing was planned*

imprison *v.* jail, lock up, confine, ★**free**

improbable *adj.* doubtful, unlikely, implausible, ▷*dubious* ★**probable**

impromptu *adj.* improvised, spontaneous, ad lib, unrehearsed ★**planned**

improper [1] *adj.* erroneous, false, unsuitable [2] immoral *My parents always taught me that lying and cheating were immoral,* indecent, ▷*wrong* ★**proper**

improve *v.* make better, repair, restore, improve upon, refine ★**diminish**

impudent *adj.* impertinent, audacious, brazen, cocky, ▷*cheeky* ★**polite**

impulse *n.* motive, drive, force, inclination, urge

impulsive *adj.* sudden, unexpected, reckless, ▷*impetuous* ★**cautious**

impure *adj.* contaminated, corrupted, foul, corrupt ★**pure**

inaccessible *adj.* remote, isolated, unattainable ★**accessible**

inaccurate *adj.* erroneous, incorrect, imprecise, ▷*faulty* ★**accurate**

inactive *adj.* inert, static, dormant, quiet, unoccupied ★**active**

inadequate *adj.* deficient, unequal, incapable, ▷*unfit* ★**adequate**

inane *adj.* absurd, ridiculous, stupid, senseless, ▷*silly* ★**sensible**

inappropriate *adj.* improper, wrong, incorrect, unsuitable, unfitting ★**appropriate**

inattentive *adj.* unheeding, indifferent, careless, neglectful ★**attentive**

incapable *adj.* helpless, inadequate, unable, unfit, weak ★**capable**

incense [1] (in-*cense*) *v.* enrage, infuriate, annoy [2] (in-cense) *n.* fragrance *We walked through fields where the fragrance of wild flowers was wonderful*, aroma, perfume

incentive *n.* motive, impulse, drive, spur, lure

incident *n.* event, happening, episode, circumstance, occurrence

incidental *adj.* casual, chance, accidental, random, minor

incite *v.* encourage, urge, drive, goad, impel, provoke, ▷*prompt* ★**restrain**

incline [1] (in-cline) *n.* slant, slope, grade, gradient [2] (in-*cline*) *v.* tend, verge, lean to, bias, favour

inclined *adj.* liable, prone, disposed, favourable

include *v.* contain, cover, incorporate, embody, comprise ★**exclude**

inclusive *adj.* comprehensive, all-embracing ★**exclusive**

income *n.* earnings, royalty, revenue, receipts, profits ★**expenses**

incomparable *adj.* brilliant, first-class, superb, ▷*unrivalled* ★**ordinary**

incompetent *adj.* incapable, inadequate, inept, helpless, ▷*clumsy* ★**competent**

incomplete *adj.* unfinished, partial, imperfect, wanting ★**complete**

incomprehensible *adj.* unintelligible, perplexing, puzzling ★**comprehensible**

inconceivable *adj.* incredible, unlikely, strange, ▷*extraordinary* ★**comprehensible**

inconsiderate *adj.* tactless, careless, insensitive, ▷*thoughtless* ★**considerate**

inconsistent *adj.* incongruous, unstable, unpredictable ★**consistent**

inconspicuous *adj.* indistinct, faint, hidden, ordinary ★**conspicuous**

inconvenient *adj.* annoying, awkward, difficult, troublesome ★**convenient**

incorrect *adj.* erroneous, imprecise, mistaken, ▷*wrong* ★**correct**

increase [1] *v.* add to, boost, magnify, heighten [2] *n.* addition *We heard the news today that Emily has had an addition to her family*, rise, enhancement ★**decrease**

incredible *adj.* unbelievable, amazing, far-fetched, wonderful ★**ordinary**

incriminate *v.* implicate, accuse, indict, ▷*blame* ★**acquit**

indecent *adj.* immodest, improper, impure, coarse ★**decent**

indeed *adv.* actually, truly, really, very much, positively

indefinite *adj.* uncertain, unsure, unreliable, dubious, ▷*vague* ★**certain**

indelicate *adj.* coarse, immodest, tasteless, ▷*unseemly* ★**delicate**

independent *adj.* free, self-reliant, separate, self-governing ★**dependent**

indicate *v.* show, point out, denote, suggest, symbolize, token

indifference *n.* disinterest, unconcern, apathy, coldness ★**interest**

indifferent *adj.* careless, cold, casual, apathetic, listless ★**interested**

indignant *adj.* annoyed, resentful, wrathful, ▷*angry* ★**pleased**

indirect *adj.* devious, roundabout, incidental ★**direct**

indiscreet *adj.* incautious, thoughtless, ill-advised, ▷*hasty* ★**discreet**

indiscriminate *adj.* confused, bewildered, careless, ▷*random* ★**deliberate**

indispensable *adj.* necessary, crucial, vital, ▷*essential* ★**unnecessary**

indistinct *adj.* faint, dim, unclear, obscure, murky, ▷*vague* ★**distinct**

individual [1] *adj.* single, odd, special, exclusive [2] *n.* person, being *The inhabitants of the planet were strange green beings*, creature

indulge *v.* gratify, humour, pamper, satisfy, spoil

industrious *adj.* busy, hard-working, diligent, conscientious, ▷*lazy*

inedible *adj.* deadly, poisonous, harmful, uneatable ★**edible**

inefficient *adj.* negligent, incapable, ▷*incompetent* ★**efficient**

inelegant *adj.* awkward, ungainly, crude, coarse, ▷*clumsy* ★**elegant**

inept *adj.* awkward, absurd, unskilled, ▷*clumsy* ★**skilful**

inert *adj.* inactive, passive, static, sluggish, listless, dead ★**alive**

inevitable *adj.* unavoidable, certain, sure, necessary ★**uncertain**

inexact *adj.* imprecise, inaccurate, ▷*erroneous* ★**exact**

inexpensive *adj.* low-priced, reasonable, economical, ▷*cheap* ★**expensive**

inexperienced *adj.* inexpert, unskilled, untrained, ▷*inept* ★**experienced**

infallible *adj.* perfect, unerring, faultless, ▷*reliable* ★**faulty**

infamous *adj.* notorious, shady, scandalous, shameful, disgraceful ★**glorious**

infant *n.* baby, child, little one, bairn

infatuated *adj.* in love, beguiled, fascinated, smitten ★**indifferent**

infect *v.* contaminate, blight, defile, pollute

infectious *adj.* catching, contagious

infer *v.* reason, conclude, judge, understand

inferior *adj.* second-rate, lesser, lower, poor, mediocre, imperfect ★**superior**

infinite *adj.* eternal, unending, endless, immense, unbounded

infirm *adj.* weak, feeble, frail, senile, decrepit ★**healthy**

inflame *v.* inspire, provoke, excite, stimulate, arouse ★**cool**

inflate *v.* expand, dilate, swell, pump up, blow up ★**deflate**

inflict *v.* apply, burden, deal, deliver, force

influence ⓵ *n.* authority, control, guidance, force ⓶ *v.* affect, impress, inspire *After Annie visited the old city, she was inspired to write a poem*, prejudice

inform *v.* tell, let know, acquaint, warn, enlighten

informal *adj.* casual, easy, familiar, relaxed, simple ★**formal**

information *n.* knowledge, news, intelligence, advice

infrequent *adj.* unusual, uncommon, occasional, ▷*rare* ★**frequent**

infringe *v.* disobey, violate, encroach, trespass, flout

infuriate *v.* anger, enrage, madden, incense, vex, ▷*annoy* ★**calm**

ingenious *adj.* clever, resourceful, shrewd, adroit, inventive ★**clumsy**

ingenuous *adj.* honest, open, simple, trusting, sincere ★**artful**

ingratiate *v.* curry favour, flatter, grovel, toady *We all disliked the new schoolmate, for she was always toadying to the teacher*

Ingratiate

We all disliked our new classmate. She was always toadying up to the teacher.

ingredient *n.* component, element, part, factor

inhabit *v.* live in, dwell in, reside in, dwell, habitate, occupy

inhale *v.* breathe in, inspire, sniff, suck in ★**exhale**

inherit *v.* succeed to, acquire, take over, receive

inhospitable *adj.* unfriendly, desolate, unkind, unsociable ★**hospitable**

inhuman *adj.* barbaric, brutal, beastly, heartless, savage

inhumane *adj.* callous, cruel, pitiless, ruthless, ▷*inhuman* ★**humane**

initiate *v.* start, launch, teach, instruct, train, ▷*begin*

initiative *n.* ambition, drive, enterprise, resourcefulness

inject *v.* inoculate, infuse, jab, vaccinate

injure *v.* hurt, mar, spoil, wound, blemish, deform, disfigure

inkling *n.* suspicion, impression, notion, clue

inlet *n.* bay, gulf, basin, bight, estuary, harbour

inn *n.* hotel, hostelry, pub IN

innocent *adj.* guiltless, faultless, stainless, virtuous, blameless ★**guilty**

inoffensive *adj.* harmless, safe, gentle, quiet, ▷*innocent* ★**malicious**

inquire *see* **enquire**

inquisitive *adj.* nosy, snooping, eager, enquiring, ▷*curious*

insane *adj.* demented, mad, frenzied, crazy, wild, lunatic ★**sane**

inscribe *v.* write, stamp, cut, carve, etch

inscription *n.* heading, caption, legend, epitaph, label

insecure *adj.* perilous, unsafe, hazardous, dangerous, unconfident, uncertain ★**secure**

insensible 1 *adj.* unconscious, stunned, knocked out *The reigning champion was knocked out in the third round* 2 insensitive, numb, stupefied

insensitive *adj.* impassive, indifferent, thick-skinned, unruffled, insensible ★**sensitive**

inseparable *adj.* undividable, devoted, intimate, close

insert *v.* put in, inset, introduce, place, interleave ★**remove**

inside *adv.* indoors, inner, inward, within ★**outside**

insight *n.* awareness, intelligence, judgment, knowledge, ▷*wisdom*

insignificant *adj.* unimportant, non-essential, meagre, irrelevant, ▷*humble* ★**important**

insincere *adj.* pretended, deceptive, dishonest, two-faced, false ★**sincere**

insinuate *v.* suggest, imply, signify, get at, intimate

insipid *adj.* tasteless, flat, flavourless, bland, banal ★**tasty**

insist *v.* assert, maintain, request, require, demand, persist ★**waive**

insolent *adj.* impudent, impertinent, discourteous, insulting, ▷*cheeky* ★**respectful**

inspect *v.* examine, check, oversee, supervise, superintend

inspiration *n.* motive, stimulus, brain-wave, ▷*encouragement*

inspire *v.* hearten, prompt, provoke, excite, ▷*encourage* ★**deter**

instal *v.* establish, plant, set, position, fix, introduce

instance *n.* example, case, occasion, occurrence INSTANTS

instant 1 *adj.* immediate, instantaneous *I pressed the button and there was an instantaneous explosion*, rapid 2 *n.* moment, minute, flash, jiffy

instantly *adv.* at once, right away, immediately, now, ▷*forthwith* ★**presently**

instead *adv.* alternatively, preferably, rather

instead of *adv.* in place of, in one's place, on behalf of

instinct *n.* ability, knack, intuition, feeling, sixth sense

institute 1 *n.* association, college, establishment, organization 2 *v.* begin, start *The people raised enough money to start a new social club*, found, open

instruct *v.* teach, direct, order, educate, coach, drill, train

Musical Instruments

Accordion	Fife	Piano
Alpen horn	Flute	Piccolo
Bagpipes	Glockenspiel	Recorder
Balalaika	Guitar	Shofar
Banjo	Harmonium	Saxophone
Bassoon	Harp	Tambourine
Bells	Harpsichord	Triangle
Bugle	Horn	Trombone
Castanets	Hurdy-gurdy	Trumpet
Cello	Kettledrum	Tuba
Clarinet	Lute	Ukelele
Cornet	Lyre	Viola
Cymbals	Mandolin	Violin
Didgeridoo	Mouth organ	Virginal
Drum	Oboe	Whistle
Dulcimer	Ocarina	Xylophone
Fiddle	Organ	Zither

instrument *n.* device, gadget, implement, contraption, tool

insufferable *adj.* unbearable, intolerable, impossible ★**tolerable**

insufficient *adj.* inadequate, lacking, scanty, wanting, ▷*sparse* ★**sufficient**

insulate *v.* protect, shield, isolate, set apart

insult *n. & v.* slander, slight, snub, abuse, outrage ★**compliment**

insure *v.* guarantee, protect, warrant, assure

intact *adj.* whole, unharmed, uncut, complete, in one piece, sound ★**damaged**

integrity *n.* honour, uprightness, honesty, goodness, purity ★**dishonesty**

intellectal *adj.* scholarly, studious, thoughful, ▷*intelligent* ★**foolish**

intelligent *adj.* acute, astute, brainy, brilliant, intellectual, ▷*clever* ★**foolish**

intend *v.* mean, aim, determine, ordain, plan, project

intense *adj.* extreme, ardent, earnest, forcible, passionate, ▷*keen* ★**mild** INTENTS

intention *n.* aim, intent, project, design, notion, end, goal

intercept *v.* stop, arrest, delay, obstruct, ▷*thwart*

interest *n.* appeal, fascination, zest, activity, concern ★**boredom**

interesting *adj.* appealing, fascinating, absorbing, entertaining ★**boring**

interfere *v.* meddle, intrude, interrupt, butt in, tamper ★**assist**

interior *adj.* internal, innermost, inside, inward ★**exterior**

interlude *n.* pause, interval, intermission, spell, 'recess

internal *adj.* inner, inward, ▷*interior* ★**external**

interpret *adj.* explain, define, construe

interrogate *v.* question, query, ask, enquire, quiz, ▷*investigate*

interrupt *adj.* break in, butt in, interject, disturb, hold up

interval *n.* space, period, term, intermission, ▷*interlude*

intervene *v.* break in, interrupt, intrude, ▷*interfere*

interview *n.* conference, enquiry, consultation, talk

intimate [1] *adj.* near, close, familiar, private, secret ★**distant** [2] *v.* hint at, suggest *I started to play the violin at school, and my teacher suggested I should take it up for a living*, ▷*insinuate*

intimidate *v.* daunt, overawe, cow, bully, frighten, browbeat ★**persuade**

intolerant *adj.* bigoted, unfair, small-minded, dogmatic ★**tolerant**

intoxicated *adj.* drunk, inebriated, tipsy

intrepid *adj.* fearless, heroic, unafraid, bold, gallant, ▷*fearless*

intricate *adj.* complex, complicated, elaborate, tricky ★**simple**

intrigue [1] *n.* plot, scheme, affair, liaison [2] *v.* attract, enchant *The hotel's location was enchanting*, captivate, scheme

introduce [1] *v.* put in, insert, inject [2] acquaint, present

intrude *v.* interrupt, interfere, invade, trespass ★**withdraw**

inundate *v.* flood, deluge, engulf, immerse, submerge, swamp *We advertised for a new assistant, and were swamped with replies*

invade *v.* break in, penetrate, assault, assail, ▷*enter* ★**withdraw** INVEIGHED

invalid [1] *adj.* (in-*val*-id) null, void *These tickets are void, for they were left over from last year*, false, useless [2] *n.* (*in*-valid) patient, sufferer, sick person

invaluable *adj.* precious, costly, priceless, valuable ★**worthless**

invent *v.* fabricate, conceive, devise, make up, originate

invention *n.* creation, gadget, contrivance, discovery

investigate *v.* explore, examine, research, enquire, search, study

invisible *adj.* hidden, concealed, out of sight, unseen, masked ★**visible**

invite *v.* ask, beckon, attract, summon, urge, encourage ★**force**

involve *v.* comprise, complicate, entangle, include, take in

inward *adj.* hidden, inner, internal, secret, inside ★**outward**

irate *adj.* incensed, cross, annoyed, furious, infuriated, ▷*angry* ★**calm**

irksome *adj.* annoying, aggravating, disagreeable ★**pleasing**

ironic *adj.* satirical, derisive, mocking, scornful

irregular *adj.* uncertain, unsettled, disordered, singular, ▷*odd* ★**regular**

irrelevant *adj.* immaterial, unnecessary, unrelated ★**relevant**

irresistible *adj.* charming, compelling, overpowering, fascinating ★**resistible**

irresponsible *adj.* undependable, unreliable, feckless, flighty ★**responsible**

irritable *adj.* bad-tempered, edgy, fretful, peevish, ▷*cross* ★**cheerful**

irritate *v.* annoy, vex, irk, offend, provoke, ▷*bother* ★**please**

island *n.* isle, islet, key, atoll, cay

issue [1] *v.* flow, ooze, bring out, circulate, publish [2] *n.* edition, printing, publication *My book of poems was ready for publication*, impression [3] problem, question

itch [1] *v.* prickle, tingle, irritate [2] *n.* impulse, motive, desire *I have always had a strong desire to work on the land*

item *n.* point, particular, thing, object, article

J j

jab *v.* poke, prod, push, stab, dig

jabber *v.* chatter, gabble, mumble, babble

jacket *n.* coat, jerkin, cover, case, sheath

jagged *adj.* rough, broken, snagged, notched, uneven **★smooth**

jail *n.* prison, lock-up, penitentiary, brig

jam 1 *n.* conserve, jelly, preserve, marmalade 2 *v.* crowd, pack *All the buses were full, and we were packed in like sardines!*, crush, squeeze

jar 1 *n.* jug, beaker, ewer, vase, pitcher, pot 2 *v.* jog, rattle, grate *That singer's voice really grates on me*, grind

jaunt *n. & v.* cruise, travel, trip, journey, tour

jaunty *adj.* cheeky, showy, dapper, spruce, debonair

jealous *adj.* envious, covetous, grudging, possessive

jealousy *n.* envy, covetousness, distrust, spite

jeer *v.* laugh at, deride, mock, ridicule, insult, ▷*taunt*

jeopardy *n.* peril, risk, hazard, plight, ▷*danger* **★safety**

jerk *n. & v.* yank, pull, drag, jog, jolt, tug

jersey *n.* pullover, sweater, jumper, woolly

jest *n.* joke, jape, spoof, banter, chaff

jester *n.* clown, buffoon, merry-andrew, japer, comedian

jet *n. & v.* spurt, squirt, flow, gush

jetty *n.* wharf, dock, quay, pier

jewel *n.* gem, stone, trinket, charm, locket

jibe *v.* mock, scoff, scorn, sneer, taunt, ▷*jeer*

jiffy *n.* instant, flash, minute, moment, tick

jilt *v.* abandon, brush off, desert, drop, forsake

jingle *v.* tinkle, clink, chink, ring, jangle

job *n.* task, work, chore, place, office, post, situation

jocular *adj.* gleeful, hilarious, witty, humorous, jolly, ▷*funny* **★serious**

jog 1 *v.* prod, nudge, shove, shake 2 canter, trot, run, sprint

join 1 *v.* unite, link, combine, connect, attach **★separate** 2 enlist, sign up *Gaby and Bill have signed up for tennis lessons*

joint 1 *n.* junction, knot, union, connection 2 *adj.* shared, united, mutual *After we were married, we opened a mutual bank account*

joke *n.* gag, trick, frolic, lark, jape, game, prank, ▷*jest*

jolly *adj.* jovial, cheerful, blithe, frisky, ▷*merry* **★sad**

jolt *n. & v.* jar, shock, shove, rock, jerk, bump

jostle *v.* push, shove, shoulder, thrust, elbow

jot 1 *n.* atom, bit, grain, particle 2 *v.* note, scribble, take down

journal 1 *n.* ledger, account-book 2 diary, newspaper, magazine *I've just become editor of the natural history society's magazine*

journey *n.* excursion, trip, tour, jaunt, ramble

jovial *adj.* jolly, festive, cordial, affable, cheery, ▷*merry* **★sad**

joy *n.* rapture, enchantment, delight, pleasure, charm, ▷*bliss* **★sorrow**

joyful *adj.* joyous, enjoyable, pleasurable, happy, jovial, delighted **★sorrowful**

jubilant *adj.* exultant, gleeful, happy, overjoyed, excited **★depressed**

judge 1 *n.* justice, magistrate, referee, umpire 2 *v.* assess *We can ask the jeweller to assess the value of the pearls and bracelets*, decide, find, appraise, estimate

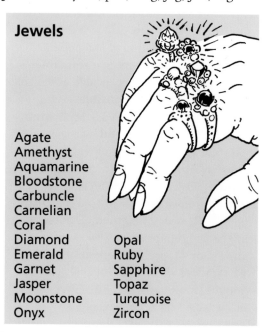

Jewels

Agate
Amethyst
Aquamarine
Bloodstone
Carbuncle
Carnelian
Coral
Diamond
Emerald
Garnet
Jasper
Moonstone
Onyx
Opal
Ruby
Sapphire
Topaz
Turquoise
Zircon

Jog

judgment [1] *n.* decision, opinion, verdict *The jury gave a verdict of 'not guilty'*, decree, finding [2] intelligence, understanding, valuation

judicious *adj.* prudent, discreet, expedient, wise ★**indiscreet**

jug *n.* beaker, ewer, urn, vase, ▷*jar*

juggle *v.* conjure, manipulate

juice *n.* essence, extract, sap, fluid, nectar

jumble *n.* medley, mixture, muddle, tangle, clutter

jump *v.* spring, bound, hop, skip, vault, ▷*leap*

jumper *n.* sweater, pullover, ▷*jersey*

junction [1] *n.* intersection, combination, joint, connection [2] crossroads, railway connection

jungle *n.* forest, bush, wilderness

junior *adj.* lesser, lower, younger, subordinate ★**senior**

junk *n.* rubbish, trash, debris, waste, clutter, litter, scrap, garbage

just [1] *adj.* sound, regular, orderly, exact, fair, honest, impartial [2] *adv.* exactly, precisely *Our meal cost 46 francs precisely*

justice *n.* equity, impartiality, fairness, right ★**injustice**

justify *v.* vindicate, acquit, condone, uphold, legalize

jut *v.* bulge, extend, stick out, overhang, project ★**recede**

juvenile [1] *adj.* adolescent, youthful, young, childish ★**mature** [2] *n.* boy, girl, child, youngster, youth

K k

keen [1] *adj.* eager, ardent, earnest, diligent [2] sharp, acute, fine *This razor has a very fine blade* ★**dull**

keep [1] *v.* hold, retain, collect, possess ★**abandon** [2] care for, maintain, shelter *We have arranged to shelter the refugees* [3] *n.* castle, fort, stronghold

keeper *n.* jailer, warden, attendant, caretaker, janitor

keeping *n.* compliance, obedience, accord *Your behaviour is not in accord with our rules*

keep on *v.* continue, go on, endure, persist ★**give up**

keepsake *n.* souvenir, token, memento, reminder

keg *n.* barrel, cask, tub, drum, container

ken *n.* grasp, grip, understanding, mastery, knowledge

kerchief *n.* scarf, headscarf, shawl, neckcloth

kernel *n.* core, heart, hub, centre, gist, nub COLONEL

kettle *n.* boiler, cauldron, cooking-pot, tea-kettle

key [1] *n.* opener [2] solution, clue, answer [3] cay, isle, inlet atoll [4] *adj.* essential, fundamental QUAY

kick [1] *v.* boot, strike with foot, hit [2] complain, grumble, rebel *The country folk rebelled against the building of the new road*, resist

kidnap *v.* abduct, capture, seize, snatch, steal

kill *v.* slay, assassinate, destroy, massacre, slaughter, ▷*murder*

killjoy *n.* spoil-sport, wet blanket *I'm not asking Pete to the party, he's such a wet blanket*, grouch, complainer ★**optimist**

kin *n.* race, kindred, offspring, kind, family, sort, relation

kind [1] *adj.* gentle, kindly, genial, good-natured, amiable ★**unkind** [2] *n.* style, character, sort, variety

kindle [1] *v.* light, ignite, set fire to [2] inflame *The mayor's words only inflamed the people even more*, excite, provoke, rouse

A Little Knowledge is a Dangerous Thing – and Other Misquotes

Many of the familiar quotations we use from literature, history or the world of entertainment are incorrect or adaptations of the original. Greta Garbo did not say 'I want to be alone'. Her true words were: 'I like to be alone'. Shakespeare did not say 'Discretion is the better part of valour'. The correct quotation is: 'The better part of valour is discretion'. Here are some more, with the correct original version printed in italic type:

From the King James Bible
Pride goes before a fall
Pride goeth before destruction and an haughty spirit before a fall

Money is the root of all evil
For the love of money is the root of all evil
(Timothy)

To go the way of all flesh
And, behold, this day I am going the way of all earth.
(Joshua)

From Shakespeare
Alas, poor Yorick: I knew him well.
Alas, poor Yorick; I knew him, Horatio....
(Hamlet)

O Romeo. Romeo! wherefore art thou, Romeo?
O Romeo. Romeo! wherefore art thou Romeo?
(Romeo and Juliet)
(Note the position of the comma. 'Wherefore' means 'why' not 'where'.)

To gild the lily
... to gild refined gold, to paint the lily....
(King John)

Screw your courage to the sticking-point
But screw your courage to the sticking-place

Lead on, Macduff ...
Lay on, Macduff....
(Macbeth)

All that glitters is not gold
All that glisters is not gold
(The Merchant of Venice)

---

kindness *n.* good nature, charity, amiability, affection, tenderness ***cruelty**

king *n.* monarch, sovereign, majesty, ruler, emperor

kink 1 *n.* knot, loop, bend, coil 2 freak, eccentricity, whim *This strange tower was built as the result of a whim by the old lady*

kiss *v.* salute, embrace, buss

kit *n.* set, outfit, baggage, effects, gear, rig

knack *n.* flair, talent, ability, genius, gift, ▷skill

knave *n.* cheat, rascal, villain, scamp, scoundrel, ▷*rogue* NAVE

knead *v.* form, squeeze, mould, shape NEED

kneel *v.* bend the knee, genuflect, bow down, worship

knickers *n.* breeches, shorts, briefs, drawers, panties

knife *n.* scalpel, blade, dagger, cutter

knight *n.* cavalier, baronet, champion, soldier, warrior NIGHT

knit *v.* weave, crochet, spin, twill, link, loop

knob *n.* boss, bump, handle, opener, button

knock *v.* hit, slap, punch, bang, smite, strike

knock out *v.* stun, make insensible, render unconscious

L l

knoll *n.* barrow, hill, mound, hillock

knot 1 *n.* tie, bond, join, loop, kink, 2 cluster, group NOT

know *v.* perceive, discern, notice, identify, ▷*understand* NO

know-how *n.* skill, knowledge, talent

knowing *adj.* astute, knowledgeable, intelligent, perceptive ★**ignorant**

knowledge *n.* understanding, acquaintance, learning, wisdom, scholarship, information, sapience ★**ignorance**

kudos *n.* prestige, distinction, fame, glory, recognition

label *n.* badge, tag, docket, slip, ticket, sticker

laborious 1 *adj.* hard-working, diligent 2 strenuous, arduous *Digging potatoes is arduous work*, hard ★**easy**

labour *n. & v.* toil, work, drudge, strain, struggle

lack 1 *n.* need, want, absence, deficiency, scarcity *During the hot weather, there was a scarcity of water* 2 *v.* need, require, want, miss

laconic *adj.* terse, curt, brief, concise ★**wordy**

lad *n.* boy, chap, fellow, kid, youth

laden *adj.* loaded, burdened, hampered, weighed down ★**empty**

ladle *v.* dip, scoop, dish, shovel

lady *n.* woman, female, dame, damsel, matron, mistress

lag *v.* dawdle, loiter, tarry, saunter, ▷*linger* ★**lead**

lagoon *n.* pool, pond, lake, basin

lair *n.* den, nest, retreat, hideout, hole

lake *n.* lagoon, loch, pond, spring, reservoir

lam *v.* beat, hit, clout, knock, ▷*strike*

lame 1 *adj.* crippled, hobbled, disabled 2 weak *That's a weak excuse for forgetting my birthday!*, inadequate, unconvincing

lament *v.* deplore, mourn, grieve, sorrow, ▷*regret* ★**rejoice**

lamp *n.* lantern, light, flare, torch

lance 1 *n.* spear, pike, javelin, shaft 2 *v.* puncture, pierce, cut

land 1 *n.* country, district, tract, area, nation, region 2 *v.* alight, arrive, carry, touch down *We had engine trouble, and the aircraft touched down in the desert*

landlord *n.* host, hotelier, innkeeper, owner

landmark *n.* milestone, milepost, beacon, monument, signpost

landscape *n.* scenery, view, prospect, countryside

lane *n.* alley, court, passage, way LAIN

language *n.* tongue, speech, utterance, dialect, jargon

languid *adj.* leisurely, unhurried, sluggish, slow, easy ★**lively**

languish *v.* decline, droop, flag, pine, suffer, yearn ★**flourish**

lanky *adj.* tall, rangy, gangling, scrawny ★**squat**

lantern *n.* flashlight, torch, lamp

lap 1 *v.* lick, drink, sip, sup 2 *n.* circuit, course, distance 3 thighs

lapse *v.* expire, die, pass, elapse, go by, deteriorate LAPS

larder *n.* pantry, storeroom, buttery, cellar

large *adj.* big, ample, substantial, great, broad, ▷*huge* ★**small**

lark *n.* adventure, escapade, spree, joke, frolic, gambol

lash 1 *v.* beat, cane, whip, flay, flog 2 *n.* prod, goad, drive, whip

lass *n.* girl, maiden, maid, young woman

last 1 *adj.* final, concluding, latest, utmost, aftermost ★**first** 2 *v.* remain, linger *The foggy weather lingered for most of the morning*, endure, stay

latch *n.* bolt, bar, padlock, fastener

late *adj.* tardy, behindhand, departed, slow ★**early**

lately *adv.* recently, latterly, formerly

lather *n.* suds, foam, bubbles, froth

latter *adj.* final, last, latest, recent, closing ★**former**

laud *v.* compliment, praise, applaud, glorify ★**blame**

laugh *v.* chuckle, giggle, guffaw, snigger ★**cry**

launch 1 *v.* start, begin, commence, establish, initiate 2 *n.* motorboat

lavish 1 *adj.* abundant, generous, liberal, extravagant 2 *v.* waste, squander *My parents left me a small fortune, but I squandered it all*, give

law *n.* rule, ordinance, regulation, edict, decree

lawful *adj.* legal, legitimate, rightful ★**illegal**

lawyer *n.* attorney, counsel, jurist, barrister, solicitor, advocate

lax *adj.* careless, casual, slack, relaxed, vague ★**strict** LACKS

lay 1 *v.* put, set *It's time for dinner: let's set the table*, deposit, place, spread 2 impute, charge 3 *adj.* non-professional, amateur *It was a very good play, performed by amateur actors*

layer *n.* seam, sheet, thickness, tier

lazy *adj.* idle, inactive, slothful, slow, sluggish ★**active**

lead *v.* conduct, guide, escort, direct, command ★**follow**

leader *n.* guide, pilot, conductor, chief, head, master

leaf *n.* frond, blade, sheet LIEF

league *n.* band, association, society, guild, group

leak *v.* trickle, ooze, seep, exude, flow out LEEK

lean 1 *adj.* spare, slim, thin, skinny *Lina has no flesh on her, she is very skinny*, 2 *v.* bend, curve, tilt, incline LIEN

leap *v.* spring, bound, jump, hop, skip

learn *v.* find out, ascertain, determine, acquire knowledge, understand

learned *adj.* cultured, educated, scholarly, literate ★**ignorant**

learning *n.* scholarship, education, knowledge, ▷*wisdom* ★**ignorance**

least *adj.* fewest, smallest, slightest, lowest, tiniest ★**most** LEASED

leave 1 *v.* abandon, desert, forsake, quit, go 2 bequeath, bestow 3 *n.* holiday, furlough *Jack's on a furlough from the Army*, permission

lecture *n.* talk, speech, address, sermon

ledge *n.* shelf, ridge, step

legacy *n.* bequest, inheritance, gift

legal *adj.* legitimate, lawful, valid, sound ★**illegal**

legend 1 *n.* fable, myth, tale, fiction 2 inscription *The box bore a brass plate with an inscription*, heading, caption

legible *adj.* clear, readable, understandable, distinct ★**illegible**

legitimate *adj.* legal, lawful, proper, rightful, ▷*genuine* ★**illegal**

leisurely *adj.* unhurried, slow, easy, carefree, tranquil ★**hectic**

lend *v.* load, advance, provide, supply, grant, lease ★**borrow**

Lights

Arc
Bedlamp
Candle
Chandelier
Desk lamp
Electric light
Flashlamp
Fluorescent tube
Footlights
Gaslight
Headlight
Lantern
Limelight
Reading light
Spotlight
Standard lamp
Sunlamp
Table lamp
Torch

lengthen *v.* extend, elongate, stretch, draw out, prolong ★**shorten**

lengthy *adj.* long, drawn out, long-winded, ▷*tedious* ★**short**

lenient *adj.* tolerant, merciful, sparing, forbearing, indulgent ★**severe**

less *adj.* lesser, smaller, inferior, lower

lessen *v.* reduce, cut, become smaller, diminish, decrease ★**increase** LESSON

lesson *n.* instruction, lecture, information, teaching, exercise LESSEN

let 1 *v.* allow, permit, suffer, authorize, grant 2 hire *The owners hired the launch to us for the summer*, lease

let down 1 *v.* lower, take down 2 betray, abandon, disappoint ★**satisfy**

letter 1 *n.* dispatch, communication, epistle, message 2 character *The book was printed in Hebrew characters*, sign, symbol

level 1 *n.* plane, grade 2 *adj.* even, flat, smooth ★**uneven** 3 *v.* aim, direct, point 4 demolish *Many houses were demolished during the earthquake*, destroy

liable 1 *adj.* answerable, accountable, responsible 2 apt *My parents are apt to be annoyed if I play music too loud*, prone, inclined

liar *n.* deceiver, fibber, teller of tales LYRE

libel *v.* slander, malign, blacken, defame, slur ★**praise**

liberal *adj.* open-handed, generous, open-hearted, free, lavish ★**mean**

liberate *v.* set free, save, release, ★**restrict**

liberty *n.* freedom, independence ★**slavery**

license *v.* allow, permit, entitle ★**ban**

lie 1 *n.* untruth, falsehood 2 *v.* recline *I shall recline on the sofa for the afternoon*, lounge, repose, ▷*loll* 3 tell a lie, fib, invent LYE

life *n.* being, existence, activity, energy, ★**death**

lift *v.* raise, erect, hoist, elevate, hold up ★**lower**

light 1 *n.* radiance, glow, shine, glare, brightness 2 lamp, beacon, flame 2 *v.* ignite, illuminate, kindle *The scouts kindled a fire to cook our food* 3 *adj.* fair, light-coloured, sunny ★**dark** 4 lightweight, buoyant, airy ★**heavy**

like [1] *adj.* similar, resembling, akin ★**unlike**
[2] *v.* admire, love, adore, cherish, prize
★**dislike**

likely *adj.* probable, expected, possible

likeness [1] *n.* resemblance, appearance [2]
photograph *That's a wonderful photograph of my
grandmother*, portrait

likewise *adv.* also, too, furthermore, further

limb *n.* leg, arm, extension, branch, shoot,
bough

limit [1] *n.* barrier, boundary, border, edge,
end, restraint [2] *v.* reduce, restrict *The heavy
rain was restricted to the hilly country*, confine
★**free**

limited *adj.* restricted, reduced, narrow,
confined ★**unrestricted**

limp [1] *adj.* flabby, flimsy, flexible [2] *v.*
hobble, falter, shuffle

line [1] *n.* stripe, streak, dash, bar [2] cord,
thread [3] row, queue *We stood in a queue
awaiting the arrival of the bus*, file [4] calling,
occupation

linger *v.* loiter, lag, dally, tarry, delay,
▷*dawdle* ★**speed**

link *n.* bond, tie, connection, joint, *v.* unite,
join, couple, bracket ★**separate**

liquefy *v.* liquidize, melt

liquid *n.* fluid, liquor, solution

list *n.* schedule, table, catalogue, register, *v.*
tilt, lean, heel *The yacht heeled over as it turned
into the wind*, careen, slope

listen *v.* hear, hearken, hark, heed

listless *adj.* languid, dull, lethargic, lifeless,
▷*sluggish* ★**lively**

literally *adv.* actually, faithfully, precisely,
really ★**loosely**

literate *adj.* educated, well- educated,
learned, lettered ★**illiterate**

lithe *adj.* agile, nimble, flexible, supple ★**stiff**

litter *n.* clutter, jumble, rubbish, mess, refuse

little [1] *adj.* small, tiny, short, slight, trivial,
petty, ▷*small* ★**large** [2] *adv.* hardly, rarely,
seldom

live [1] *adj.* alive, living, existing, active,
alert ★**dead** [2] *v.* be, subsist, breathe, exist

lively *adj.* active, brisk, vivacious, animated,
agile ★ **listless**

livid [1] *adj.* angry, enraged, furious, mad [2]
ashen *We were really scared, and Bob's face was
ashen*, greyish, pale, leaden

living [1] *adj.* alive, existing [2] *n.* job,
occupation, work

load [1] *n.* freight, cargo, goods, burden [2] *v.*
fill, pack, burden, pile up, stack LODE,
LOWED

loaf [1] *v.* waste time, idle, dally, dawdle [2] *n.*
mass of bread, cake, piece

loan [1] *n.* credit, advance, allowance [2] *v.*
allow, lend, advance *The bank advanced me
the money to pay the mortgage* LONE

loath or **loth** *adj.* reluctant, disinclined,
opposed

loathe *v.* abhor, detest, despise, dislike,
▷*hate* ★**like**

lobby *n.* hallway, entrance, vestibule, foyer

local *adj.* regional, district, parish, provincial

locate *v.* find, discover, detect, unearth

lock [1] *n.* bolt, fastener, latch, clasp [2] *v.*
bolt, fasten, secure [3] *n.* floodgate, weir [4]
curl, plait, tress *I kept a tress of her hair in a
locket*

lodge [1] *v.* stay at, put up, shelter, get stuck
A fishbone got stuck in his throat, remain [2] *n.*
inn, hotel, country seat

lofty [1] *adj.* tall, high, noble, great [2] proud,
exalted, arrogant ★**modest**

logical *adj.* fair, justifiable, reasonable,
sound ★**illogical**

loiter *v.* lag, trail, linger, dally, dawdle, hang
about

loll *v.* recline, sprawl, lounge, lie, rest, flop

lone *adj.* single, sole, lonely, separate,
unaccompanied LOAN

lonely *adj.* alone, forsaken, friendless, remote,
forlorn, lonesome

long [1] *adj.* lengthy, extended, expanded
★**short** [2] *v.* crave, hanker, yearn, desire

look [1] *v.* appear, seem, [2] peer, glance,
watch, behold [3] *n.* appearance, glance, gaze
*Her gaze fell upon me, and I had to answer the
next question*

loom *v.* menace, portend, rise, emerge,
appear

loop *n.* bend, circle, coil, noose, twist

loophole *n.* escape, way out, excuse, get-out

loose 1 *adj.* slack, separate, apart, flimsy, flabby, baggy 2 free, relaxed, 3 vague, indefinite

loosely *adv.* freely, separately, vaguely

loosen *v.* slacken, relax, undo, detach, release, unfasten ★**tighten**

loot *n.* booty, haul, sway, spoils, plunder LUTE

Loot **Lute**

lord *n.* noble, ruler, baron, viscount, earl, marquess

lose 1 *v.* mislay, misplace, miss ★**find** 2 be defeated, suffer defeat *The rebels suffered defeat at the hands of the army*, fail ★**win**

loser *n.* failure, dud, flop ★**winner**

loss *n.* damage, harm, forfeit, ruin, misfortune ★**gain**

lost *adj.* mislaid, missing, gone, vanished, strayed, ruined ★**found**

lot 1 *n.* group, batch, assortment 2 fate, portion, fortune 3 plot, patch, land

lotion *n.* balm, salve, ointment, cream, liniment

loud 1 *adj.* noisy, blatant, shrill, blaring, deafening 2 gaudy, vulgar, tasteless ★**quiet**

lounge 1 *v.* recline, lie, loll, sprawl, laze 2 *n.* bar, parlour *Tea was served in the charming little parlour*, sitting room

lout *n.* oaf, clod, boor, lummox

lovable *adj.* winsome, charming, attractive, fascinating ★**hateful**

love 1 *v.* adore, idolize, worship, dote on, cherish, treasure 2 *n.* affection, passion, devotion, ardour ★**hate**

lovely *adj.* charming, delightful, beautiful, adorable ★**hideous**

low 1 *adj.* base, vulgar, crude, improper 2 not high, flat, level 3 soft, faint, muffled, deep 4 humble, modest, lowly 5 cheap, inexpensive ★**high** LO

lower 1 *v.* let down, fall, descend 2 debase, disgrace, degrade 3 *adj.* inferior, lesser, smaller, minor

loyal *adj.* constant, staunch *Bill was Kathy's staunch friend for years*, true, ▷*faithful* ★**disloyal**

lucid *adj.* clear, obvious, intelligible, bright, ▷*transparent* ★**murky**

luck *n.* chance, fortune, success, windfall ★**misfortune**

lucky *adj.* fortunate, successful, blessed, charmed, favoured ★**unlucky**

ludicrous *adj.* absurd, foolish, silly, outlandish, ▷*ridiculous*

lug *v.* pull, draw, drag, haul, tow, heave

luggage *n.* baggage, cases, trunks, boxes

lull 1 *v.* calm, dwindle, cease, slacken, subside 2 *n.* calm, hush, respite

lumber 1 *n.* clutter, jumble, junk, rubbish, trash 2 timber

luminous *adj.* shining, radiant, bright

lump *n.* bit, piece, chunk, block, knob, swelling *I noticed a rather nasty swelling on my arm*

lunatic *n.* mad person, maniac, psychopath

lunge *v.* push, thrust, plunge, charge, pounce

lurch *v.* lean, list, reel, rock, stagger, stumble

lure *v.* attract, draw, decoy, ensnare, invite, ▷*tempt* ★**repulse**

lurid *adj.* ghastly, disgusting, grim, grisly, melodramatic, sensational

lurk *v.* slink, skulk, crouch, hide, prowl, snoop

luscious *adj.* juicy, succulent, mellow, delicious, scrumptious ★**nauseous**

lush *adj.* wild, luxuriant, green, rich, abundant

lust *n.* desire, greed, passion, craving

lustre *n.* brightness, brilliance, gleam, sheen

lusty *adj.* hale, hearty, vigorous, energetic, rugged, tough ★**weak**

luxury *n.* affluence, wealth, richness, comfort, bliss

lyre *n.* harp, lute, zither LIAR

M m

macabre *adj.* ghastly, grisly, hideous, horrible, ▷*ghostly*

machine *n.* engine, contrivance, device

mad [1] *adj.* lunatic, crazy, ▷*insane* [2] angry, furious ★**sane**

madcap *adj.* flighty, reckless, thoughtless, impulsive

magazine [1] *n.* periodical, publication [2] storehouse, depot, arsenal

magic [1] *n.* wizardry, witchcraft, sorcery, conjuring [2] *adj.* bewitching *She greeted me with a bewitching smile*, fascinating, miraculous

magician *n.* conjuror, wizard, witch, sorcerer, juggler

magistrate *n.* judge, justice, bailiff

magnanimous *adj.* forgiving, generous, charitable, liberal ★**paltry**

magnate *n.* industrialist, merchant, tycoon, VIP, leader MAGNET

magnet *n.* lodestone, attraction, bait, draw MAGNATE

magnetic *adj.* attracting, attractive, absorbing, entrancing, ▷*charming* ★**repulsive**

magnificent *adj.* majestic, noble, grand, brilliant, superb, ▷*splendid* ★**modest**

magnify *v.* enlarge, increase, exaggerate, ▷*enhance* ★**diminish**

maid [1] *n.* maiden, virgin, miss, damsel [2] maidservant, domestic help, waitress MADE

mail [1] *n.* letters, post, correspondence, epistles [2] armour *The knight's armour was of breastplates and chain mail*, shield MALE

maim *v.* mutilate, injure, mangle, crush, ▷*disable* ★**heal**

main [1] *adj.* leading, principal, head *Such important matters are dealt with at our head office*, chief, central [2] *n.* channel, duct, line, pipe

mainly *adv.* chiefly, generally, mostly, on the whole, usually

maintain [1] *v.* sustain, keep, support, provide for [2] affirm, advocate *The director advocated an increase in charges*, assert

Mail

majestic *adj.* dignified, grand, noble, august, elevated, ▷*magnificent* ★**unimportant**

major [1] *adj.* senior, chief, leading, more important, greater ★**minor** [2] *n.* officer, soldier

majority *n.* greater number, most part, bulk, mass ★**minority**

make [1] *v.* build, construct, fabricate, fashion [2] compel, drive, coerce [3] designate *Liz was designated as next head of the department*, appoint

make up [1] *v.* invent, fabricate, create [2] forgive and forget, bury the hatchet *At last, my brother and sister stopped arguing and decided to bury the hatchet*

makeshift *adj.* improvised, temporary, stop-gap *I fixed the car engine, but it was only a stop-gap repair* ★**permanent**

malady *n.* illness, sickness, ailment, affliction, disease

malevolent *adj.* malign, baleful, venomous, malicious, ▷*hostile* ★**benevolent**

malice *n.* bitterness, rancour, spite, enmity, ▷*hatred* ★**kindness**

malicious *adj.* malignant, spiteful, resentful, bitter, ▷*hateful* ★**kind**

maltreat *v.* bully, harm, abuse, injure, ▷*hurt* ★**assist**

mammoth *adj.* giant, colossal, enormous, ▷*huge* ★**small**

man [1] *n.* male, sir, mankind, gentleman [2] valet, manservant [3] *v.* equip, fit out, arm, crew

manage [1] *v.* direct, control, administer [2] get along *I get along quite well on my own*, fare, cope with ★**fail**

manager *n.* director, superintendent, overseer, foreman, boss

mandate *n.* authority, command, instruction, warrant

mangle *v.* crush, deform, destroy, maul, ▷*maim*

mania *n.* madness, delirium, craze, fad, enthusiasm, passion

manifest *v.* signify, suggest, demonstrate, display, ▷*show* ★**hide**

manipulate *v.* work, handle, wield, conduct, ▷*operate*

manly *adj.* male, masculine, brave, bold, strong, ▷*fearless*

manner *n.* fashion, style, form, mode, demeanour, bearing, way MANOR

manoeuvre *v.* direct, drive, guide, handle, ▷*manipulate*

manor *n.* estate, country house, château, hall MANNER

mansion *n.* house, castle, residence, ▷*manor*

mantle *n.* canopy, cape, covering, hood, shroud MANTEL

mantel *n.* fireplace shelf, mantelpiece MANTLE

manual [1] *adj.* hand-operated, physical [2] *n.* guide, guide-book, handbook *This washing-machine comes with its own handbook*

manufacture *v.* make, build, fabricate, ▷*construct*

manuscript [1] *n.* script, article, essay, theme [2] handwriting, autograph

many *adj.* numerous, varied, various, frequent, countless ★**few**

map *n.* chart, plan, diagram, outline

mar *v.* deface, disfigure, injure, blemish, damage, ▷*spoil* ★**enhance**

march *v.* stride, walk, pace, step, file, trek

margin *n.* edge, border, rim, side, boundary, brim, brink ★**centre**

mariner *n.* seaman, sailor, seafarer, deckhand, tar, seadog

mark [1] *n.* feature, emblem, impression *The letter had a handstamped impression on it*, blemish [2] *v.* scratch, blemish, stain [3] take notice of, observe

marked *adj.* noticeable, conspicuous, apparent, clear, striking ★**slight**

market *n.* bazaar, market-place, mart, fair

maroon *v.* desert, beach, strand, abandon, cast away ★**rescue**

marry *v.* wed, get married, espouse, mate, unite ★**separate**

marsh *n.* swamp, mire, moor, morass, bog

marshal *v.* gather, group, deploy, assemble MARTIAL

martial *adj.* military, militant, hostile, warlike ★**peaceful** MARSHAL

marvel *n.* miracle, wonder, spectacle, sensation

marvellous *adj.* wonderful, wondrous, fabulous, spectacular, ▷*remarkable* ★**ordinary**

masculine *adj.* male, manlike, manly, robust, strapping, ▷*strong* ★**feminine**

mash *v.* crush, squash, pulverize, grind

mask [1] *n.* camouflage, veil, domino [2] *v.* conceal, disguise *Aladdin went to the market-place disguised as a beggar*, shield ★**uncover**

mass *n.* batch, combination, hunk, load, quantity, lump

massacre *v.* exterminate, butcher, murder, slaughter, kill

massive *adj.* big, large, bulky, enormous, ▷*huge* ★**small**

master [1] *n.* controller, director, leader, captain, champion [2] *v.* tame *Our job on the ranch was to tame the wild horses*, control, defeat, subdue

match [1] *n.* light, fuse, taper, lucifer [2] *v.* copy, pair, equal, tone with

mate [1] *n.* spouse, husband, wife, companion, chum, comrade [2] *v.* breed, join, wed, yoke

material ⬚1 *n.* fabric, textile, cloth, stuff,
matter ⬚2 *adj.* actual, real, concrete *There was
concrete evidence of the prisoner's innocence*

maternal *adj.* motherly, parental, kind,
affectionate, protective

matter ⬚1 *n.* affair, concern, subject, topic
⬚2 stuff, material, substance *This rock contains
some sort of mineral substance* ⬚3 trouble,
distress ⬚4 *v.* signify, count, affect

mature *adj.* ripe, mellowed, seasoned,
developed, grown-up, adult ★**immature**

maul *v.* batter, beat, molest, paw, ▷*mangle*

maxim *n.* saying, motto, axiom, proverb

maximum *adj.* supreme, highest, most,
greatest, top, largest ★**minimum**

maybe *adv.* possibly, perhaps, perchance

maze *n.* labyrinth, puzzle, tangle, confusion,
▷*muddle* MAIZE

meadow *n.* grassland, field, mead, pasture

meagre *adj.* thin, spare, slight, flimsy, sparse,
▷*scanty* ★**substantial**

meal *n.* repast, dinner, lunch, breakfast,
supper, ▷*feast*

mean ⬚1 *v.* signify, denote, express, suggest
⬚2 *adj.* base, low, paltry, miserly
★**generous** ⬚3 average, medium MIEN

meaning *n.* significance, explanation, sense

means ⬚1 *n.* resources, money, wealth ⬚2
technique, ability *She has the ability to become
a professional player*, method

measure ⬚1 *n.* meter, gauge, rule ⬚2 limit,
extent, amount ⬚3 *v.* estimate, value,
quantify *It is hard to quantify how much damage
has been done*

meat *n.* flesh, viands, victuals, food MEET
METE

mechanical ⬚1 *adj.* automatic, machine-
driven ⬚2 routine, unthinking

medal *n.* award, decoration, ribbon, prize,
trophy MEDDLE

meddle *v.* interfere, intervene, intrude,
tamper MEDAL

medicine *n.* remedy, cure, physic,
medicament, nostrum, drug

mediocre *adj.* average, common, inferior,
middling, ▷*ordinary* ★**excellent**

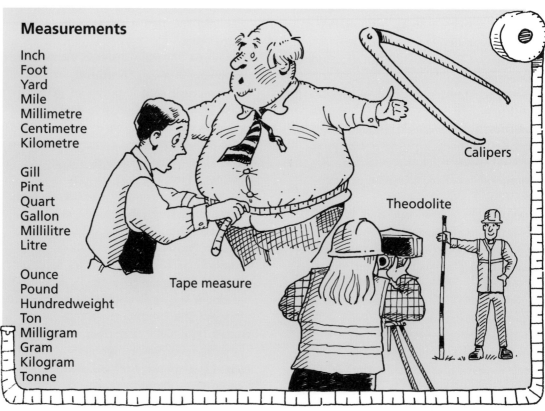

Measurements

Inch
Foot
Yard
Mile
Millimetre
Centimetre
Kilometre

Gill
Pint
Quart
Gallon
Millilitre
Litre

Ounce
Pound
Hundredweight
Ton
Milligram
Gram
Kilogram
Tonne

Tape measure

Calipers

Theodolite

meditate *v.* ponder, puzzle over, think, reflect, contemplate

medium [1] *n.* means, agency, centre [2] conditions, setting, atmosphere *I like school because it has such a wonderful atmosphere of learning* [3] *adj.* average, fair, ▷*mediocre*

medley *n.* assortment, jumble, collection, hotchpotch

meek *adj.* docile, humble, quiet, patient, uncomplaining, ▷*mild* ★**arrogant**

meet *v.* come together, converge, join, flock, assemble, encounter MEAT METE

meeting *n.* gathering, assembly, convention

melancholy *adj.* glum, gloomy, unhappy, sad, ▷*miserable* ★**cheerful**

mellow [1] *adj.* ripe, rich, full-flavoured ★**unripe** [2] jovial, cheerful [3] smooth, soothing, delicate *The wine had a smooth, delicate flavour*

melodious *adj.* sweet, mellow, silver-toned, rich, resonant ★**harsh**

melody *n.* tune, air, lay, song, chant, theme

melt *v.* dissolve, liquefy, soften, thaw ★**solidify**

member [1] *n.* fellow, associate, representative [2] limb, part, portion, leg, arm

memorable *adj.* unforgettable, fresh, indelible, noticeable, striking, ▷*conspicuous*

memorial *n.* monument, memento, relic, mausoleum *The old emperor was buried in the state mausoleum*

memorize *v.* learn, commit to memory, remember

memory *n.* recall, recapture, recollection, renown, ▷*fame*

menace *v.* threaten, intimidate, frighten, alarm, ▷*bully*

mend *v.* restore, correct, promote, improve, rectify, heal, ▷*repair* ★**damage**

menial [1] *adj.* servile, ignoble, base [2] *n.* flunkey, skivvy, underling, lackey

mental [1] *adj.* intellectual, theoretical, abstract ★**physical** [2] crazy, lunatic, ▷*mad* ★**sane**

mention *v.* declare, announce, observe, disclose, speak of, say

mercenary [1] *adj.* acquisitive, grasping, greedy, ▷*selfish* [2] *n.* soldier of fortune *The men who were killed were not Austrians, but soldiers of fortune*, freelance, hireling

merchandise *n.* wares, goods, commodities, cargo, freight, stock

merchant *n.* dealer, trader, marketeer, vendor, retailer, tradesman

merciful *adj.* humane, clement, lenient, compassionate, sparing, forgiving ★**merciless**

merciless *adj.* callous, cruel, pitiless, unrelenting, inhuman ★**merciful**

mercy *n.* compassion, clemency, forgiveness, forbearance, grace, ▷*pity* ★**cruelty**

mere *adj.* pure, unmixed, absolute, unaffected, simple, paltry

merge *v.* mix, mingle, combine, fuse, blend, weld, ▷*unite*

merit [1] *n.* excellence, quality, virtue, worth, calibre, ▷*talent* ★**failing** [2] *v.* deserve, be worthy of

merry *adj.* jolly, gleeful, cheerful, mirthful, sunny, ▷*happy* ★**melancholy**

mesh *n.* net, lattice, snare, netting, tangle, trap

mess [1] *n.* muddle, confusion, clutter, jumble, chaos, ▷*plight* ★**order** [2] dining-hall, eating-place

message *n.* communication, letter, missive, notice, note, dispatch *The reporter sent a dispatch to her paper in Lisbon*

messenger *n.* courier, runner, agent, bearer, carrier, herald

Metals

Aluminium	Nickel
Brass	Platinum
Bronze	Silver
Chromium	Tin
Copper	Zinc
Gold	
Iron and Steel	
Lead	
Manganese	
Mercury	

Nuggets

Girder

mete *v.* measure, apportion, distribute, divide, deal MEAT MEET

method *n.* routine, usage, way, means, system, rule, manner, ▷*mode*

metre 1 *n.* measure, gauge, rule 2 cadence *He recited some of his poems, which had a peculiar cadence to them*, rhythm, lilt, swing

mettle *n.* spirit, life, fire, animation, ardour, boldness, ▷*courage*

middle 1 *n.* centre, heart, midst 2 *adj.* medium, average, normal

midget 1 *n.* dwarf, gnome, pygmy 2 *adj.* little, miniature, small, ▷*tiny* ★**giant**

mien *n.* appearance, air, look, manner, expression MEAN

miffed *adj.* annoyed, nettled, offended, hurt, ▷*upset* ★**delighted**

might 1 *n.* strength, ability, power, force, energy 2 *v.* past tense of **may** *She might not have gone had she known it would snow* MITE

mighty *adj.* strong, powerful, potent, stupendous, ▷*hefty* ★**weak**

mild *adj.* moderate, calm, gentle, genial, docile, ▷*meek* ★**harsh**

military *adj.* martial, soldierly, warlike

mill 1 *n.* grinder, works, factory, plant 2 crush, grind, pulverize *The rock was pulverized and used for making roads*, grate

mimic *v.* impersonate, copy, simulate, imitate

mince *v.* shred, chop, crumble, grind, hash MINTS

mind 1 *n.* brain, intellect, soul, spirit 2 *v.* listen to, obey, follow orders 3 take care of, look after 4 be careful, watch out for

mine 1 *n.* quarry, colliery, shaft, deposit, tunnel 2 bomb, explosive 3 *v.* excavate, dig out 4 *pron.* belonging to me *This shop is mine*

mingle *v.* mix, blend, combine, ▷*merge*

miniature 1 *adj.* tiny, small, dwarf, midget, minute 2 *n.* small portrait

mimimum *adj.* least, smallest, lowest, slightest ★**maximum**

minister 1 *n.* clergyman, vicar, priest 2 ambassador, diplomat *My aunt was a diplomat and was a minister in the embassy* 3 government official, secretary

minor *adj.* lesser, smaller, lower, junior, trivial, trifling ★**major** MINER

mint 1 *v.* stamp, forge, cast 2 *adj.* new, perfect, untarnished 3 *n.* peppermint, plant

minute 1 (*min*-it) *n.* flash, instant, moment 2 (my-*nyute*) *adj.* slight, tiny, small, ▷*miniature* ★**huge**

miracle *n.* marvel, wonder, phenomenon

miraculous *adj.* supernatural, amazing, wondrous, prodigious ★**ordinary**

mire *n.* slime, muck, ooze, mud

mirror 1 *n.* looking-glass, reflector 2 *v.* imitate, simulate, reflect *The essay reflected my feelings about my old home*, copy

mirth *n.* hilarity, laughter, jocularity, fun, frolic, jollity ★**melancholy**

misbehave *v.* do wrong, disobey, offend, be naughty

miscellaneous *adj.* various, varied, divers, sundry, mixed, jumbled

mischief *n.* roguery, pranks, damage, hurt, annoyance, harm

mischievous *adj.* rascally, villainous, naughty, destructive, spiteful ★**good**

misconduct *n.* misbehavour, wrong-doing, naughtiness, rudeness

miser *n.* niggard, skinflint, Scrooge, penny-pincher, tightwad ★**spendthrift**

miserable *adj.* forlorn, wretched, pitiable, desolate, suffering ★**cheerful**

misery *n.* sorrow, woe, grief, anguish, distress, ▷*unhappiness* ★**happiness**

misfit *n.* eccentric *Professor Jones is something of an eccentric and comes to college in her slippers*, drop-out, oddball, nonconformist

misfortune *n.* adversity, bad luck, hardship, evil, calamity, ▷*disaster* ★**luck**

misgiving *n.* distrust, mistrust, doubt, apprehension, anxiety, ▷*qualm* ★**confidence**

mishap *n.* misadventure, blow, accident, ▷*misfortune*

misjudge *v.* underestimate, overestimate, overrate, underrate, ▷*mistake*

mislay *v.* lose, misplace, miss

mislead *v.* deceive, lead astray, hoodwink, take in, outwit, ▷*bluff*

miss [1] *v.* fail, fall short of, skip, pass over, mistake [2] grieve over, yearn for, lament [3] *n.* girl, young woman, damsel

missile *n.* projectile, arrow, dart, pellet, shot, rocket

mission *n.* errand, task, assignment, object, objective, end, aim, ▷*quest*

mist *n.* moisture, dew, vapour, fog, cloud MISSED

mistake [1] *n.* error, fault, lapse, blunder, oversight [2] *v.* slip up, misunderstand, confuse

mistaken *adj.* erroneous, untrue, false, fallacious, ▷*wrong* *★correct

mistrust *v.* disbelieve, distrust, doubt, fear, ▷*suspect* *★trust

misunderstand *v.* mistake, misinterpret, take wrongly *★grasp

misuse *v.* exploit, abuse, corrupt, harm

mite [1] *n.* grain, atom, morsel, particle [2] spider-like creature *The plants were infested with mites* MIGHT

mitigate *v.* allay, ease, abate, moderate, justify *★aggravate

mix *v.* blend, whip, mingle, combine, ▷*stir*

mix up *v.* confuse, confound, muddle, jumble, ▷*bewilder*

mixture *n.* miscellany, medley, jumble, blend

moan *v.* wail, groan, grouse, grumble, grieve, whinge *★rejoice

mob *n.* crowd, mass, gang, flock, rabble, company, throng

mobile *adj.* active, portable, wandering, movable *★immobile

mock [1] *v.* mimic, imitate, jeer at, laugh at, ridicule, ▷*flatter* [2] *adj.* pretended, artificial

mode *n.* fashion, style, vogue, manner, way, form, ▷*method* MOWED

model [1] *n.* pattern, original, prototype *This car is a prototype, and we shall soon produce many like it* [2] mannequin [3] replica, representation

moderate *adj.* reasonable, medium, gentle, mild, quiet, modest, ▷*fair*

modern *adj.* new, up-to-date, modish, stylish, recent

modest *adj.* bashful, demure, diffident, unassuming, humble *★vain

modesty *n.* humility, diffidence, reserve, shyness, decency *★vanity

modify *v.* transform, convert, change, alter, revise, redesign

moist *adj.* damp, humid, watery, clammy, dank, ▷*wet* *★dry

moisture *n.* damp, dampness, liquid, wetness

molest *v.* annoy, bother, pursue, attack, torment, ▷*harry*

moment [1] *n.* second, instant, twinkling [2] importance, worth, weight *I think your argument has some weight, and I agree with you*

momentous *adj.* notable, outstanding, decisive, important *★insignificant

monarch *n.* king, sovereign, ruler, emperor, prince *The head of state in Monaco is a prince*

Mode   **Mowed**

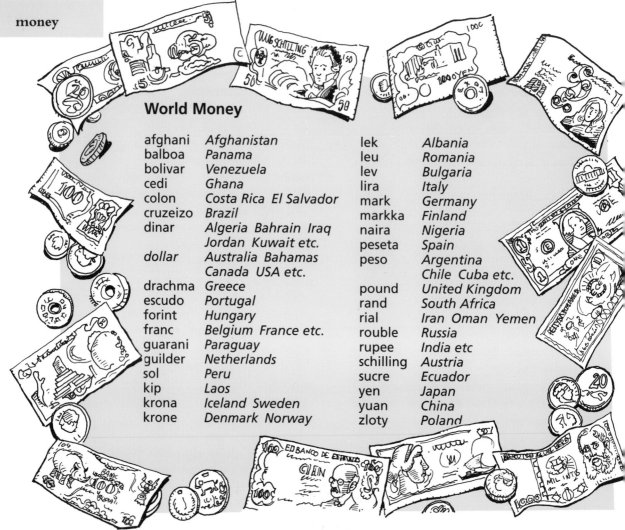

World Money

afghani	*Afghanistan*	lek	*Albania*
balboa	*Panama*	leu	*Romania*
bolivar	*Venezuela*	lev	*Bulgaria*
cedi	*Ghana*	lira	*Italy*
colon	*Costa Rica El Salvador*	mark	*Germany*
cruzeizo	*Brazil*	markka	*Finland*
dinar	*Algeria Bahrain Iraq Jordan Kuwait etc.*	naira	*Nigeria*
		peseta	*Spain*
dollar	*Australia Bahamas Canada USA etc.*	peso	*Argentina Chile Cuba etc.*
drachma	*Greece*	pound	*United Kingdom*
escudo	*Portugal*	rand	*South Africa*
forint	*Hungary*	rial	*Iran Oman Yemen*
franc	*Belgium France etc.*	rouble	*Russia*
guarani	*Paraguay*	rupee	*India etc*
guilder	*Netherlands*	schilling	*Austria*
sol	*Peru*	sucre	*Ecuador*
kip	*Laos*	yen	*Japan*
krona	*Iceland Sweden*	yuan	*China*
krone	*Denmark Norway*	zloty	*Poland*

money *n.* wealth, cash, coin, legal tender

mongrel *n.* hybrid, mixed, crossbreed, dog

monitor ☐1 *n.* listener, auditor, watchdog, prefect ☐2 *v.* check, supervise, oversee

monologue *n.* lecture, sermon, oration, speech, recitation

monopolize *v.* control, take over, appropriate, ▷*dominate* ★**share**

monotonous *adj.* tedious, uninteresting, dull, prosaic *His speech was so prosaic that I almost dropped off to sleep!*, repetitive, ▷*tiresome*

monster *n.* beast, fiend, wretch, villain, brute

monstrous *adj.* hideous, frightful, dreadful, terrible, criminal, ▷*wicked*

mood *n.* humour, temper, disposition, state of mind

moody *adj.* morose, sulky, sullen, peevish, cantankerous *I didn't like Uncle Harry; he was a cantankerous old man* ★**cheerful**

moor ☐1 *v.* tether, picket, tie, chain, anchor, secure ☐2 *n.* heath, moorland

mop ☐1 *n.* sponge, swab, towel ☐2 hair, tresses, locks, mane

mope *v.* be dejected, grieve, moon, pine, sulk

moral *adj.* virtuous, good, honest, honourable, ▷*upright* ★**immoral**

morbid *adj.* gruesome, macabre, melancholy, grisly, putrid

more ☐1 *adj.* in addition, also, beyond, extra, further ☐2 *adv.* better, again, longer

morning *n.* dawn, daybreak, daylight, cockcrow *I rose at cockrow, saddled my horse and was off to York*, sunrise ★**evening** MOURNING

morose *adj.* glum, sullen, sulky, broody, taciturn, ▷*moody* ★**cheerful**

morsel *n.* bit, bite, piece scrap, nibble

mortal ☐1 *adj.* human, feeble, ephemeral ☐2 fatal, final, deadly, severe

most [1] *adj.* greatest [2] *adv.* mostly, chiefly, mainly, utmost

mostly *adv.* as a rule, principally, usually, normally

mother [1] *n.* female parent, ma, mama, mummy [2] *v.* nurse, protect, rear, care for

motherly *adj.* caring, comforting, loving, maternal, gentle

motion [1] *n.* movement, locomotion, action, passage [2] proposal *I vote that we accept the proposal,* suggestion

motionless *adj.* stationary, still, transfixed, stable, inert ★**moving**

motive *n.* reason, purpose, occasion, impulse, cause, ▷*spur*

mottled *adj.* speckled, spotted, pied, piebald

motto *n.* saying, slogan, watchword, maxim *My mother's maxim was "always look on the bright side",* proverb

mould [1] *v.* form, shape, fashion, cast, create [2] *n.* pattern, matrix [3] earth, loam

mouldy *adj.* mildewed, putrid, bad

mound *n.* hillock, pile, knoll, rise, mount

mount *v.* ascend, climb, rise, vault

mourn *v.* lament, deplore, sorrow, regret, weep, ▷*grieve* ★**rejoice**

mournful *adj.* doleful, sombre, cheerless, sorrowful, ▷*melancholy* ★**joyful**

mouth *n.* aperture, opening, entrance, orifice, inlet, jaws

mouthful *n.* bite, morsel, sample, taste, titbit

move [1] *v.* march, proceed, walk, go [2] propose, suggest, recommend [3] propel, drive, impel

moving *adj.* touching, affecting, stirring, emotional

much [1] *adj.* abundant, considerable, ample [2] *adv.* considerably, greatly, often [3] *n.* loads, lots, heaps, plenty

muck *n.* dirt, filth, mire, ooze, mud, scum

muddle [1] *n.* confusion, clutter, jumble, mix-up [2] *v.* bungle, tangle, confound, ▷*bewilder*

muff *v.* botch, mismanage, miss, spoil, ▷*muddle*

muffle [1] *v.* deaden, mute, muzzle, silence [2] wrap, envelop, wind, swaddle

mug [1] *n.* innocent, fool, simpleton [2] cup, beaker, tankard [3] *v.* attack, beat up, rob

muggy *adj.* clammy, dank, damp, humid, close ★**dry**

mull *v.* meditate *I meditated over the weekend before deciding what to do,* consider, study, think about

multiply *v.* increase, spread, grow, extend, intensify ★**decrease**

multitude *n.* crowd, legion, throng, swarm, horde ★**handful**

mum *adj.* dumb, silent, quiet, mute

munch *v.* crunch, chew, bit, nibble, ▷*eat*

murder *v.* slay, assassinate, butcher, destroy, slaughter, ▷*kill*

murky *adj.* foggy, cloudy, dark, gloomy, dull, misty ★**bright**

murmur *n. & v.* whisper, mutter, mumble, drone

muscular *adj.* brawny, athletic, burly, beefy, powerful, ▷*robust* ★**puny**

muse *v.* meditate, ponder, puzzle over, brood, deliberate

must [1] *v.* ought to, should, be obliged to [2] *n.* duty, necessity, requirement

muster *v.* marshal, collect, assemble, rally *The soldiers rallied and prepared to attack again,* enrol

musty *adj.* mouldy, rank, mildewy, decayed

mute *adj.* silent, speechless, voiceless, soundless ★**loud**

mutilate *v.* injure, hurt, cut, damage, hack, ▷*maim*

mutiny *n. & v.* protest, revolt, strike, riot

mutter *v.* mumble, grouse, grumble, ▷*murmur* ★**exclaim**

mutual *adj.* common, reciprocal, interchangeable, ▷*joint* ★**one-sided**

mysterious *adj.* obscure, unrevealed, unexplained, secret, ▷*hidden* ★**clear**

mystery *n.* puzzle, enigma, secrecy, riddle, problem

mystify *v.* confuse, bamboozle, hoodwink, puzzle, mislead, ▷*baffle* ★**enlighten**

myth *n.* fable, legend, supposition, fabrication, tradition, fantasy ★**fact**

mythical *adj.* fabulous, fabled, legendary, traditional, imaginary ★**true**

N n

nab v. arrest, apprehend, seize, catch, capture, grab

nag [1] v. pester, hector, heckle, badger, annoy, henpeck, scold *My parents scolded me for coming home late* [2] n. horse, hack, pony

nail [1] n. brad, peg, pin, spike, tack [2] v. hammer, fix, tack, peg [3] capture, catch, seize

naïve adj. innocent, unworldly, unsophisticated, simple, trusting ★**cunning, sophisticated**

naked adj. nude, bare, unclothed, undressed ★**clothed**

name [1] n. title, description, designation [2] character, reputation *A good reputation is very important to me*, distinction [3] v. christen, style, term, entitle

nap [1] v. sleep, doze, drowse, rest [2] n. down, fibre, fuzz *Velvet is a cloth with a kind of fuzz to the surface*

narrate v. describe, tell, recite, yarn

narrow adj. slender, fine, small, ▷*thin* ★**wide**

nasty adj. dirty, mucky, foul, offensive, unpleasant, ▷*squalid We walked through several streets of dirty, squalid hovels* ★**nice**

national adj. civil, governmental, public, general

native adj. natural, inborn, aboriginal, domestic, local

natural adj. frank, genuine, innate, instinctive, ordinary, usual

naturally adj. absolutely, certainly, frankly, normally

nature [1] n. temper, personality, disposition

naughty adj. mischievous, rascally, wicked, disobedient, ▷*bad* ★**well-behaved**

nauseous adj. nauseated, queasy, squeamish, sick, disgusting ★**pleasant**

nautical adj. maritime *Ancient Greece was a great maritime nation*, seamanlike, naval, sailing

navigate v. voyage, cruise, sail, guide, pilot

navy n. ships, fleet, armada, flotilla

near adj. close, nearby, adjacent, bordering, beside, ▷*nigh The old lady was nigh on ninety years of age* ★**remote**

nearly adv. about, almost, all but, thereabouts, roughly

neat [1] adj. tidy, spruce, smart, stylish ★**untidy** [2] accurate, adept *Jim wants to be a juggler: he's already very adept*, agile, clever

necessary adj. needed, essential, basic, required, compulsory ★**optional**

need [1] v. require, want, crave, ▷*demand* ★**have** [2] n. distress, want, necessity, deprivation *After the long war, the people suffered many deprivations* KNEAD

needed adj. wanted, desired, lacking, ▷*necessary* ★**unnecessary**

needless adj. pointless, unnecessary, superfluous, useless ★**necessary**

needy adj. destitute, down-and-out, deprived, ▷*poor* ★**well-off**

neglect v. overlook, ignore, scorn, slight, disregard, ▷*spurn Charlie wanted to marry Bella, but she spurned him* ★**cherish**

neglected adj. unkempt, abandoned, dilapidated, uncared for ★**cherished**

negligent adj. neglectful, forgetful, slack, indifferent, ▷*careless* ★**careful**

negotiate v. bargain, deal, treat, haggle, mediate

neighbourhood n. vicinity, surroundings, district, area, locality *There are many fine houses in this locality*

neighbourly adj. hospitable, friendly, kind, obliging, ▷*helpful*

nerve [1] n. mettle, guts, pluck, audacity [2] cheek, sauce, impudence *Mr Thompson already owes us money, and has the impudence to ask for more!*

nervous adj. tense, taut, jumpy, flustered, anxious, timid ★**confident**

nest n. den, burrow, haunt, refuge, resort

nestle adj. cuddle, snuggle, huddle, nuzzle

net [1] v. catch, trap, lasso, capture [2] n. mesh, lattice, trap, web, lace *I have some new lace curtains* [3] adj. clear *Your bill comes to ten pounds clear*, final, lowest

National and Religious Holidays

Advent All Saints' Day
Anzac Day Ascension Day
Ash Wednesday Australia
    Day
Bastille Day Boxing Day
Canada Day Candlemas
    Carnival Christmas
Diwali Day of the Dead
Easter
Father's Day Fourth of July
Gandhi's Birthday Good
    Friday Guy Fawkes Day
Halloween Hanukkah
Kenyatta Day Kwanza
Labor Day Lent Lincoln's
    Birthday
Mardi Gras May Day
Memorial Day Midsummer
    Day Mother's Day
    Muhammad's
    Birthday New Year's Day
Palm Sunday Passover
    Pentecost

Purim
Ramadan Rosh Hashanah
Saint Patrick's Day
    Saint Valentine's Day
    Shauvot Sukko
Thanksgiving Day
Washington's Birthday
Yom Kippur

A puppet from Mexican Day of the Dead Festival

nettle *v.* exasperate, annoy, ruffle, pique, ▷*vex*

neutral *adj.* impartial, unbiased, fair-minded, unprejudiced ★**biased**

never *adv.* at no time, not at all, under no circumstances ★**always**

new *adj.* recent, just out, current, latest, fresh, unused, ▷*novel* ★**old** GNU KNEW

news *n.* information, intelligence, tidings, account

next 1 *adj.* following, succeeding, after, later 2 adjacent, adjoining *I live in Park Street and my friend lives in the street adjoining,* beside

nibble *v.* bite, peck, gnaw, munch, ▷*eat*

nice 1 *adj.* pleasant, agreeable, amiable, charming, delightful ★**nasty** 2 precise, accurate, fine, subtle

niche *n.* compartment, hole, corner, recess, place

nick *v.* dent, score, mill, cut, scratch

nigh *adj.* next, close, adjacent, adjoining, ▷*near* ★**distant**

night *n.* dark, darkness, dusk, evening ★**day** KNIGHT

nimble *adj.* active, agile, spry, lithe, skilful, ▷*deft* ★**clumsy**

nip *v.* cut, snip, pinch, twinge, bite

no 1 *adj.* not any, not one, none 2 *adv.* nay, not at all KNOW

noble *adj.* dignified, lofty *My aunt is very important, and has a lofty position on the council,* generous, grand, stately, elevated ★**mean**

nod 1 *v.* beckon, signal, indicate, salute 2 sleep, doze, nap

noise *n.* din, discord, clamour, clatter, hubbub, tumult, uproar ★**silence**

noisy *adj.* loud, boisterous, turbulent, rowdy, clamorous ★**quiet**

nominate *v.* appoint, assign, elect, choose, propose, suggest

nonchalant *adj.* casual, unperturbed, calm, blasé. *We enjoyed the new musical but Sue has been to numerous shows and is very blasé,* cool, detached ★**anxious**

nondescript *adj.* commonplace, colourless, dull, ordinary, ▷*plain* ★**unusual**

none *pron.* not one, not any, not a part, nil, nobody NUN

nonsense *n.* absurdity, balderdash, drivel, rot, rubbish, twaddle ★**sense**

nook *n.* compartment, hole, corner, alcove, crevice, ▷*niche*

noose *n.* loop, bight, snare, rope, lasso

normal *adj.* usual, general, average, sane, lucid, rational, standard ★**abnormal**

nose ①︎ *n.* beak, bill, neb, snout ②︎ prow, stem, bow, front

nosy *adj.* inquisitive, curious, prying, snooping, intrusive

nostalgia *n.* homesickness, longing, pining, regret, remembrance

notable *adj.* eventful, momentous, outstanding, great, ▷*famous* ★**commonplace**

notch *n.* dent, nick, score, cut, cleft, indentation

note ①︎ *n.* letter, message, communication ②︎ remark, record, report ③︎ fame, renown, distinction ④︎ banknote, bill

noted *adj.* eminent, renowned, celebrated, great, ▷*famous* ★**obscure**

nothing *n.* nil, zero, naught, null ★**something**

notice ①︎ *n.* announcement, advice, sign, poster ②︎ *v.* note *After noting the darkening sky, we decided it would rain*, remark, observe, perceive, make out, see ★**ignore**

Notice

After noting the darkening sky, we decided it would rain.

notify *v.* inform, tell, intimate, announce, declare ★**withhold**

notion *n.* idea, conception, opinion, belief, judgment

notorious *adj.* infamous, questionable, scandalous, blatant ★**shameful**

notwithstanding *adv.* nevertheless, nonetheless, however, despite

nourish *v.* feed, sustain, nurture, comfort, support ★**starve**

nourishing *adj.* beneficial, heathful, nutritious, wholesome

novel ①︎ *adj.* fresh, unusual, original, unique, rare, uncommon ②︎ *n.* fiction, story, book, romance, tale

novice *n.* beginner, tyro, learner, apprentice, pupil ★**expert**

now *adv.* at this moment, at present, at once, instantly, right away

now and then *adv.* from time to time, sometimes, occasionally

nude *adj.* bare, naked, unclothed, stripped, undressed

nudge *v.* poke, push, prod, jog, shove, dig

nuisance ①︎ *n.* offence, annoyance, plague, trouble, bore, pest, irritation

nullify *v.* annul, invalidate, cancel, quash, ▷*abolish* ★**establish**

numb *adj.* deadened, insensible, dazed, stunned, unfeeling ★**sensitive**

number ①︎ *n.* figure, amount, volume, quantity, sum ②︎ crowd, throng, multitude *The country's president was visiting the town, watched by a multitude of people* ③︎ figure, symbol, ▷*numeral* ④︎ *v.* count, reckon, tally

numeral *n.* symbol, figure, character, cipher

numerous *adj.* many, divers, several, plentiful, ▷*abundant* ★**few**

nun *n.* sister, religious, abbess, prioress NONE

nurse ①︎ *v.* attend, care for, foster, support, sustain ②︎ *n.* hospital sister, matron

nursery ①︎ *n.* crèche, children's room ②︎ greenhouse, hothouse, garden

nurture *v.* feed, nourish, cherish, foster, ▷*nurse*

nutritious *adj.* healthful, substantial, health-giving, ▷*nourishing* ★**bad**

O o

oaf *n.* brute, lout, blockhead, dolt, ruffian, lummox

obedient *adj.* respectful, obliging, law-abiding, servile, dutiful ★**rebellious**

obey *v.* comply, conform, submit, heed, mind, behave ★**disobey**

object 1 *v.* protest, complain, argue, oppose, refuse ★**agree** 2 *n.* thing, article, commodity, item 3 mission, purpose *The purpose of my visit is to end this conflict*, end, objective

objection *n.* dislike, exception, opposition, protest, ▷*complaint* ★**assent**

objectionable *adj.* displeasing, distasteful, disagreeable, repugnant ★**pleasant**

obligation *n.* responsibility, liability, commitment ★**choice**

oblige 1 *v.* require, compel, force, make 2 gratify, please, help, ▷*assist* ★**displease**

obliging *adj.* helpful, polite, agreeable, courteous, ▷*willing* ★**unkind**

obliterate *v.* blot out, efface, erase, wipe out, destroy

oblivious *adj.* unmindful, absent-minded, heedless, unaware ★**aware**

obnoxious *adj.* repulsive, revolting, offensive, ▷*unpleasant* ★**pleasant**

obscene *adj.* dirty, unclean, vile, filthy, nasty, immoral, indecent ★**decent**

obscure 1 *adj.* indistinct, dim, vague, hidden, confusing *Chaucer wrote in old English, which I find confusing*, ▷*doubtful* ★**clear** 2 *v.* conceal, hide, cloud, darken, cover, ▷*hide* ★**clarify**

observant *adj.* attentive, watchful, heedful, ▷*alert* ★**inattentive**

observation 1 *n.* attention, study, supervision 2 utterance, comment, remark, statement *The police issued a statement.*

observe 1 *v.* abide by *I intend to abide by the laws of the country*, adhere to, carry out, keep up 2 *v.* note, notice, perceive, watch, ▷*see* 3 utter, remark, mention

obsolete *adj.* dated, outmoded, unfashionable, out of date ★**current**

obstacle *n.* obstruction, barrier, bar, hindrance, ▷*drawback* ★**advantage**

obstinate *adj.* determined, dogged, unyielding, perverse *As a child I upset my parents by my perverse behaviour*, ▷*stubborn* ★**docile**

obstruct *v.* hinder, impede, block, bar, choke, ▷*restrain* ★**help**

obstruction *n.* hindrance, restraint, impediment, snag

obtain *v.* acquire, achieve, gain, procure, attain, ▷*get* ★**lose**

obtuse *adj.* dull, stupid, unintelligent, stolid, thick, blunt ★**bright**

obvious *adj.* plain, evident, self-evident, explicit, apparent, ▷*clear* ★**obscure**

occasion 1 *n.* affair, episode, occurrence, circumstance 2 reason, purpose, motive

occasional *adj.* casual, rare, infrequent, periodic ★**frequent**

occult *adj.* hidden, unrevealed, secret, mysterious, supernatural *Edgar Allan Poe wrote tales of the supernatural* ★**open**

occupant *n.* owner, resident, proprietor, tenant

occupation 1 *n.* activity, employment, calling, job 2 possession, tenancy, residence

occupied 1 *adj.* busy, employed, active 2 settled, populated, peopled ★**unoccupied**

occupy 1 *v.* inhabit, live in, reside, dwell in, own, possess, hold

occur *v.* take place, befall, turn out, come to pass, result, ▷*happen*

occurrence *n.* happening, affair, circumstance, incident, occasion, ▷*event*

ocean *n.* sea, main *The pirates of the Spanish Main were the curse of shipping*, deep, tide

Oceans and Seas

Antarctic	Bay	Sound
Arctic	Fjord	Straits
Atlantic	Gulf	
Indian	Lagoon	
Pacific	Sea loch	

odd [1] *adj.* single, unmatched [2] singular, peculiar, quaint, queer ***ordinary** [3] surplus, left over, remaining

odds and ends *n.* leavings, debris *The police found the debris of the crashed aircraft*, leftovers, oddments, remains

odious *adj.* hateful, offensive, detestable, ▷*abominable* ***pleasant**

odorous *adj.* fragrant, perfumed, aromatic, sweet-smelling

odour [1] *n.* scent, aroma, ▷*fragrance* [2] stink, stench, reek, ▷*smell*

off [1] *adv.* away from, over, done [2] *prep.* along, against, opposite, distant ***on** [3] *adj.* bad, mouldy, rotten

offence *n.* insult, outrage, attack, crime, hurt

offend [1] *v.* insult, hurt, wound, outrage, displease [2] transgress, sin ***please**

offensive *adj.* insulting, offending, rude, repugnant. hurtful, distasteful

offer [1] *v.* propose, proffer, present, tender, attempt [2] *n.* bid, endeavour, proposal

offering *n.* sacrifice, donation, gift, present

offhand [1] *adj.* brusque, casual, curt, informal, abrupt [2] informal, improvised, impromptu *My sister, who is a singer, gave an impromptu performance* ***planned**

office [1] *n.* bureau, department, room [2] position, appointment, post

officer [1] *n.* official, administrator, functionary, executive [2] military rank, policeman, minister *A minister from the French Embassy called*

official [1] *adj.* authorised, authentic, proper, formal ***unofficial** [2] *n.* executive, office-holder, bureaucrat *The city bureaucrats take months to get a job done*

officious *adj.* interfering, meddlesome, self-important

offspring *n.* child, children, descendant, heir, family

often *adv.* frequently, regularly, recurrently, time after time, repeatedly ***seldom**

ointment *n.* salve, cream, balm, embrocation, liniment, lotion

old [1] *adj.* ancient, antique, aged, antiquated [2] crumbling, decayed *Beneath the ivy were the decayed remains of the castle wall*, decrepit ***new** [3] out-of-date, old-fashioned, passé [4] aged, mature, elderly ***young**

ominous *adj.* menacing, threatening, foreboding, sinister

omit *v.* leave out, neglect, let go, overlook, miss out, skip ***include**

once *adv.* formerly, at one time, previously

one [1] *adj.* sole, alone, lone, whole [2] *n.* unit, single thing

one-sided *adj.* unequal, unfair, unjust, biased

only [1] *adj.* exclusive, single, sole, lone, solitary [2] *adv.* solely, barely, exclusively

onset *n.* start, outbreak, assault, attack, onslaught

onslaught *n.* charge, attack, bombardment

ooze [1] *n.* mire, muck, slime [2] *v.* bleed, discharge, emit, exude, leak

open [1] *v.* uncover, unlock, unfasten [2] start, commence, begin [3] *adj.* uncovered, clear, evident, apparent ***closed** [4] frank, honest, candid, fair

opening [1] *n.* aperture, mouth, crevice, recess, hole [2] commencement, beginning

openly *adv.* candidly, frankly, plainly, sincerely ***secretly**

operate *v.* function *Despite its age, the old millwheel continued to function*, work, manipulate, drive, ▷*perform*

operation *n.* performance, movement, action, motion, proceeding

opinion *n.* view, concept, judgment, belief, point of view

opponent *n.* antagonist, rival, competitor, contestant, foe, ▷*enemy* ***ally**

opportune *adj.* timely *Since it had started to rain, the timely arrival of the bus was welcome*, convenient, fortunate, suitable ***untimely**

opportunity *n.* occasion, chance, opening, scope, moment

oppose *v.* withstand, resist, obstruct, confront, hinder, ▷*defy* ***support**

opposite [1] *adj.* facing, fronting [2] conflicting, opposing, contrary, adverse ***same**

opposition *n.* antagonism, defiance, hostility, difference, ▷*resistance* ***co-operation**

oppress *v.* crush, depress, harass, overpower, overwhelm

optimist *n.* hopeful person, perfectionist ★**pessimist**

optimistic *adj.* hopeful, cheerful, confident, positive ★**pessimistic**

option *n.* preference, choice, alternative

optional *adj.* possible, voluntary, unforced, open ★**compulsory**

opulent *adj.* rich, affluent, prosperous, well-to-do, ▷*wealthy* ★**poor**

oration *n.* sermon, lecture, speech, discourse

orb *n.* globe, ball, sphere

orbit 1 *n.* path, passage, trajectory 2 province, realm, domain *The river, the forest and the castle were within her domain*

ordeal *n.* trial, nightmare, torment, agony

order 1 *n.* arrangement, pattern, grouping, organization 2 command, law, rule, decree *A royal decree was issued forbidding the killing of deer* 3 shipment, consignment 4 *v.* direct, instruct, command 5 arrange, control, conduct

orderly *adj.* regular, methodical, trim, neat, well-mannered ★**untidy**

ordinary *adj.* common, usual, commonplace, general, customary ★**extraordinary**

organization 1 *n.* association, group, institute, establishment 2 structure, arrangement, system

organize *v.* arrange, form, structure, establish, classify ★**disorganize**

origin *n.* beginning, start, basis, foundation, root, source ★**end**

original 1 *adj.* first, aboriginal, ancient, former, primary 2 fresh, new, novel *Travelling in a horse-drawn carriage was a novel experience*

originate 1 *v.* create, conceive, compose 2 arise, begin, ▷*start* ★**end**

ornament 1 *n.* decoration, adornment, tracery, pattern 2 trinket, curio, knick-knack

ornate *adj.* decorated, adorned, flowery, embellished, showy, garish ★**plain**

oust *v.* expel, eject, evict, dismiss, propel, ▷*overthrow*

Original

Travelling in a horse-drawn carriage was a novel experience.

out 1 *adj.* away, outside, away, absent ★**in** 2 open, revealed, uncovered 3 *adv.* loudly, aloud, audibly

out of order *adj.* broken, not working

out of sorts *adj.* sick, ill, poorly, gloomy, fed up

outbreak *n.* epidemic *An epidemic of cholera had hit the village*, rebellion, eruption, explosion, flare-up

outburst *n.* eruption, explosion, ▷*outbreak*

outcast *n.* exile *Robinson Crusoe was an exile on a desert island*, castaway, derelict, refugee

outcome *n.* effect, consequence, conclusion, result

outcry *n.* commotion, row, uproar, tumult, shouting, hue and cry, ▷*clamour*

outdated *adj.* old, antique, old-fashioned, unfashionable, obsolete ★**modern**

outdo *v.* surpass, excel, beat, outclass, surpass, eclipse

outfit *n.* ensemble, set *My mother presented me with a new train set*, rig, rig-out, equipment, gear

outing *n.* excursion, picnic, expedition, trip, ramble

outlandish *adj.* strange, erratic, odd, queer, quaint, bizarre *★ordinary*

outlaw *n.* bandit, highwayman, hooligan, desperado *Ned Kelly was a desperado of the Australian bush*, robber

outlet *n.* exit, egress, way out, vent, spout, nozzle, opening *★inlet*

outline ⒈ *n.* diagram, plan, blue-print, sketch, framework, summary ⒉ *v.* draw, sketch, describe

outlook *n.* view, prospect, forecast, attitude, aspect

output *n.* yield, product, produce, achievement, manufacture

outrage ⒈ *n.* disgrace, injury, offence, affront ⒉ *v.* offend, insult, shock, violate

outrageous *adj.* insulting, offensive, exorbitant, monstrous *★acceptable*

outright ⒈ *adj.* complete, thorough, absolute, wholesale ⒉ *adv.* at once, completely, entirely, altogether

outset *n.* first, opening, beginning, ▷*start* *★finish*

outside ⒈ *n.* exterior, surface, front ⒉ *adj.* exterior, external, outward, surface

outsider *n.* stranger, foreigner, alien, misfit *Gulliver was something of a misfit in the land of the tiny Lilliputians*

outskirts *n.* limits, bounds, boundary, outpost, suburb

outspoken *adj.* frank, open, straightforward, blunt, direct, ▷*candid* *★tactful*

outstanding *adj.* striking, pronounced, conspicuous, notable ▷*exceptional* *★ordinary*

outward *adj.* exterior, outside, outer, superficial *At a distance, my father and Bill Jones look alike, but it's really just superficial*

outwit *v.* get the better of, swindle, defraud, dupe, ▷*cheat*

over ⒈ *adj.* concluded, ended, done with, settled ⒉ *prep.* above, more than, exceeding ⒊ *adv.* aloft, above, beyond, extra

overall ⒈ *adj.* complete, inclusive, total, broad ⒉ *adv.* by and large, on the whole

overbearing *adj.* domineering, dictatorial, haughty, pompous, ▷*arrogant* *★modest*

overcast *adj.* cloudy, heavy, dark, murky, dull *★bright*

overcome *adj.* overwhelm, conquer, crush, defeat, vanquish, ▷*subdue*

overdo *v.* overwork, exaggerate, go too far *I didn't mind you eating one of my apples, but taking all four was going too far!*

overdue *adj.* delayed, belated, late, behindhand *★early*

overflow *v.* swamp, deluge, inundate, submerge, soak, spill

overhaul ⒈ *v.* repair, mend, fix, inspect, examine ⒉ overtake, pass, gain on

overhead *adv.* above, upward, aloft, on high *★below*

overhear *v.* listen, eavesdrop, snoop, spy

overjoyed *adj.* elated, jubilant, rapturous, ▷*delighted* *★disappointed*

overlap *v.* overrun, go beyond, coincide, overlay

overlook ⒈ *v.* disregard, pardon, condone, ignore ⒉ neglect, miss, pass over ⒊ inspect, check, examine

overpower *v.* conquer, crush, master, subdue, vanquish, ▷*defeat*

overseas *adj.* abroad, foreign *★home*

overseer *n.* inspector, foreman, boss, manager, master, mistress

oversight *n.* omission, blunder, error, fault, lapse, ▷*mistake*

overtake *v.* catch up, pass, outdo, outstrip, pass, ▷*overhaul*

overthrow *v.* defeat, beat, topple, ▷*overpower*

overture *n.* ⒈ (in music) prelude, opening, introduction. ⒉ offer, proposal, invitation

overwhelm *v.* overcome, stun, shock, overpower, deluge, inundate *The reply to our advertisement was huge: we were inundated with letters*

overwhelming *adj.* all-powerful, formidable, breathtaking, shattering *★insignificant*

owe *v.* be in debt, incur, be due

own ⒈ *v.* possess, occupy, hold ⒉ admit, confess, grant ⒊ *adj.* individual, personal, private

owner *n.* proprietor, possessor, landlord, master

P p

pace [1] *n. & v.* step, tread, stride [2] *n.* speed, rate, velocity, tempo

pacify *v.* appease, calm, moderate, tranquillize, ▷*soothe* ★**aggravate**

pack [1] *n.* bundle, bunch, swarm, crowd, group [2] *v.* cram, load, fill, throng

package *n.* parcel, packet, bundle, box, carton

packet *n.* bag, pack, container, parcel, ▷*package*

pact *n.* contract, treaty, agreement, arrangement PACKED

pad [1] *n.* tablet, notepad, jotter [2] foot, paw [3] *v.* fill, pack, shape, stuff, cushion

paddle [1] *n.* oar, sweep, scull [2] *v.* row, steer, propel [3] wade, splash, swim

pagan *n.* heathen, idol-worshipper, infidel

page [1] *n.* sheet, leaf, paper [2] boy, attendant, bellhop, messenger

pageant *n.* fair, parade, procession, exhibition, masque, ▷*show*

pail *n.* bucket, churn, tub, container PALE

pain [1] *n.* ache, pang, throb, twinge, spasm, cramp [2] *v.* hurt, sting, ache, torment, ▷*ail* ★**please** PANE

painful *adj.* aching, throbbing, sore, agonizing ★**painless**

painstaking *adj.* scrupulous *Carly kept a scrupulous record of all she spent*, careful, diligent, particular ★**negligent**

paint *v.* colour, draw, daub, varnish, stain

painting *n.* drawing, illustration, picture, mural, design

pair *n.* couple, brace, two, twins, twosome PARE PEAR

pal *n.* chum, friend, mate, buddy, crony, ▷*comrade* ★**enemy**

palace *n.* castle, château, stately home, mansion

pale *adj.* pallid, ashen, pasty, colourless, faint, feeble, white ★**ruddy** PAIL

pallid *adj.* ashen, colourless, livid *The man had a livid scar across his forehead*, waxen, ▷*pale*

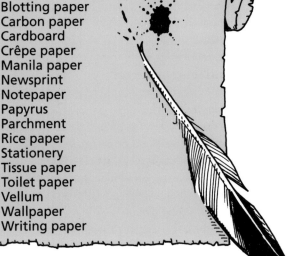

Paper

Blotting paper
Carbon paper
Cardboard
Crêpe paper
Manila paper
Newsprint
Notepaper
Papyrus
Parchment
Rice paper
Stationery
Tissue paper
Toilet paper
Vellum
Wallpaper
Writing paper

paltry *adj.* petty, mean, shabby, trifling, pitiable, trashy ★**significant**

pamper *v.* humour, indulge, coddle, fondle, ▷*spoil* ★**neglect**

pan *n.* pannikin, container, ▷*pot*

pandemonium *n.* uproar, clatter, row, rumpus, din, chaos *You haven't tidied your room: it's in utter chaos!*, ▷*noise* ★**calm**

pander *v.* indulge, pamper, please, give in to

pane *n.* panel, glass, window PAIN

panel [1] *n.* pane, rectangle, insert [2] jury, group, committee, forum *There will be a forum of all parties before the election*

pang *n.* ache, throe, twinge, throb, ▷*pain*

panic [1] *n.* fright, alarm, fear, terror [2] *v.* scare, frighten, startle, stampede ★**relax**

pant *v.* puff, snort, blow, gasp, heave

pantry *n.* larder, buttery, storeroom, cupboard

paper *n.* stationery, document, deed, article, dossier *The police have a dossier of all known criminals in this town*

parade [1] *n.* procession, march, display, ▷*pageant* [2] *v.* display, exhibit, flaunt, show off

paralyze *v.* cripple, disable, incapacitate, deaden, stun

paramount *adj.* leading, chief, supreme, outstanding, ▷*foremost* ★**minor**

paraphernalia *n.* baggage, equipment, gear

parasite *n.* sponger, hanger-on, leech, scrounger

parcel *n.* batch, bundle, lot, ▷*package*

parched *v.* arid, scorched, withered, dry, thirsty

pardon *v.* excuse, forgive, acquit, condone, absolve **★condemn**

pare *v.* skin, peel, uncover, strip, scrape, shave
PAIR PEAR

parent *n.* father, mother, guardian, originator

park [1] *n.* garden, green, grounds, pleasure garden, woodland [2] *v.* leave *You can leave your car outside our house*, position, station

parlour *n.* drawing-room, lounge, living-room, sitting-room

parody *n.* caricature, burlesque, satire, imitation

parry *v.* avoid, avert, fend off, rebuff, repel

parsimonious *adj.* niggardly *The fruit-pickers received a niggardly sum for their work*, sparing, mean, stingy, ▷*frugal* **★generous**

part [1] *n.* piece, fragment, portion, scrap [2] character, rôle *My sister has a leading rôle in the play*, duty [3] *v.* separate, divide, detach [4] depart, quit, leave

partial [1] *adj.* imperfect, limited, part, unfinished [2] biased, favourable to, inclined

partially *adv.* incompletely, somewhat, in part

participate *v.* take part, share, co-operate

particle *n.* morsel, atom, bit, seed, crumb, grain, scrap

particular [1] *adj.* choosy, fastidious, scrupulous [2] strange, odd, peculiar [3] special, distinct, notable *Old John Cotton was one of the notable citizens of our city*

partly *adv.* in part, incompletely, to some degree, up to a point **★totally**

partner *n.* colleague, associate, ally, helper

party [1] *n.* function, celebration, festivity, social [2] group, faction *A small faction on the committee wanted the park to be closed*, body

pass [1] *v.* exceed, overstep, outstrip [2] experience *He experienced little pain after the operation*, suffer, undergo [3] neglect, ignore [4] *n.* permit, ticket, passport [5] gorge, passage, canyon

passage [1] *n.* corridor, pathway, alley [2] journey, cruise, voyage [3] sentence, paragraph, clause

passenger *n.* traveller, commuter, wayfarer

passing *adj.* casual, fleeting, hasty, temporary, brief **★permanent**

passion *n.* desire, ardour, warmth, excitement, zeal, ▷*emotion* **★calm**

passionate *adj.* ardent, impetuous, fiery, earnest, enthusiastic **★indifferent**

past [1] *adj.* finished, ended, former, gone **★present** [2] *prep.* after, exceeding, beyond [3] *n.* history, yesterday **★tomorrow**
PASSED

paste *n.* glue, cement, gum, adhesive

pastime *n.* recreation, sport, fun, hobby, amusement

pasture *n.* grass, field, meadow, mead

pat [1] *v.* tap, caress, fondle, stroke, touch [2] *adv.* timely, exactly *Celia arrived at exactly the right moment*, precisely

patch *v.* mend, patch up, sew, darn, cobble

path *n.* way, track, road, route, course, footway

Paths and Passageways

Alley	Highway	Path
Autobahn	Lane	Pavement
Autoroute	Motorway	Road
Avenue	Pass on	Sidewalk
Boulevard	mountain	Street
Drive	Passage	Thoroughfare

pathetic *adj.* pitiable, sad, wretched, miserable, poor, puny *Our dog Sally had puppies, but they were small and puny*

patience *n.* endurance, perseverance, composure, calmness ★**impatience** PATIENTS

patient *adj.* forbearing, long-suffering, persevering, understanding ★**impatient**

patriotic *adj.* loyal, nationalistic, public-spirited

patrol *v.* police, watch, guard, protect, tour

patronize [1] *v.* assist, encourage, foster, buy from [2] talk down to, condescend

pattern [1] *n.* model, standard, prototype [2] arrangement, decoration, ornament

pause [1] *v.* halt, cease, suspend, stop, delay [2] *n.* lull, intermission, break, interruption PAWS

pay [1] *v.* reward, award, support, compensate, discharge [2] *n.* payment, salary, wages, compensation

peace *n.* harmony, calm, concord, serenity, quiet, tranquility *We spent the day in total tranquility down by the lake* ★**tumult** PIECE

peaceful *adj.* serene, quiet, restful, harmonious, ▷*tranquil* ★**disturbed**

peak *n.* summit, apex, top, crown, pinnacle

peal *v.* ring, strike, clamour, chime, resound PEEL

peasant *n.* rustic, bumpkin, countryman, yokel

peculiar [1] *adj.* singular, odd, curious, unusual, uncommon, strange [2] unique, private, special

peddle *v.* sell, hawk, canvas, trade, vend, retail

pedestal *n.* base, stand, plinth, support

pedlar *n.* hawker, street-trader, trader, vendor

peel [1] *v.* skin, strip, pare, scale [2] *n.* skin, covering, rind, coat PEAL

peep *n. & v.* glimpse, blink, look, ▷*peer*

peer [1] *v.* peep, stare, look, gaze [2] *n.* aristocrat, lord, noble [3] equal, fellow, counterpart PIER

peerless *adj.* unequalled, unique, beyond compare, unbeatable

peevish *adj.* cross, childish, grumpy, crusty, irritable, ▷*testy* ★**good-tempered**

peg *n.* hook, knob, pin, post, hanger, fastener

pelt [1] *v.* beat, bombard, thrash, throw [2] rain cats and dogs, teem, pour [3] *n.* skin, hide, fleece, fur

pen [1] *n.* quill, stylo, ballpoint [2] cage, coop, hutch, stall [3] *v.* write, autograph, scribble

penalty *n.* fine, forfeit, punishment, price ★**reward**

pending *adj.* awaiting, unfinished, doubtful, uncertain

penetrate [1] *v.* pierce, perforate, stab, permeate *The aroma of the sweet peas permeated the house* [2] discern, see through, comprehend

penetrating [1] *adj.* sharp, perceptive, understanding [2] shrill, stinging

pennant *n.* flag, streamer, bunting, banner

penniless *adj.* destitute, needy, poverty-striken, ▷*poor* ★**wealthy**

pensive *adj.* thoughtful, reflective, wistful, preoccupied

people [1] *n.* folk, society, the public, populace, inhabitants [2] *v.* populate, inhabit, settle

pep *n.* punch, energy, high spirits, vigour, ▷*vitality*

peppery [1] *adj.* biting, caustic *I'm afraid your essay wasn't any good; the teacher made some very caustic comments!* hot-tempered, angry [2] hot, pungent, sharp

perceive *v.* feel, sense, observe, notice, make out, understand, ▷*see*

perch [1] *v.* alight, light, sit, squat [2] *n.* rod, pole, staff, roost [3] fish

perfect [1] *adj.* absolute, ideal, sublime, excellent, splendid, faultless ★**imperfect** [2] *v.* complete, finish, fulfil, refine

perforate *v.* puncture, drill, punch, penetrate

perform [1] *v.* carry out, do, fulfil, accomplish [2] play, act, stage, present *The local drama group is to present a new play next week*

performer *n.* actor, player, singer, entertainer, artiste

perfume *n.* scent, essence, aroma, odour

perhaps *adv.* possibly, perchance, maybe, conceivably

peril *n.* hazard, jeopardy, menace, risk, insecurity, ▷*danger* ★**safety**

period *n.* spell, time, duration, term, interval, course, span, age

periodical [1] *n.* magazine, publication, journal, gazette, review [2] *adj.* regular, routine, recurring, repeated

perish *v.* die, pass away, wither, disintegrate, expire, shrivel

perky *adj.* bouncy, bright, cheerful, lively, ▷*sprightly* ★**dull**

permanent *adj.* endless, ageless, timeless, constant, ▷*durable* ★**fleeting**

permission *n.* authorization, sanction, privilege, warrant *The police have a warrant for your arrest!* ★**prohibition**

permit [1] (per-*mit*) *v.* allow, grant, agree, empower [2] (*per*-mit) *n.* warrant, licence, pass

perpendicular *adj.* upright, erect, sheer, steep, vertical ★**horizontal**

perpetrate *v.* commit, do, inflict, perform, practise

perpetual *adj.* everlasting, ceaseless, eternal, never-ending, ▷*endless* ★**fleeting**

perplex *v.* mystify, baffle, bewilder, confound, ▷*puzzle* ★**enlighten**

persecute *v.* harass, plague, molest, badger, ▷*bother* ★**pamper**

persevere *v.* persist, hold out, hang on, endure, continue ★**give up**

persist *v.* remain, stand fast, abide, carry on, ▷*persevere* ★**stop**

persistent *adj.* tenacious, relentless, stubborn, obstinate ★**weak**

person *n.* individual, human, being, somebody, personage

personal *adj.* individual, intimate, private, special, peculiar

personality *n.* individuality, character, disposition, nature

perspective *n.* outlook, aspect, proportion

perspire *v.* sweat, exude, ooze

persuade *v.* convince, wheedle, blandish, entice, cajole *I cajoled my mother into buying me a new swimsuit*, induce, ▷*coax* ★**discourage**

pert *adj.* saucy, flippant, cheeky, brash, jaunty ★**shy**

perturb *v.* upset, disturb, trouble, distress, fluster, ▷*bother* ★**reassure**

peruse *v.* read, study, pore over, browse, inspect

pervade *v.* penetrate, permeate, spread, saturate

perverse *adj.* contrary, wayward, opposite, disobedient, ▷*stubborn* ★**reasonable**

pessimist *n.* defeatist, killjoy, wet blanket, cynic *Uncle Bert is a real cynic: he thinks the prize draws are fixed!* ★**optimist**

pessimistic *adj.* cynical, dismal, fatalistic, defeatist, downhearted ★**optimistic**

pest *n.* nuisance, plague, blight, curse, vexation, bug

pester *v.* nag, hector, badger, annoy, disturb, harass, ▷*bother*

pet [1] *v.* fondle, caress, baby, cosset, cuddle [2] *n.* favourite, beloved, dear [3] *adj.* endearing, cherished, dearest

petition *n.* plea, appeal, entreaty, round robin, request

petrified *adj.* spellbound, frighted, scared, terrified

petty [1] *adj.* paltry, cheap, inferior, trifling, ▷*trivial* ★**important** [2] mean, measly, stingy

petulant *adj.* fretful, displeased, querulous, irritable, ▷*peevish*

phantom [1] *n.* apparition, spectre, spook, ghost [2] *adj.* spooky, ghostly, imaginary

phase *n.* aspect, appearance, angle, view, period, point FAZE

phenomenal *adj.* remarkable, outstanding, marvellous, miraculous

phenomenon *n.* marvel, rarity, curiosity, sensation, spectacle

philanthropic *adj.* charitable, kind, generous, humane, benevolent, bountiful, public-spirited ★**selfish**

philosophical *adj.* calm, cool, logical, thoughtful, impassive, unruffled

phobia *n.* dread, fear, awe, neurosis, hang-up *My father has a hang-up about bats: he can't stand them!*, horror

Phobia

My Father has a hang-up about bats; he can't stand them.

phrase *n.* expression, idiom, saying, utterance, sentence FRAYS

physical [1] *adj.* material, substantial, solid, concrete [2] bodily, personal, sensible

pick [1] *v.* select, choose, single out, gather [2] *n.* pike, pickaxe

picket [1] *n.* patrol, scout, sentinel, lookout, guard [2] post, rail, panel, fence

pickle [1] *n.* preserve [2] difficulty, predicament [3] *v.* cure, salt, preserve, souse

picture [1] *n.* painting, tableau, portrait, illustration, drawing [2] movie, film [3] *v.* illustrate, imagine, fancy

picturesque *adj.* attractive, artistic, pictorial, scenic

piece *n.* portion, fragment, lump, morsel, bit, ▷*scrap* PEACE

pier *n.* wharf, dock, quay, jetty PEER

pierce *v.* perforate, drill, bore, ▷*penetrate*

piercing [1] *adj.* loud, deafening, shrill, penetrating [2] keen, sharp, cutting

pigment *n.* colour, dye, hue, paint, stain

pile *n.* & *v.* heap, mass, stack, load, store

pilfer *v.* purloin, rifle, rob, filch, ▷*steal*

pilgrim *n.* traveller, wanderer, wayfarer

pilgrimage *n.* excursion, journey, mission, tour, trip

pillage *v.* plunder, ravage, loot, ransack *Thieves broke into the museum and ransacked all the cases,* rifle

pillar *n.* column, shaft, tower, obelisk, monument

pillow *n.* cushion, bolster, support

pilot [1] *n.* guide, steersman, coxswain, helmsman [2] aviator, flyer, airman

pimple *n.* spot, blemish, swelling, boil

pin [1] *n.* fastener, clip, spike, peg [2] *v.* fix, fasten, attach, join, tack

pinch [1] *v.* nip, squeeze, crush, tweak [2] pilfer, steal [3] *n.* dash, drop, splash [4] crisis, difficulty, jam

pine *v.* hanker, yearn, long for, languish *The flowers in the garden are languishing for want of water,* sicken

pinnacle *n.* summit, top, crest, peak, apex

pioneer *n.* founder, leader, trail-blazer, explorer, innovator

pious *adj.* devoted, godly, holy, moral, religious

pipe [1] *n.* tube, duct, passage, hose, conduit [2] whistle, flute

piquant *adj.* appetizing, spicy, tangy, savoury, pungent

pique *v.* annoy, displease, irritate, affront, vex PEAK

pirate [1] *n.* corsair *In days of old the ships in the Mediterranean were often raided by corsairs,* buccaneer, privateer, sea-rover [2] *v.* copy, plagiarize, steal

pistol *n.* revolver, automatic, gun PISTIL

pit [1] *n.* hole, hollow, crater, trench, mine [2] dent, dimple, depression

pitch [1] *v.* fling, throw, cast, sling, toss [2] fall, drop, descend [3] raise, set up, erect [4] *n.* angle, slope, degree [5] playing-field, sports-ground

pitcher *n.* jar, beaker, crock, jug, ewer, vessel

piteous *adj.* pitiful, heartbreaking, mournful, ▷*pathetic*

pitiless *adj.* merciless, unmerciful, cruel, unrelenting ★**merciful**

pity [1] *n.* mercy, compassion, charity, tenderness [2] *v.* spare, forgive, grieve for, sympathize with

pivot [1] *n.* axle, axis, hinge, turning point, spindle, swivel [2] *v.* revolve, rotate, turn, spin

Planets

The nine planets of our solar system travel around a star we call the Sun.

Earth
Jupiter
Mars
Mercury
Neptune
Pluto
Saturn
Uranus
Venus

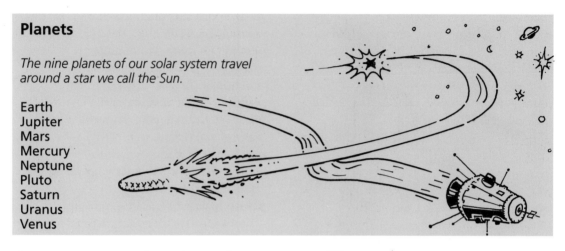

placate *v.* appease, pacify, soothe, satisfy, ▷*humour* ★**infuriate**

place [1] *n.* spot, locality, site, situation, position [2] house, flat, residence [3] *v.* put, deposit, establish, allocate, arrange PLAICE

placid *adj.* peaceful, quiet, serene, mild, ▷*restful* ★**ruffled**

plague [1] *n.* epidemic, disease, contagion, pest, blight [2] *v.* persecute, pester *Our picnic was pestered by flies*, infest, annoy, ▷*badger*

plain [1] *adj.* unadorned, simple [2] obvious, clear, apparent [3] blunt, direct, candid [4] smooth, level, flat [5] *n.* prairie, plateau, tableland PLANE

plan [1] *n.* design, chart, diagram, drawing [2] project, proposal, arrangement, scheme [3] *v.* design, prepare, arrange, invent

plane [1] *adj.* level, even, flat, smooth [2] *n.* aircraft [3] smoothing tool PLAIN

planned *adj.* prepared, ready, arranged

plant [1] *v.* sow, scatter, implant [2] place, set, establish [3] *n.* herb, shrub, vegetable [4] equipment, machinery

plaster [1] *n.* cement, mortar, paste [2] *n.* bandage, dressing [3] *v.* spread, smear, daub

plastic [1] *adj.* mouldable, pliable, malleable, soft, supple [2] *n.* thermoplastic, polythene

plate [1] *n.* dish, platter, palette [2] sheet, panel [3] *v.* laminate, cover, gild, anodize

platform *n.* rostrum *I was called up to the rostrum to receive my prize*, stage, stand, dais

plausible *adj.* believable, credible, convincing, glib, persuasive ★**unlikely**

play [1] *v.* sport, gambol, frisk, romp, frolic [2] perform, act, represent [3] *n.* drama, performance [4] sport, amusement, recreation

player *n.* actor, sportsman, artiste, musician, performer, contestant

playful *adj.* frisky, frolicsome, larky, lively, sportive ★**serious**

plead *v.* appeal, argue, ask, implore, request, beseech

pleasant *adj.* affable, agreeable, cheerful, nice, ▷*charming* ★**unpleasant**

please [1] *v.* gratify, enchant, amuse, entertain, ▷*delight* [2] like, choose, wish, prefer

pleased *adj.* delighted, gratified, satisfied, ▷*contented* ★**annoyed**

pleasing *adj.* agreeable, enchanting, entertaining, ▷*satisfying* ★**unpleasant**

pleasure *n.* delight, joy, amusement, entertainment, enjoyment, ▷*fun* ★**trouble**

pledge [1] *n.* promise, vow, undertaking, warrant, oath [2] *v.* bind, contract, promise, undertake

plentiful *adj.* lavish, ample, profuse, bountiful, ▷*abundant* ★**scanty**

plenty *n.* enough, profusion, affluence, ▷*abundance* ★**scarcity**

pliable *adj.* supple, flexible, pliant, mouldable, bendy ★**rigid**

plight *n.* predicament, difficulty, condition, dilemma *When the rain started we were in a dilemma: should we wait for it to stop, or run for it?*, jam

plod *v.* toil, labour, drudge, slog. grind

plot [1] *n.* scheme, plan, intrigue [2] story, narrative [3] *v.* hatch, intrigue, scheme

pluck [1] *v.* gather, pick, pull, yank, catch [2] *n.* courage, determination, bravery

plucky *adj.* courageous, daring, heroic, hardy, ▷*brave* ✱**feeble**

plug [1] *n.* stopper, cork, bung [2] *v.* stop, block, choke, cork [3] publicize, boost, promote

plum [1] *n.* prize, bonus, treasure [2] *adj.* best, choice, first-class

plump *adj.* buxom, stout, chubby, rotund, podgy ✱**skinny**

plunder [1] *n.* booty, loot, swag, spoils [2] *v.* fleece, rob, ransack, pillage, loot

plunge *v.* dive, pitch, submerge, duck, immerse, swoop, hurtle

poach [1] *v.* pilfer, steal, filch, purloin [2] cook

pocket [1] *n.* compartment, pouch, sack, bag [2] *v.* filch, pinch, steal

poem *n.* ode, verse, rhyme, ballad, lyric

poetic *adj.* artistic, elegant, graceful, flowing, lyrical

poignant *adj.* moving, touching, pathetic, biting, penetrating

point [1] *n.* spike, barb, pike, prong, end, tip [2] locality, place, spot [3] aspect, object, aim, purpose [4] headland, cape, ness [5] *v.* aim, direct, level, train

pointless *adj.* meaningless, senseless, silly, vague, feeble, ▷*absurd* ✱**significant**

poise [1] *n.* confidence, assurance, dignity, self-possession, balance [2] *v.* stand, hover, brood over

poison [1] *n.* venom, virus, toxin [2] *v.* taint, fester, corrupt, infect

poisonous *adj.* deadly, evil, lethal *Don't even touch those red berries: they're lethal!*, noxious, toxic, venomous

poke *v.* jab, push, nudge, jostle, ram, thrust, ▷*shove*

pole *n.* stick, stave, stake, rod, post, bar, mast, shaft, spar

policy *n.* discretion, course, action, practice, rule, procedure

polish [1] *v.* burnish, buff, smooth, brighten, clean [2] *n.* gloss, glaze, shine [3] refinement, grace, culture

polished [1] *adj.* glossy, burnished, shiny [2] refined, cultivated, cultured

polite *adj.* courteous, attentive, civil, well-bred, elegant, discreet ✱**impolite**

poll [1] *n.* election, vote, count, census [2] *v.* clip, shear, trim

pollute *v.* adulterate, debase, befoul, taint, poison, corrupt ✱**purify**

pomp *n.* ceremony, show, splendour, pageantry, magnificence ✱**simplicity**

pompous *adj.* showy, self-important, bombastic, ▷*pretentious* ✱**modest**

ponder *v.* meditate, consider, reflect, deliberate, think about

pool [1] *n.* lagoon, pond, lake [2] accumulation, funds, reserve, kitty [3] *v.* combine, contribute, share

poor [1] *adj.* destitute, penniless, miserable ✱**rich** [2] low quality, faulty, feeble, shoddy *The goods in the market may be cheap, but they're just shoddy rubbish* ✱**superior** PORE POUR

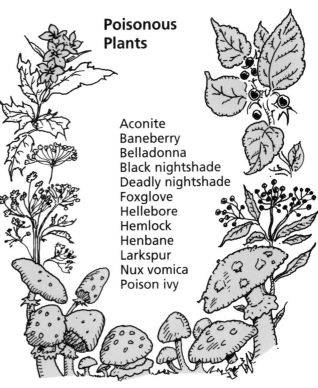

Poisonous Plants

Aconite
Baneberry
Belladonna
Black nightshade
Deadly nightshade
Foxglove
Hellebore
Hemlock
Henbane
Larkspur
Nux vomica
Poison ivy

poorly [1] *adj.* ailing, ill, sick, seedy [2] badly, inexpertly, crudely ★**well**

pop [1] *v.* bang, burst, crack, explode [2] slide, slip, insert

popular [1] *adj.* well-liked, favourite, in favour, fashionable [2] current, common, vulgar, prevailing

pore *v.* scan, examine, peruse, scrutinize POOR POUR

portable *adj.* lightweight, convenient, transportable, ▷*handy* ★**awkward**

portion *n.* piece, fragment, share, fraction, ▷*part*

portly *adj.* plump, stout, fat, burly, bulky

portrait *n.* likeness, painting, picture, profile

portray *v.* describe, depict, represent, picture, illustrate, impersonate

pose [1] *v.* stand, poise, posture, position [2] *n.* position, stand, guise, stance *I think you will learn to play golf well; you have a good stance*

position [1] *n.* spot, situation, location, place, site [2] job, post, situation [3] posture, attitude [4] rank, standing, status

positive [1] *adj.* certain, sure, confident ★**doubtful** [2] real, true, absolute ★**negative** [3] precise, definite, unmistakable

possess *v.* have, own, hold, occupy ★**lose**

possessions *n.* wealth, assets, property, goods

possible *adj.* conceivable, imaginable, likely, feasible, attainable ★**impossible**

possibly *adv.* perhaps, maybe, perchance hopefully

post [1] *n.* rail, pole, beam, bannister, stake [2] place, position, employment, job [3] mail

poster *n.* placard, bill, advertisement, sign

posterior *adj.* hind, behind, after, rear ★**front**

postpone *v.* put off, defer, shelve, adjourn, ▷*delay* ★**advance**

posture *n.* bearing, stance, attitude, carriage

pot *n.* basin, bowl, pan, vessel, container, jar

potential [1] *adj.* possible, probable, latent *The professor discovered that I had a latent talent for languages*, dormant, budding [2] *n.* ability, talent, capacity, ▷*flair*

potion *n.* beverage, medicine, mixture, tonic, brew

potter *v.* dabble, fiddle, tinker, mess about

pouch *n.* bag, poke, sack, purse, pocket, wallet

pounce *v.* strike, lunge, spring, swoop, fall upon, ▷*attack*

pound [1] *v.* beat, batter, crush, hammer [2] *n.* enclosure, compound, pen [3] weight [4] currency *In Britain, the currency is based on the pound sterling*

pour *v.* spout, jet, gush, spill, cascade, rain PORE POUR

pout *v.* grimace, glower, sulk, scowl, mope ★**smile**

poverty [1] *n.* distress, need, bankruptcy, privation, ▷*want* [2] scarcity, shortage ★**plenty**

powder [1] *n.* dust, sand, ash, grit, bran [2] *v.* pulverize, crunch, grind

power [1] *n.* authority, command, control, ability [2] energy, force, strength

powerful *adj.* mighty, vigorous, forceful, ▷*strong* ★**weak**

practical [1] *adj.* useful, effective, workable [2] experienced, qualified, trained, ▷*skilled* ★**impractical**

practice [1] *n.* custom, habit, usage [2] work, conduct, performance, action ★**theory**

practise *v.* carry out, apply, do, execute, ▷*perform*

praise [1] *v.* acclaim, applaud, glorify, exalt ★**criticize** [2] *n.* applause, flattery, compliment, approval ★**criticism** PRAYS PREYS

prance *v.* gambol *I love to watch the lambs gambol in the spring*, frolic, romp, caper, swagger

prank *n.* trick, joke, antic, lark, jape, stunt

prattle *n. & v.* chatter, jabber, gossip, drivel, witter

pray *v.* beg, beseech, entreat, implore, request PREY

prayer *n.* petition, entreaty, worship, devotion

preach *v.* lecture, moralize, advocate, urge, proclaim

precarious *adj.* perilous, hazardous, insecure, dangerous, ▷*risky* ★**safe**

Prey

Pray

precaution *n.* forethought, provision, anticipation, care, providence, ▷*prudence*

precede *v.* lead, head, usher, go before, preface ***follow**

precious *adj.* valuable, costly, cherished, treasured, dear, beloved, ▷*costly* ***worthless**

precise [1] *adj.* definite, exact, pointed, accurate [2] formal, particular, strict ***vague**

precisely *adv.* absolutely, just so, exactly, correctly

precision *n.* exactitude, accuracy, care, detail

precocious *adj.* over-forward, fast, smart, clever ***backward**

predicament *n.* situation, state, condition, embarrassment, fix, ▷*plight*

predict *v.* foresee, foretell, prophesy, presage, divine

predominant *adj.* leading, main, powerful, superior, ruling, controlling ***minor**

preen *v.* prance, swagger, strut, spruce up, doll up, groom

preface *n.* introduction, prelude, prologue, preamble, foreword

prefer *v.* choose, select, fancy, desire, like better, ▷*favour* ***reject**

prejudice [1] *n.* bigotry, intolerance, bias, discrimination [2] *v.* influence, warp, twist, distort, undermine ***benefit**

prejudiced *adj.* biased, bigoted *The people in this town are very bigoted against strangers*, one-sided, unfair, intolerant ***fair**

preliminary *adj.* introductory, preparatory, opening, initial ***final**

premature *adj.* untimely, previous, early, immature ***late**

premeditated *adj.* calculated, planned, prearranged, intentional ***spontaneous**

premier [1] *n.* prime minister, first minister, head of government [2] *adj.* chief, first, head, leading, principal

premises *n.* grounds, house, building, lands

prepare *v.* arrange, adapt provide, get ready, concoct, plan ***demolish**

preposterous *adj.* absurd, unreasonable, ridiculous, laughable, ▷*unreasonable* ***reasonable**

prescribe *v.* indicate, order, propose, recommend, specify

presence [1] *n.* existence, appearance, aspect [2] nearness, neighbourhood, proximity
PRESENTS

present [1] *n.* gift, donation, bounty, favour [2] *v.* offer, tender, bestow, award, exhibit [3] *adj.* here, on the spot, ready, current

presently *adv.* soon, shortly, before long, immediately

preserve [1] *v.* protect, safeguard, conserve, shield, ▷*keep* [2] *n.* jam, jelly, pickle

press [1] *v.* bear down, depress, clamp, jam, compress, flatten [2] *n.* printing machine [3] newspapers, reporters, journalism

pressure [1] *n.* strain, tension, stress, urgency [2] weight, compression, force

prestige *n.* repute, authority, weight, power

presume *v.* infer, suppose, grant, take for granted, assume

presumptuous *adj.* arrogant, bold, audacious, insolent, ▷*forward* ***modest**

pretend [1] *v.* make believe, simulate, sham, feign, masquerade [2] aspire, claim, strive for

pretext *n.* excuse, pretence, guise, device

pretty *adj.* attractive, beautiful, comely, dainty, bonny, ▷*lovely* ★**ugly**

prevail *v.* obtain, overcome, predominate, ▷*triumph* ★**lose**

prevalent *adj.* current, common, popular, in use, accepted ★**uncommon**

prevent *v.* avert, forestall, ward off, discourage, stop, ▷*hinder* ★**help**

previous *adj.* former, prior, earlier, premature, untimely ★**later**

prey *n.* quarry, chase, booty, victim

prey on *v.* plunder, fleece, oppress, terrorize

price *n.* cost, amount, expense, payment, value, worth

priceless [1] *adj.* invaluable, precious, cherished, costly [2] amusing, comic, humorous, hilarious *The clown's antics were hilarious*

prick *v.* jab, jag, puncture, stab, pierce

pride *n.* conceit, vanity, egotism, self-importance, honour, exaltation, pleasure PRIED

prim *adj.* puritanical, demure, starchy, priggish ★**informal**

primary *adj.* first, original, chief, essential, fundamental

prime [1] *adj.* principal, chief, basic, original [2] best, finest, choice

primitive [1] *adj.* simple, austere, crude [2] uncivilized, savage, barbarous

principal [1] *adj.* main, chief, head, leading, foremost [2] *n.* head, leader, boss, director PRINCIPLE

principle [1] *n.* law, regulation, rule, doctrine [2] virtue, worth, integrity, rectitude *The headteacher of our school was given the freedom of the city as a 'person of high moral rectitude'.* ★**wickedness** PRINCIPAL

print [1] *v.* impress, stamp, brand, publish [2] *n.* impression, printing, imprint

prior [1] *adj.* previous, former, earlier [2] *n.* abbot, monk

prise *v.* force, lever, pry, lift, raise PRIES PRIZE

prison *n.* jail, gaol, dungeon, lock-up, penitentiary

private [1] *adj.* particular, personal, special, own [2] solitary, remote, quiet ★**public**

Printing

Collotype
Computer-setting
Cylinder press
Flatbed press
Intaglio
Letterpress
Linotype
Lithography
Monotype
Photogravure
Rotary press
Silk screen
Type
Web offset

privilege [1] *n.* advantage, benefit, exemption [2] right, authority, entitlement, prerogative *It was the emperor's prerogative to pardon offenders against the state*

prize [1] *n.* reward, premium, trophy, honour [2] booty, spoils, plunder [3] *adj.* best, champion, winning [4] *v.* value, appreciate, cherish PRIES PRISE

probable *adj.* likely, presumable, reasonable, possible ★**improbable**

probe [1] *v.* poke, prod [2] examine, investigate, scrutinize

problem [1] *n.* puzzle, question, riddle, poser, quandary [2] difficulty, dilemma, predicament

proceed [1] *v.* advance, continue, go on, progress ★**recede** [2] arise, flow, spring, emanate *A strong sulphurous odour emanated from the crater of the volcano*

process [1] *n.* procedure, operation, movement, system, method [2] *v.* convert, alter, handle, refine

procession *n.* parade, pageant, march, cavalcade

proclaim *v.* declare, announce, advertise, publish, expound

procure *v.* secure, acquire, win, gain, attain, get ★**lose**

prod *v.* goad, poke, nudge, incite, urge, shove

prodigal *adj.* extravagant, reckless, lavish, ▷*spendthrift* ★**thrifty**

prodigious [1] *adj.* miraculous, abnormal, amazing, remarkable, ▷*extraordinary* *ordinary* [2] huge, mighty, ▷*enormous* *tiny*

produce [1] (*pro*-duce) *n.* product, output, yield, crop, harvest [2] (pro-*duce*) *v.* provide, yield, create, deliver, put forward

product *n.* output, crop, harvest, merchandise, commodity

profane *adj.* impious, blasphemous, unholy, worldly, sinful *sacred*

profess *v.* declare, avow, acknowledge, own

profession [1] *n.* occupation, career, job, calling, employment [2] avowal, admission

professional *adj.* skilled, efficient, experienced, ▷*expert* *amateur*

proffer *v.* tender, present, offer, submit

proficient *adj.* competent, able, skilled, ▷*expert* *clumsy*

profit [1] *n.* benefit, gain, advantage, acquisition *loss* [2] *v.* improve, gain, reap, acquire *lose* PROPHET

profound [1] *adj.* deep, penetrating, fathomless [2] wise, shrewd, learned, sagacious *The leader of the tribe was old, wise and sagacious* *shallow*

profuse *adj.* bountiful, extravagant, exuberant, prolific, sumptuous, ▷*lavish* *sparse*

progress [1] (*pro*-gress) *n.* advancement, growth, development [2] (pro-*gress*) *v.* advance, proceed, go, forge ahead, travel *decline*

prohibit *v.* forbid, bar, deny, ban, obstruct, hinder, ▷*prevent* *permit*

project [1] (*pro*-ject) *n.* work, affair, plan, scheme, undertaking [2] (pro-*ject*) *v.* propel, hurl, jut, protrude [3] contrive, scheme, plan

prolific *adj.* fruitful, creative, productive, fertile *scarce*

prolong *v.* lengthen, stretch, draw out, spin out, ▷*extend* *shorten*

prominent [1] *adj.* famous, notable, distinguished *minor* [2] projecting, standing out, bulging, jutting

promise [1] *n.* commitment, undertaking, warrant, pledge [2] *v.* agree, guarantee, vow

promote [1] *adj.* cultivate, advance, assist, ▷*encourage* [2] dignify, elevate, upgrade, honour *degrade*

prompt [1] *adj.* punctual, timely, quick, smart, ready *slothful* [2] *v.* hint, remind, urge, ▷*encourage* *deter*

prone [1] *adj.* inclined, apt, liable, disposed *unlikely* [2] prostrate *The poor fellow lay prostrate on the ship's deck,* face down, recumbent *upright*

pronounce [1] *v.* speak, utter, say, articulate [2] declare, decree, proclaim

pronounced *adj.* outstanding, striking, noticeable, ▷*distinct* *vague*

proof *n.* evidence, testimony, confirmation, criterion, scrutiny *failure*

prop *n.* & *v.* stay, brace, truss, support

propel *v.* start, push, force, impel, send, ▷*drive* *stop*

proper [1] *adj.* correct, without error, accurate, exact [2] respectable, decent, becoming, seemly *improper* [3] personal, own, special *common*

property [1] *n.* possessions, wealth, chattels, buildings, wealth [2] quality, virtue, characteristic, peculiarity

prophecy (*prof*-essee) *n.* forecast, divination, prediction

prophesy (*prof*-esseye) *v.* predict, foretell, foresee

proportion [1] *n.* ratio, percentage, part, fraction [2] adjustment, arrangement

proposal *n.* proposition, offer, outline

propose [1] *v.* put forward, offer, suggest [2] ask for the hand of *Sir, I have the honour to ask you for the hand of your daughter in marriage,* pop the question

proprietor *n.* owner, possessor, landlady, landlord

prosaic *adj.* tedious, uninteresting, boring, dull, mundane, ordinary *interesting*

prosecute [1] *v.* indict, put on trial, summon, sue [2] continue, pursue, carry on, conduct *abandon*

prospect [1] *n.* outlook, forecast, promise, expectation [2] view, landscape, vista, aspect

prosper *v.* succeed, flourish, grow *fail*

prosperous *adj.* affluent, wealthy, rich, successful, thriving ★**unsuccessful**

protect *v.* defend, preserve, guard, secure, shelter, support ★**endanger**

protest [1] (pro-*test*) *v.* complain, object, dispute, challenge ★**accept** [2] (*pro*-test) *n.* objection, complaint, dissent

protracted *adj.* extended, drawn out, lengthy, prolonged ★**shortened**

protrude *v.* project, bulge, jut ★**recede**

proud [1] *adj.* arrogant, haughty, supercilious, boastful ★**humble** [2] lofty, majestic, noble, splendid ★**mean**

prove *v.* show, demonstrate, authenticate, confirm, verify ★**disprove**

provide *v.* supply, furnish, equip, contribute, afford ★**withhold**

province [1] *n.* realm, sphere, orbit, place, department [2] region, state, county

provoke *v.* prompt, incite, excite, enrage, inflame, ▷*aggravate* ★**appease**

prowess *n.* ability, strength, might, bravery, ▷*valour* ★**clumsiness**

prowl *v.* stalk *Somewhere in the darkness a large grey animal stalked its prey*, roam, prey, slink

prudent *adj.* careful, cautious, discreet, shrewd, ▷*thrifty* ★**rash**

prudish *adj.* strait-laced, narrow-minded, demure, priggish, ▷*prim*

prune [1] *v.* cut, shorten, trim, crop [2] *n.* dried plum

pry *v.* snoop, peep, meddle, intrude

public [1] *adj.* communal, civil, popular, social, national [2] *n.* the people, the populace, society

publish *v.* broadcast, distribute, circulate, communicate, bring out

pucker *v.* fold, crease, cockle, furrow, wrinkle ★**straighten**

puerile *adj.* callow, immature, juvenile

puff *v.* inflate, swell, blow, pant, distend

pull [1] *v.* haul, drag, tow, heave ★**push** [2] gather, pluck, detach, pick

pump [1] *v.* inflate, expand, swell [2] interrogate, question, query

punch [1] *v.* strike, beat, hit, cuff [2] puncture, pierce, perforate, bore

punctual *adj.* prompt, on time, precise, timely ★**tardy**

puncture *n.* perforation, hole, leak, wound

pungent *adj.* sharp, bitter, poignant, biting, ▷*acrid* ★**mild**

punish *v.* chastise, correct, discipline, chasten, reprove, scold

puny *adj.* feeble, weak, frail, small, petty, stunted, insignificant ★**large**

pupil *n.* student, scholar, schoolchild, learner

puppet [1] *n.* doll, marionette [2] catspaw *The prisoner was not the true villain, but only a catspaw*, figurehead, pawn

purchase [1] *v.* buy, procure, secure, obtain, get, ▷*buy* ★**sell** [2] *n.* bargain, investment

pure [1] *adj.* immaculate, spotless, stainless, clear, ▷*clean* ★**impure** [2] virtuous, chaste, honest, blameless

purely *adv.* simply, barely, merely, only

purge [1] *v.* purify, clean, cleanse [2] liquidate, exterminate, kill

purify *v.* clean, clarify, wash, purge

purloin *v.* rob, thieve, take, filch, pilfer, ▷*steal*

purpose *n.* intent, design, will, goal, target

purse [1] *n.* wallet, pouch, reticule, handbag [2] *v.* pucker, crease, compress, wrinkle

pursue [1] *v.* follow, track, trace, ▷*chase* [2] *v.* practise, maintain, work for

pursuit [1] *n.* hunt, chase, hue and cry [2] occupation, hobby, interest *Stamp collecting has always been one of my main interests*

push [1] *v.* shove, thrust, press, drive, propel [2] *n.* advance, assault, drive [3] vigour, vitality, endeavour

put [1] *v.* set, place, deposit, repose, lay [2] express, propose, state

put down [1] *v.* write, jot down, record, note [2] crush, humiliate, subdue [3] kill

put off [1] *v.* postpone, defer, delay, adjourn [2] dishearten, unsettle, perturb

putrid *adj.* decomposed, rotten, rancid, rank, stinking ★**wholesome**

puzzle [1] *v.* baffle, confuse, mystify, perplex, ▷*bewilder* [2] *n.* conundrum, brain-teaser, problem, dilemma

puzzling *adj.* baffling, curious, strange, bewildering, ▷*peculiar*

Q q

quack *n.* impostor, charlatan *She pretended to tell fortunes by cards, but she was nothing but a charlatan*, mountebank, humbug, fake

quaff *v.* imbibe, swallow, ▷*drink*

quagmire *n.* bog, mire, marsh, ▷*swamp*

quail *v.* tremble, flinch, shrink, cower, succumb **★withstand**

quaint *adj.* curious, whimsical, fanciful, singular, old-fashioned, droll

quake 1 *v.* tremble, quaver, shiver, quiver, shudder 2 *n.* shock, convulsion *The convulsions from the earthquake were felt hundreds of miles away*

qualification 1 *n.* fitness, capacity, ability, accomplishment 2 restriction, limitation, modification *The engineer's design was accepted with certain modifications*

qualify 1 *v.* empower, enable, fit, suit 2 moderate, limit, restrict

quality 1 *n.* characteristic, condition, power 2 excellence, worth, goodness

qualm *n.* doubt, misgiving, hesitation

quandary *n.* difficulty, doubt, ▷*dilemma*

quantity *n.* amount, number, volume, sum

quarrel 1 *n.* dispute, squabble, wrangle, disagreement **★harmony** 2 *v.* argue, bicker, brawl, squabble **★agree**

quarry 1 *n.* game, prey, object, victim, target 2 mine, excavation, pit

quarter 1 *n.* area, territory, place, district 2 one-fourth 3 mercy *The commander of the invading army showed no mercy to the local defenders*, grace, lenience

quarters *n.* lodgings, dwelling, billet, rooms

quash *v.* abolish, nullify, suppress, overthrow, subdue

quaver 1 *v.* shake, tremble, shiver, shudder, vibrate 2 *n.* musical note

quay *n.* pier, dock, wharf, landing, jetty KEY

queasy *adj.* bilious, squeamish, sick, faint

queer *adj.* strange, odd, whimsical, peculiar

quell *v.* crush, stifle, extinguish, defeat

quench 1 *v.* douse *We carefully doused our campfire before leaving the site*, put out, cool, check 2 slake *The cattle rushed to the river and slaked their thirst*, cool, allay

query 1 *n.* question, doubt, objection 2 *v.* ask, enquire, question, doubt **★accept**

quest *n.* chase, hunt, search, pursuit, venture

question 1 *n.* query, enquiry, interrogation, 2 topic, problem, issue 3 *v.* ask, enquire, interrogate **★answer**

questionable *adj.* doubtful, uncertain, undecided, unbelievable **★certain**

queue 1 *n.* row, line, procession, line-up 2 pigtail, coil, braid CUE

quibble *v.* argue, trifle, split hairs, carp *If you like our plan, don't carp about the details*

quick 1 *adj.* speedy, rapid, express, swift, ▷*fast* 2 alert, active, agile, lively **★slow** 3 clever, intelligent, acute **★dull** 4 hasty, sharp, touchy **★mild**

quicken *v.* accelerate, ▷*hasten* **★delay**

quiet 1 *adj.* silent, soundless, noiseless, hushed **★noisy** 2 placid, smooth, undisturbed **★busy** 3 *n.* peace, rest, tranquillity, silence **★tumult**

quilt *n.* blanket, cover, eiderdown, duvet

quip *n.* joke, gag, gipe, jest, wisecrack, retort

quirk *n.* pecularity, curiosity, foible *Despite his age and one or two foibles, old Uncle Fred was very agile*, mannerism, ▷*habit*

quit 1 *v.* cease, desist, stop 2 leave, depart, relinquish 3 give up, surrender

quite *adv.* absolutely, altogether, wholly

quits *adj.* even *If I pay what I owe, it makes us even*, all square, level, equal

quiver 1 *v.* tremble, quake, shiver, shudder 2 *n.* holster, scabbard, sheath

quiz 1 *v.* question, ask, examine, grill 2 *n.* test, examination, contest *Barbara was the winner in the radio spelling contest*

quizzical 1 *adj.* incredulous, sceptical, suspicious 2 whimsical, teasing, amused

quota *n.* allowance, allocation, ration

quotation 1 *n.* extract, selection, passage 2 cost, estimate, price

quote *v.* recite, recollect, tell, instance, mention **★contradict**

R r

rabble *n.* crowd, mob, scum, riffraff

race [1] *n.* competition, contest, chase, dash [2] people, nation, folk, stock, breed, tribe [3] *v.* run, speed, hurry, scamper, gallop, sprint

rack [1] *n.* shelf, stand, frame, framework [2] *v.* distress, strain, torment, pain WRACK

racket [1] *n.* uproar, noise, hubbub, tumult, ▷*din* [2] fraud, deception, swindle

racy [1] *adj.* pungent, piquant, zestful [2] spirited, smart, lively

radiant [1] *adj.* brilliant, bright, luminous, shining [2] splendid, glorious, happy ★**dull**

radiate [1] *v.* gleam, sparkle, beam, shine [2] emit, spread, diffuse

radical [1] *adj.* extreme, fanatical, deep-seated [2] original, fundamental *The new head teacher made some fundamental changes in our lessons*, natural ★**superficial**

raffle *n.* draw, sweepstake, lottery

rafter *n.* joist, girder, beam, support

ragamuffin *n.* scarecrow, urchin, ▷*waif*

rage [1] *n.* wrath, fury, ferocity, passion, madness, ▷*anger* [2] *v.* rave, fret, fume *The mad bull was fuming with rage as we leaped over the fence*, storm, flare up

ragged *adj.* shabby, seedy, shaggy, rough, torn ★**smart**

raid [1] *n.* invasion, attack, strike, sortie [2] *v.* attack, invade, ransack, plunder *The ship was attacked and plundered by pirates* RAYED

rail [1] *n.* post, picket, fence, railing [2] *v.* scold, rant, blast, reproach

rain *n. & v.* deluge, drizzle, flood, shower, torrent REIGN REIN

raise [1] *v.* elevate, lift, erect, hoist *The flag was hoisted as the ship came into port* ★**lower** [2] excite, awaken, rouse [3] promote, increase, advance [4] cultivate, grow, breed RAZE

rake *v.* grope, scrape, collect, gather, assemble

rally [1] *v.* meet, assemble, convene *The members of the club will convene next month* ★**disperse** [2] encourage, restore, reunite

ram [1] *v.* cram, crowd, push, pack, stuff, poke, wedge [2] charge, beat, crash, drive

ramble [1] *v.* stroll, meander, saunter, roam, rove [2] chatter, digress *Joe's speech was very long, as he kept digressing from the point*, dodder

ramp [1] *n.* gradient, slope, incline, grade [2] swindle, fraud, ▷*racket*

rampage [1] *n.* storm, rage, riot, uproar, tumult [2] rave, rush, run wild *Someone left the gate open, and the pigs ran wild in the cabbage patch*

ramshackle *adj.* unstable, shaky, unsteady, flimsy, rickety, ▷*decrepit* ★**stable**

rancid *adj.* sour, curdled, rank, putrid, musty

rancour *n.* spite, grudge, animosity, hatred, ▷*malice* RANKER

random *adj.* haphazard, vague, casual, accidental, ▷*chance* ★**deliberate**

range [1] *n.* extent, length, span, magnitude, area [2] kind, sort, class, order [3] *v.* wander, rove, roam, stray

rank [1] *n.* grade, class, position, level [2] *adj.* foul, musty, offensive, coarse [3] luxuriant, fertile, dense *The whole country was covered with dense forest*

rankle *v.* burn, smoulder, fester, be embittered

ransack *v.* plunder, pillage, search, scour

ransom [1] *n.* release, deliverance, pay-off, price [2] *v.* rescue, redeem *Jill was lazy at school to begin with, but redeemed herself with hard work*, liberate

rant *v.* rave, declaim, bluster, roar, shout

rap *v.* tap, pat, strike, knock

rape *v.* abuse, assault, violate, attack

rapid *adj.* speedy, quick, swift, ▷*fast* ★**slow**

rapt *adj.* engrossed, intent, captivated, fascinated, delighted RAPPED WRAPPED

rapture *n.* bliss, ecstasy, delight, ▷*joy* ★**sorrow**

rare [1] *adj.* unusual, uncommon, scarce, occasional [2] valuable, fine, precious ★**common** [3] underdone *I would like my steak to be underdone and rather rare*, lightly cooked

rascal *n.* rogue, knave, villain, scamp, scoundrel, blackguard ★**gentleman**

rash 1 *adj.* headstrong, audacious, hasty, foolhardy, ▷*reckless* ★**cautious** 2 *n.* eruption, outbreak, epidemic *There has been an epidemic of house-breaking in our town*

rashness *n.* audacity, carelessness, hastiness, recklessness ★**carefulness**

rasp 1 *v.* file, grate, grind 2 irk, irritate, vex 3 *n.* file, tool

rate 1 *n.* pace, tempo *It took us some time to get used to the tempo of life in the city*, velocity, speed 2 tax, charge, cost 3 *v.* appraise, assess, estimate, merit, value

rather 1 *adv.* somewhat, to some extent, sort of 2 first, preferably, sooner

ration 1 *n.* portion, share, allotment, helping 2 *v.* allocate, allot, restrict, control

rational 1 *adj.* sensible, sound, wise, intelligent, sane ★**crazy** 2 reasonable, fair, proper ★**absurd**

rattle 1 *v.* jangle, jingle, vibrate 2 muddle, confuse, daze, ▷*bewilder*

ratty *adj.* cross, snappy, touchy *Craig is very touchy on the subject of his bad spelling*, irritable ★**calm**

raucous *adj.* harsh, hoarse, rough, strident

ravage *v.* devastate, destroy, pillage, ransack, desolate, wreck

rave 1 *v.* rant, ramble, roar, rage, storm 2 enthuse, favour, be ecstatic about

ravenous *adj.* hungry, starving, famished, voracious, ▷*greedy*

ravishing *adj.* beautiful, bewitching, delightful, charming, ▷*enchanting*

raw 1 *adj.* uncooked 2 unripe, green *I was pretty green during the first six months in the job*, inexperienced 3 sensitive, painful, tender 4 cold, exposed, chilly

ray *n.* beam, gleam, glimmer, shaft, stream, spark

raze *v.* demolish, destroy, flatten, obliterate, ruin RAISE RAYS

reach 1 *v.* arrive at, gain, get to, attain, grasp 2 stretch, extend 3 *n.* extent, length, grasp, distance, scope

react *v.* respond, reverberate *The sound of the church bell reverberated through the village*, behave, respond

Read

Reed

read *v.* peruse, pore over, study, browse, understand REED

readily *adv.* easily, eagerly, freely, gladly, promptly ★**reluctantly**

ready 1 *adj.* prepared, alert, prompt, willing ★**reluctant** 2 convenient, handy ★**remote** 3 skilful, facile, expert ★**clumsy**

real 1 *adj.* genuine, authentic, factual ★**false** 2 substantial, existent, actual ★**imaginary** REEL

realistic 1 *adj.* authentic, lifelike 2 practical, down-to-earth *Sue is a real romantic type, but her boyfriend is much more down-to-earth*, unromantic ★**fanciful**

realize 1 *v.* understand, comprehend, feel 2 earn, gain, obtain, acquire

really *adv.* truly, indeed, actually, absolutely

realm *n.* domain, province, sphere *My mother has taken up writing and is much involved in the sphere of books*, region, territory

reap *v.* harvest, gather, obtain, realize, derive, gain ★**squander**

rear 1 *n.* back, end, tail, behind, posterior 2 *adj.* hind, after, following 3 *v.* foster, breed, educate 4 lift, raise, elevate

reason 1 *n.* purpose, motive, basis, cause, explanation 2 wisdom, sense, intellect 3 *v.* consider, think, argue

reasonable 1 *adj.* sensible, valid, rational ★**absurd** 2 moderate, fair, just 3 cheap, low-priced *Everything in our new supermarket is very low-priced* ★**excessive**

reassure *v.* inspire, hearten, convince, ▷*encourage* ★**discourage**

rebate *n.* refund, repayment, discount, allowance

rebel [1] (re-*bel*) *v.* revolt, mutiny, disobey, resist [2] (*reb*-el) *n.* revolutionary, mutineer *Fletcher Christian was the leader of the mutineers on the **Bounty**,* traitor

rebellious *adj.* defiant, disobedient, mutinous, resistant ★**obedient**

rebuke *v.* reprimand, reproach, scold, tell off ★**praise**

recall [1] *v.* recollect, remember [2] cancel, overrule, countermand *We were just about to pull down the building when our orders were countermanded,* call back

recede *v.* ebb, retreat, flow back, decline, shrink, withdraw, return ★**proceed**

receipt [1] *n.* acknowledgement, voucher [2] acceptance, reception, inheritance [3] formula, ▷*recipe*

recent *adj.* late, new, fresh, novel, modern ★**out-of-date**

recently *adv.* lately, currently, latterly

receptacle *n.* container, holder, vessel, bowl

reception [1] *n.* entertainment, function, party [2] acceptance, acknowledgement

recess [1] *n.* alcove, corner, socket, niche, slot, nook [2] intermission, interlude, pause

recession *n.* slump, stagnation, depression ★**boom**

recipe *n.* formula, receipt, method, prescription

recite *v.* recount, chant, speak, declaim, relate, describe

reckless *adj.* unwary, incautious, daring, brash, heedless, ▷*rash* ★**cautious**

reckon [1] *v.* calculate, figure, count, tally *I have checked the accounts, and my figures tally with yours,* account [2] judge, expect, believe

reclaim *v.* recover, redeem, reform, retrieve, restore, salvage

recline *v.* lounge, sprawl, lie, rest, loll, repose

recognize [1] *v.* recall, recollect, remember, identify, know [2] see *I will explain my idea slowly, and you will see what I mean,* comprehend, understand

recoil [1] *v.* rebound, backfire, boomerang [2] falter, flinch, shrink, quail *My little brother quailed at the sound of the thunder*

recollect *v.* recall, recognize, place, ▷*remember* ★**forget**

recommend *v.* suggest, advise, propose, commend, approve ★**veto**

recompense [1] *n.* payment, compensation, remuneration [2] *v.* reimburse, repay, ▷*reward*

reconcile [1] *v.* accept, harmonize, pacify, placate ★**estrange** [2] adjust, settle, square

record [1] (re-*cord*) *v.* note, register, enter, inscribe, list [2] (*rec*-ord) *n.* album, disc, platter, CD, LP [3] chronicle, archive, almanac *We'll get hold of the almanac and check the time of high tide,* register [4] performance, championship

recount [1] (re-*count*) *v.* relate, tell, recite, describe [2] (re-count) count again

recover [1] *v.* reclaim, retrieve, redeem, regain [2] get better, recuperate, revive ★**worsen**

recreation *n.* pastime, sport, amusement, games, fun

recruit [1] *n.* trainee, beginner, apprentice [2] *v.* enlist, enrol, draft, mobilize

rectify *v.* correct, put right, repair, remedy, restore

recuperate *v.* get better, rally, improve, mend, ▷*recover* ★**worsen**

recur *v.* return, reappear, come back, repeat, revert

redden *v.* crimson, colour, flush, ▷*blush*

redeem [1] *v.* buy back, compensate for, exchange [2] save, liberate, free

reduce [1] *v.* lessen, diminish, curtail, contract [2] overcome, defeat, humiliate

reek *v.* smell, stink, fume, exhale, smoke

reel [1] *v.* roll, rock, shake, stagger, falter, totter [2] *n.* bobbin, spool, spindle REAL

refer *v.* relate, connect, associate, assign, belong

referee *n.* umpire, arbitrator, judge

reference [1] *n.* allusion, insinuation, innuendo *From your innuendo, it seems that you think I'm joking!,* ▷*hint* [2] recommendation, testimonial, credentials

refine *v.* clarify, purify, filter, process, cultivate

refined 1 *adj.* civilized, cultivated, cultured, ▷*polite* 2 purified, pure, clarified ★**coarse**

reflect 1 *v.* think, contemplate, deliberate, consider 2 mirror, copy, imitate, image

reform 1 *v.* improve, correct, ▷*rectify* 2 remodel, reorganize ★**worsen**

refrain 1 *v.* avoid, abstain, forbear, resist, keep from 2 *n.* chorus, melody, tune

refresh *v.* rejuvenate, renew, restore, cheer, enliven ★**exhaust**

refrigerate *v.* chill, cool, freeze

refuge *n.* haven, harbour, asylum, sanctuary, ▷*shelter*

refugee *n.* exile, fugitive, emigrant

refund *v.* repay, rebate, reimburse *I must reimburse you for all you spent on my behalf*, pay back, return

refuse 1 (re-*fuze*) *v.* decline, say no, demur, repudiate 2 (*ref*-use) *n.* rubbish, garbage, trash, waste

refute *v.* deny, dispute, disprove, discredit ★**prove**

regain *v.* recover, get back, retrieve, redeem

regal *adj.* royal, princely, majestic, noble, stately

regard 1 *v.* esteem, revere, honour, respect ★**dislike** 2 notice, observe, see, gaze 3 *n.* affection, esteem, fondness, repute ★**contempt**

regardless 1 *adj.* heedless, neglectful, indifferent ★**careful** 2 *adv.* anyhow, anyway, in any case

region *n.* area, zone, territory, locality, province, country

register 1 *n.* roll, roster, record, archives *We can trace the town's history from the ancient archives* 2 *v.* enter, record, inscribe, enrol, sign on

regret 1 *v.* repent, rue, deplore, lament, mourn, apologize ★**welcome** 2 *n.* remorse, sorrow, apology, grief

regular 1 *adj.* normal, customary, periodical, formal ★**unusual** 2 orderly, steady, unchanging ★**variable**

regulate 1 *v.* control, manage, govern, determine 2 adjust, measure, time, correct

Rain

Rein

regulation 1 *n.* rule, law, command, bye-law *There is a local bye-law forbidding football on Sunday* 2 adjustment, order, control, government

rehearse *v.* repeat, practise, drill, prepare, run through

reign (pr. rain) 1 *n.* rule, sway, power, control 2 *v.* govern, rule, dominate, command RAIN REIN

rein (pr. rain) *v. & n.* bridle, hold, check, harness RAIN REIGN

reinforce *v.* support, strengthen, toughen, stiffen ★**weaken**

reject 1 (re-*ject*) *v.* discard, get rid of, refuse, repel, deny 2 (*re*-ject) *n.* cast-off, scrap, throw-out

rejoice *v.* glory, exult, cheer, please, ▷*delight* ★**lament**

relapse 1 *v.* revert, backslide, turn back, recede 2 repetition, recurrence, setback

relate *v.* describe, recount, tell, mention, detail

related *adj.* associated, allied, connected, linked, akin ★**different**

relative 1 *n.* kinsman, kinswoman, cousin, relation, sibling *I have four siblings – three sisters and one brother* 2 *adj.* comparative, approximate, relevant

relax *v.* diminish, loosen, ease, reduce, relieve, unwind ★**tighten**

relaxed *adj.* composed, cool, easy-going, mellow, ▷*casual* ★**tense**

release *v.* let go, loose, liberate, acquit, discharge, ▷*free* ★**detain**

relent *v.* relax, soften, yield, ease, give in, unbend ★**harden**

relentless *adj.* unmerciful, remorseless, grim, pitiless, ▷*cruel* ★**humane**

relevant *adj.* applicable, pertinent, appropriate, apt, ▷*suitable* ★**irrelevant**

reliable *adj.* dependable, trustworthy, responsible, honest, ▷*sound* ★**unreliable**

relic *n.* fragment, vestige, antique, keepsake, memento *This brooch is a memento of my great-grandmother: she wore it on her wedding day*

relief *n.* aid, assistance, respite, support, succour, ▷*help* ★**aggravation**

relieve *v.* release, support, comfort, lighten, relax, console ★**aggravate**

religious *adj.* pious, devout, orthodox, devoted, god-fearing, faithful

relinquish *v.* renounce, let go, waive, disclaim, give up, ▷*abandon* ★**retain**

relish [1] *v.* enjoy, like, approve, ▷*appreciate* ★**loathe** [2] *n.* savour, flavour, tang, gusto *The fried chicken was a great success; everyone ate with enormous gusto!*, zest, sauce

reluctant *adj.* hesitant, averse, loth, disinclined, squeamish ★**willing**

rely on *v.* depend on, count on, believe in

remain [1] *v.* stay, tarry, dwell, wait, rest ★**depart** [2] persist, last, endure,

remainder *n.* remnant, residue, leavings

remark [1] *v.* utter, observe, state, mention, ▷*say* [2] notice, perceive, note, ▷*see*

remarkable *adj.* unusual, surprising, curious, prominent, ▷*outstanding* ★**ordinary**

remedy [1] *n.* cure, restorative, medicine [2] relief, solution, treatment, corrective [3] *v.* relieve, heal, cure, put right

remember *v.* recollect, recognize, think back, ▷*recall* ★**forget**

remind *v.* suggest, hint, cue, prompt

remit [1] *v.* relax, desist, slacken, modify, excuse, forgive [2] pay, square, settle up

remnant *n.* residue, remains, rest ▷*remainder*

remorse *n.* sorry, regrets, contrition, pity

remote [1] *adj.* distant, far, isolated ★**near** [2] unrelated, alien, foreign ★**significant**

remove *v.* dislocate, take away, transfer, withdraw, carry off

rend *v.* split, fracture, tear apart, sever, break

render [1] *v.* give, present, surrender, deliver [2] play, execute, perform

renew [1] *v.* modernize, mend, prolong, renovate [2] reissue *Next week we start to reissue some of the old silent movies*, revive

renounce *v.* disown, disclaim, give up, repudiate, forsake ★**retain**

renowned *adj.* eminent, noted, famed, notable, ▷*celebrated* ★**obscure**

rent [1] *v.* hire, lease, let, charter [2] *n.* tear, rip, break, crack

repair [1] *v.* fix, mend, correct, remedy, rectify *We are sorry there was an error in your account; we shall rectify it right away* [2] *n.* restoration, adjustment

repast *n.* meal, food, snack, spread

repay [1] *v.* refund, reimburse, pay [2] avenge, retaliate, revenge, punish

repeal *v.* revoke, annul, abolish, quash *The man's innocent was proved and his sentence was quashed*, ▷*cancel* ★**establish**

repeat *v.* duplicate, renew, reiterate, do again

repel [1] *v.* repulse, deter, reject, push back [2] revolt, disgust, nauseate ★**attract**

repellent *adj.* distasteful, hateful, discouraging, ▷*repulsive* ★**attractive**

repent *v.* sorrow, deplore, grieve, ▷*regret*

replace [1] *v.* supersede, succeed, follow, substitute [2] put back, reinstate, restore

replenish *v.* fill, refill, restock, furnish, provide, top up ★**empty**

replica *n.* facsimile, copy, likeness, duplicate

reply [1] *v.* answer, respond, rejoin, retort, acknowledge [2] *n.* answer, response, acknowledgement, riposte

report [1] *n.* statement, account, message, communication, tidings [2] noise, explosion, bang [3] *v.* tell, disclose, reveal, expose

repose [1] *v.* rest, settle, lie down, sleep, recline [2] *n.* ease, peace, quiet, tranquility ★**tumult**

represent [1] *v.* depict, picture, portray, illustrate [2] stand for, mean, denote

representative [1] *n.* agent, delegate, envoy, deputy [2] *adj.* typical, figurative

repress *v.* restrain, suppress, bottle up, smother, stifle

reprimand [1] *v.* admonish, blame, rebuke, ▷*chide* [2] *n.* ticking-off, reproach *The service in the hotel was excellent, quite beyond reproach*, talking-to, scolding **★praise**

reproach *v.* scold, reprove, reprimand, blame, ▷*rebuke* **★approve**

reproduce [1] *v.* copy, duplicate, imitate, simulate [2] breed, multiply, generate

reprove *v.* reproach, reprimand, ▷*rebuke* **★approve**

repudiate *v.* renounce, disown, disavow, disclaim **★acknowledge**

repugnant *adj.* unattractive, disagreeable, offensive, ▷*repulsive*, **★pleasant**

repulse *v.* repel, rebuff, drive back, reject, ▷*spurn* **★attract**

repulsive *adj.* obnoxious, disgusting, loathsome, ▷*repugnant* **★attractive**

reputation *n.* standing, position, esteem, honour, good name

request [1] *v.* demand, beg, entreat, beseech, ▷*ask* [2] *n.* petition, entreaty, invitation

require [1] *v.* need, want, demand, crave [2] expect, cause, instruct

rescue [1] *v.* save, set free, liberate, recover, release [2] *n.* liberation, deliverance, salvation *Salvation for the starving islanders came when the aircraft dropped food and supplies* **★capture**

research *v.* examine, explore, investigate, enquire, ▷*study*

resemble *v.* look like, mirror, take after, be like **★differ**

resent *v.* resist, begrudge, dislike, take exception to **★like**

resentful *adj.* offended, bitter, piqued, huffy, ▷*indignant* **★contented**

reserve [1] *v.* hoard, retain, withhold, ▷*keep* [2] *n.* modesty, shyness, restraint [3] supply, backlog, stock

reservoir *n.* lake, spring, pool, container

reside *v.* live, occupy, inhabit, lodge, ▷*dwell*

residence *n.* house, home, habitation, dwelling, mansion RESIDENTS

resign *v.* retire, abdicate, step down, give notice, abandon, ▷*quit* **★join**

resign oneself to *v.* accept, comply, reconcile *Robinson Crusoe became reconciled to loneliness on his island*, yield, ▷*submit* **★resist**

Resign oneself to

Robinson Crusoe became reconciled to loneliness on his island.

resist *v.* withstand, oppose, defy, refrain, hinder, ▷*thwart* **★submit**

resistance *n.* defiance, obstruction, opposition, hindrance **★acceptance**

resolute *adj.* determined, resolved, obstinate, stubborn, dogged *Despite the bad weather, the climbers were dogged in their will to reach the peak* **★weak**

resolve [1] *v.* determine, intend, decide [2] decipher, unravel, disentangle [3] *n.* resolution, purpose, will

resort [1] *v.* frequent, haunt, visit [2] *n.* alternative, chance, course [3] spa, holiday centre

resourceful *adj.* clever, ingenious, bright, talented

respect [1] *n.* esteem, honour, regard, repute, dignity [2] *v.* esteem, honour, revere, venerate *The names of the pioneers and explorers will always be venerated*

respectable adj. decent, admirable, honest, honourable, proper ★**disreputable**

respectful adj. deferential, courteous, polite, dutiful ★**disrespectful**

respite n. break, halt, interval, lull, recess, let-up

respond v. answer, reply, retort, tally, accord, agree ★**differ**

responsible [1] adj. accountable, dependable, sensible, ▷reliable ★**unreliable** [2] liable, guilty

rest [1] n. repose, relaxation, peace, tranquillity [2] break, pause, respite, spell [3] remainder, residue, balance [4] v. repose, settle, sleep, relax WREST

restful adj. peaceful, quiet, calm, placid ★**disturbing**

restless adj. uneasy, fitful, agitated, nervous, fretful ★**calm**

restore [1] v. replace, reinstate, return [2] refurbish, recondition, renovate We renovated this old sofa which we found in a junk shop

restrain v. stop, prevent, hold back, subdue, ▷check ★**encourage**

restrict v. confine, limit, cramp, handicap, ▷regulate ★**free**

result [1] n. effect, consequence, outcome, end ★**cause** [2] v. ensue, happen, turn out, follow ★**begin**

resume v. renew, recommence, start again, go back to, ▷continue ★**interrupt**

retain v. hold, restrain, withhold, detain, ▷keep ★**relinquish**

retaliate v. avenge, reciprocate, fight back, repay, retort ★**submit**

retire [1] v. retreat, go back, ▷withdraw ★**advance** [2] abdicate, resign, relinquish

retort [1] n. riposte, reply, rejoinder [2] v. return, answer, reply

retract v. recant, deny, disavow, take back ★**maintain**

retreat [1] v. retire, depart, shrink, ▷withdraw ★**advance** [2] n. sanctuary This section of the park is being made into a bird sanctuary, shelter, den, haven

retrieve v. redeem, recover, regain, rescue, ▷salvage ★**lose**

return [1] v. rejoin, come back, reappear [2] restore, give back, repay, refund [3] n. form, document, list

reveal v. disclose, expose, show, display, uncover, divulge ★**hide**

revel [1] v. make merry, celebrate, have fun [2] n. celebration, gala, party, spree

revenge [1] n. vengeance, reprisal, retaliation [2] v. avenge, get one's own back

revenue n. income, receipts, earnings

revere v. honour, esteem, regard, adore, venerate, respect ★**despise**

reverse [1] v. cancel, change, overrule, repeal, revoke [2] n. adversity, disaster, bad luck, misfortune [3] adj. backward, contrary, opposite We turned our car around and went back in the opposite direction

review [1] v. reconsider, revise, examine, survey [2] n. inspection, examination [3] synopsis, journal, magazine REVUE

revise v. edit, amend, improve, rewrite, alter

revive v. awaken, rally, recover, refresh, ▷rouse

revoke v. repeal, abolish After the metric system was introduced, most countries abolished the old measures, cancel, quash, reverse, withdraw

revolt [1] v. rebel, mutiny, riot [2] nauseate, sicken, disgust [3] n. rebellion, uprising, revolution

revolting adj. obnoxious The chemical factory's chimney was giving off obnoxious fumes, repulsive, offensive, ▷repugnant ★**pleasant**

revolve v. rotate, spin, gyrate, turn

reward [1] n. award, payment, benefit, bonus, profit ★**punishment** [2] v. compensate, repay, remunerate ★**punish**

rhyme n. verse, poem, ditty, ode RIME

rhythm n. beat, pulse, throb, stroke, timing

ribald adj. smutty, vulgar, coarse, gross

rich [1] adj. wealthy, prosperous, affluent, opulent ★**poor** [2] fertile, loamy, fruitful, abundant ★**barren** [3] delicious, sweet, luscious, delicate

rid v. get rid of, unburden, expel, free

riddle [1] n. puzzle, cryptogram, enigma [2] v. puncture, bore, perforate, pierce

ride [1] v. sit, travel, drive, manage, journey, control [2] n. journey, jaunt, lift, trip

Rivers and Waterways

Brook
Canal
Channel
Creek
Lake
Loch
Mere
Pool
Pond
River
Spring
Strait
Stream
Surf
Tide
Waterfall

ridge [1] *n.* groove, furrow, fold [2] highland, chain, range *A range of hills could be seen in the distance*

ridicule [1] *n.* scorn, derision, travesty, sarcasm, mockery [2] *v.* deride, mock, jeer, banter *The chairperson continued to banter amusingly until the speaker was ready*, make fun of

ridiculous *adj.* laughable, absurd, foolish, preposterous, ▷*silly* ★**sensible**

rife *adj.* common, current, frequent, prevalent, ▷*widespread* ★**scarce**

rifle [1] *v.* loot, rob, plunder, ▷*ransack* [2] *n.* gun, musket, firearm

rift [1] *n.* fissure, breach, crack [2] disagreement, clash, break

right [1] *adj.* correct, proper, true ★**incorrect** [2] honest, upright, fair [3] seemly, fit, suitable, becoming ★**improper** [4] *n.* truth, justice, honesty ★**wrong** RITE WRIGHT WRITE

righteous *adj.* honourable, upright, moral

rigid [1] *adj.* stiff, firm, inflexible [2] stern, austere, harsh ★**flexible**

rigorous *adj.* stern, severe, strict, rigid

rim *n.* border, margin, edge, verge *Parking is not allowed on the grass verge of this road*, brink

ring [1] *n.* circle, band, collar [2] bell, chime, tinkle [3] *v.* chime, strike, jingle, sound WRING

riot [1] *n.* uproar, tumult, brawl, broil ★**calm** [2] *v.* revolt, rampage, rebel

ripe [1] *adj.* mellow, mature, seasoned [2] developed, adult, full-grown

rise [1] *v.* ascend, mount, soar, arise, grow ★**fall** [2] appear, occur, happen ★**vanish** [3] *n.* ascent, advance, increase ★**fall**

risk [1] *v.* chance, dare, hazard, gamble [2] *n.* adventure, peril, danger, jeopardy ★**safety**

risky *adj.* perilous, chancy, dangerous, tricky, uncertain ★**safe**

rite *n.* custom, ritual, practice RIGHT

rival [1] *adj.* opposing, competing, conflicting [2] *n.* opponent, adversary ★**associate**

river *n.* stream, waterway, brook, torrent *Before the rains came, this torrent was quite a small stream*

road *n.* street, avenue, drive, lane, motorway, route, way RODE ROWED

roam *v.* rove, ramble, range, stroll, wander

roar *v.* bellow, bawl, yell, blare, cry

rob *v.* cheat, defraud, loot, plunder, ▷*steal*

robber *n.* bandit, brigand, thief, crook

robe *n.* costume, dress, gown, habit

robust *adj.* strong, healthy, lusty, sturdy, ▷*vigorous* ★**delicate**

rock [1] *n.* stone, boulder, cobble, pebble, crag, reef [2] *v.* totter, reel, sway, falter [3] quiet, still, tranquillize, soothe

rod *n.* baton, stick, stave, pole, perch, cane

rogue *n.* rascal, blackguard, scamp, knave, ▷*scoundrel* ★**gentleman**

rôle *n.* character, post, duty, function *At the end of the party, my function will be to wash up*

roll [1] *n.* record, register, list [2] spool, scroll, reel [3] *v.* revolve, rotate, turn [4] smooth, level, press [5] lurch, reel, pitch, ROLE

romance [1] *n.* love story, novel, love affair [2] adventure, excitement, fantasy, glamour

romantic [1] *adj.* amorous, passionate, loving [2] visionary, fanciful *Many people have a fanciful idea of how things were in the old days*, fantastic, extravagant ★**ordinary**

romp v. gambol, caper, frolic, prance, play

roof n. ceiling, covering, cover, canopy

room [1] n. apartment, chamber, area, compartment, salon [2] space, capacity

root [1] n. seed, source, radicle [2] basis, element, stem, origin

rope n. cable, cord, hawser, line, lasso

rosy [1] adj. cheerful, encouraging, hopeful, optimistic [2] pink, flesh-coloured

rot [1] v. corrupt, crumble, decay, perish [2] n. bunkum *The last speaker at the meeting was talking a lot of bunkum!*, balderdash, bosh

rotate v. revolve, turn, spin, pivot, gyrate

rotten [1] adj. decayed, putrid, decomposed, fetid [2] deplorable, despicable, nasty, vicious *People have told some vicious lies about my dad*

rough [1] adj. wrinkled, craggy, coarse, shaggy, broken [2] rude, crude, imperfect [3] blunt, gruff, brusque, discourteous RUFF

round [1] adj. circular, rotund, spherical [2] n. ring, circle, loop

rouse [1] v. waken, arouse, excite, disturb [2] anger, inflame, incite ★**calm**

rout v. crush, defeat, conquer, overthrow

route n. road, track, way, journey, direction

routine n. usage, practice, formula, technique, method, habit *After being alone for so long, I have got into the habit of talking to myself*

rove v. tramp, roam, wander, stroll, drift

row [1] (ro) n. string, line, queue, rank, column [2] v. paddle, scull ROE [3] (as in *now*) n. fight, squabble, noise, quarrel ★**calm**

rowdy adj. rough, unruly, boisterous, noisy, wild ★**quiet**

royal adj. sovereign, princely, stately, majestic, ▷*regal*

rub v. stroke, brush, scrub, wipe, polish

rubbish n. debris, garbage, trash, junk

rude [1] adj. coarse, ill-bred, impolite, boorish, ▷*vulgar* [2] crude, formless, shapeless ★**polished** ROOD RUED

rue v. be sorry for, deplore, grieve, ▷*regret*

ruffian n. hooligan, lout, hoodlum, scoundrel, rogue, ▷*rascal*

ruffle [1] v. fluster, worry, excite, agitate [2] crumple, rumple, crease, cockle

Rulers, Monarchs, and Leaders

Caesar Rajah
Emperor Sultan
Empress Tsar
King Tsarina
Mikado
Mogul
Pharaoh
President
Prince
Princess
Queen

ruffled adj. upset, worried, flustered, harassed

rugged [1] adj. rough, craggy, shaggy, ragged [2] rigorous, robust, strong, strenuous

ruin [1] v. demolish, wreck, damage, smash [2] bankrupt, impoverish, overwhelm

rule [1] v. control, govern, command, manage, direct [2] decide, determine, settle, judge [3] n. law, regulation [4] straight-edge

ruler [1] n. leader, director, king, queen, monarch, governor [2] rule, straight-edge

rum [1] adj. curious, odd *There is something very odd about the old house on the hill*, strange, suspicious [2] n. spirit, liquor

rumble v. roar, thunder, boom, roll

rumour n. hearsay, report, gossip, scandal

rumpus n. uproar, racket, riot, commotion, hurly-burly ★**calm**

run [1] v. hurry, hasten, speed, sprint ★**saunter** [2] leak, flow, ooze [3] operate, propel, drive [4] n. race, course

run away v. escape, flee, bolt, abscond ★**stay**

rupture v. & n. break, burst, puncture, split

rural adj. rustic, countrified, pastoral ★**urban**

ruse n. dodge, hoax, scheme, trick, ploy RUES

rush v. & n. dash, speed, hurry, scramble, stampede, rampage ★**saunter**

rust n. mould, blight, mildew, stain

rustic adj. rural, pastoral, country, homely, simple

rustle v. crackle, swish, murmur, whisper

rut n. furrow, channel, groove, score, track

ruthless adj. cruel, savage, harsh, ferocious, pitiless ★**merciful**

S s

sack [1] *n.* bag, pouch, pack [2] *v.* rob, plunder, pillage [3] discharge, dismiss, lay off SAC

sacred *adj.* holy, blessed, hallowed, spiritual ★**profane**

sacrifice [1] *n.* offering [2] *v.* forfeit, give up, relinquish, ▷*abandon*

sad *adj.* sorrowful, melancholy, unhappy, mournful, woeful, ▷*sorry* ★**happy**

sadden *v.* mourn, grieve, distress, lament ★**please**

safe [1] *adj.* secure, protected, sure ★**unsafe** [2] *n.* vault, coffer, cash-box, strongbox

safety *n.* shelter, security, sanctuary, protection, refuge ★**danger**

sag *v.* bend, curve, bow, decline, flag, ▷*droop* ★**bulge**

sage [1] *adj.* wise, sensible, shrewd, sagacious ★**foolish** [2] *n.* wise person, savant *We were taught by an old savant of the university, Professor Hankins, philosopher* ★**fool**

said *adj.* expressed, stated, above-mentioned

sail *v.* cruise, voyage, navigate, float, skim SALE

sailor *n.* seaman, seafarer, mariner, jack tar, seadog SAILER

sake *n.* motive, reason, purpose, object, principle

salary *n.* pay, earnings, reward, wages, income

sale *n.* auction, transaction, selling, trade, disposal SAIL

sally *n.* jest, joke, crack, riposte, ▷*quip*

salute [1] *v.* greet, accost, welcome, hail, honour [2] *n.* greetings, welcome, acknowledgement

salvage *v.* save, conserve, rescue, restore, reclaim, ▷*preserve* ★**abandon**

same [1] *adj.* identical, duplicate, alike, similar [2] aforesaid, aforementioned *I leave all my possessions to my wife, the aforementioned Mrs Harriet Wellington*

sample [1] *n.* specimen, example, model, pattern, illustration [2] *v.* inspect, try, taste

sanction *v.* permit, allow, authorize, approve

sanctuary *n.* retreat, shelter, shrine, asylum, ▷*refuge*

sane *adj.* normal, rational, reasonable, lucid, ▷*sensible* ★**insane**

sap *v.* bleed, drain, exhaust, reduce, weaken ★**strengthen**

sarcastic *adj.* biting, cutting, sardonic, cynical, ironic, caustic *My cousins made some caustic comments after I played the violin*

satire *n.* invective, sarcasm, burlesque, ridicule, parody

satisfaction *n.* contentment, delight, gratification, compensation ★**grievance**

satisfy *v.* gratify, fulfil, appease, suit, please, ▷*delight* ★**disappoint**

saturate *v.* soak, steep, drench, souse, waterlog *I am afraid our old canoe is too waterlogged ever to be used again*

saucy *adj.* cheeky, forward, pert, impudent, disrespectful ★**civil**

saunter *v.* roam, loiter, wander, linger, dawdle, amble, ▷*stroll* ★**hasten**

savage [1] *adj.* barbaric, wild, uncivilized, ferocious, brutal ★**civilized** [2] *n.* brute, heathen, oaf, native

Sacred Books

Apocrypha	Gospels
Bhagavad-Gita	Granth
Bible	Hebrew Bible
Book of Mormon	Koran
Book of Common	Talmud
Prayer	Torah
	Tripitaka
	Upanishad
	Veda

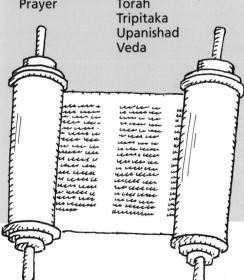

save [1] *v.* liberate, set free, rescue, protect, guard [2] keep, preserve, salvage, hoard, put aside *squander

savoury *adj.* appetizing, flavourful, luscious, agreeable *tasteless

say *v.* speak, utter, state, pronounce, talk, tell, assert

saying *n.* proverb, statement, adage, idiom, maxim

scale [1] *n.* measure, balance, calibration [2] crust, plate, flake [3] clef, key *I shall play this next piece in the key of C*, chord [4] *v.* climb, ascend, clamber up

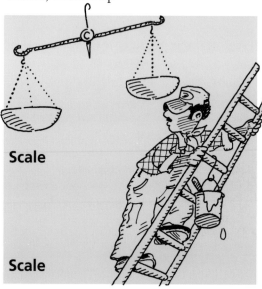

Scale

Scale

scamp *n.* knave, rogue, rascal, scoundrel, blighter *Someone rang our doorbell, but when I opened the door, the blighter had gone*

scamper *v.* hurry, run, scurry, hasten, sprint, ▷*rush*

scan *v.* examine, glance at, scrutinize, pore over, ▷*check*

scandal *n.* disgrace, libel, slander, offence, infamy, rumour, discredit *honour

scanty *adj.* meagre, insufficient, sparse, inadequate, poor, scant *plenty

scar [1] *n.* blemish, mark, stigma, wound [2] *v.* brand, damage, disfigure

scarce *adj.* rare, infrequent, sparse, scanty, uncommon *common

scarcity *n.* lack, deficiency, dearth, rarity, infreqency *abundance

scare *v.* frighten, startle, shock, alarm, dismay *reassure

scatter *v.* spread, disperse, strew, ▷*sprinkle* *collect

scene *n.* sight, spectacle, vision, view, exhibition, landscape SEEN

scent [1] *n.* aroma, tang, fragrance, smell, odour [2] *v.* detect, sniff, smell CENT SENT

sceptical (*skep*-tical) *adj.* doubtful, unbelieving, incredulous, ▷*dubious* *convinced

schedule (*shed*-ual) *n.* timetable *The buses in this town always keep to the timetable*, programme, catalogue, diary

scheme (*skeem*) *n.* plot, plan, project, design, proposal, idea

scholar [1] *n.* pupil, student, schoolchild, learner [2] intellectual, savant, academic

scholarly *adj.* learned, educated, literate, cultured *illiterate

scoff *v.* sneer, mock, deride, jeer, ridicule *respect

scold *v.* rebuke, admonish, reprove, find fault with, ▷*chide* *praise

scoop *v.* bail, ladle, spoon, excavate, gouge, hollow

scope *n.* extent, margin, compass, range, latitude, field

scorch *v.* sear, burn, singe, blister, shrivel

score [1] *v.* cut, mark, scratch [2] register, record, win

scorn [1] *n.* mockery, disdain, ridicule, disregard [2] *v.* despise, mock, spurn, slight *respect

scoundrel *n.* rascal, knave, thief, rogue, villain, ▷*vagabond* *gentleman

scour [1] *v.* cleanse, rinse, scrub, purge [2] search, seek, ransack, rake

scourge [1] *v.* beat, whip, cane, thrash [2] *n.* curse, evil, misfortune, plague *blessing

scowl *v. & n.* frown, glower, grimace, glare *smile

scramble [1] *v.* clamber, climb [2] jostle, struggle, swarm, push [3] *n.* turmoil, bustle, confusion *order

scrap [1] *n.* piece, morsel, bit, portion, fragment, grain [2] *v.* abandon, discard, junk

scrape [1] *v.* scratch, groove, abrade, file, grate, scour [2] *n.* predicament, fix, difficulty

scratch *v. & n.* wound, cut, mark, scribble, score

scream *v. & n.* screech, cry, shriek, howl, yell

screen [1] *n.* awning *Before the ceremony, an awning was erected over the entrance to the hotel,* canopy, shade, protection [2] *v.* protect, hide, conceal, veil

screw *v.* twist, turn, wrench, tighten, compress

scribble *v.* write, scrawl, scratch

scribe *n.* writer, penman, clerk, historian

script *n.* handwriting, manuscript, text, words, libretto *W.S. Gilbert wrote the librettos to the music of operettas by Sir Arthur Sullivan*

scrub [1] *v.* scour, brush, mop, cleanse [2] *n.* brushwood, undergrowth

scruffy *adj.* untidy, dirty, frowzy, seedy, shabby, ▷*slovenly* ★**neat**

scrumptious *adj.* delightful, delicious, appetizing, exquisite

scrupulous *adj.* painstaking, particular, rigorous, strict, conscientious ★**careless**

scrutinize *v.* examine, inspect, peruse, study

scuffle *v. & n.* tussle, skirmish, fight, struggle, squabble

scum *n.* dross, foam, froth, dregs, crust

scuttle [1] *v.* scramble, scamper, scoot, hurry [2] destroy, smash, wreck

seal [1] *n.* signet, stamp [2] cork, bung, closure [3] sea mammal [4] *v.* fasten, close, shut

seam [1] *n.* ridge, scar, lode, furrow [2] hem, pleat, tuck SEEM

search [1] *v.* seek, quest, hunt, trail, track, scour, explore [2] *n.* exploration, investigation, quest, pursuit

season [1] *n.* period, time, occasion, term [2] *v.* accustom, acclimatize, mature [3] flavour, spice, salt

seat [1] *n.* bench, chair, stool, sofa, couch, throne [2] headquarters, place, site [3] *v.* accommodate, locate, place

secret *adj.* mysterious, hidden, concealed, obscure, private ★**public**

section *n.* division, group, department, segment, portion

secure [1] *adj.* safe, protected [2] confident, certain, sure, stable ★**uncertain** [3] *v.* fasten, protect, close, lock ★**unfasten** [4] acquire, procure, obtain ★**lost**

sedate *adj.* staid, sober, demure, earnest, ▷*steady* ★**flippant**

see [1] *v.* behold, witness, sight, observe [2] heed, examine, watch, note [3] understand, comprehend, know SEA

seedy *adj.* shabby, squalid, poor, grubby, unkempt, ▷*slovenly* ★**spruce**

seek *v.* look for, search, enquire, endeavour, hunt

seem *v.* appear, look like, sound like, look as if SEAM

seemly *adj.* fit, suitable, proper, decent, decorous ★**unseemly**

seethe *v.* simmer, fizz, bubble, boil, foam

seize *v.* grasp, snatch, take, clutch, arrest, ▷*grab* ★**abandon** SEAS SEES

seldom *adv.* rarely, infrequently, hardly, scarcely ★**often**

select [1] *adj.* choice, chosen, fine, prime *All the fruit on the trees in the orchard are at their prime*, first-class ★**common** [2] *v.* choose, pick out, single out, prefer

selfish *adj.* greedy, self-centred, narrow, illiberal, ▷*mean* ★**generous**

sell *v.* market, vend, retail, trade, peddle ★**buy**

send *v.* transmit, dispatch, forward, mail, post, direct ★**detain**

send for *v.* command, order, summon, request ★**dismiss**

sensation [1] *n.* feeling, perception, impression, awareness [2] excitement, commotion, scandal

sensational *adj.* exceptional, scandalous, lurid, ▷*exciting* ★**ordinary**

sense [1] *n.* sensation, impression, feeling [2] understanding, mind, tact, intellect [3] wisdom, significance, meaning CENTS SCENTS

senseless *adj.* silly, stupid, absurd, ▷*foolish* ★**sensible**

sensible [1] *adj.* wise, intelligent, astute, shrewd [2] reasonable, rational [3] conscious, aware, mindful ★**senseless**

sensitive [1] *adj.* susceptible, responsive, acute [2] thin-skinned, touchy

sentence [1] *n.* phrase, clause [2] judgment, decision, condemnation, doom

sentimental *adj.* romantic, tender, emotional, impressionable *Because Rachel is at such an impressionable age her mother does not want her to see the film*

separate [1] *adj.* disconnected, apart, detached ★**united** [2] *v.* detach, part, divide, break, disconnect ★**unite**

sequel *n.* continuation, consequence, result, outcome

serene *adj.* tranquil, calm, peaceful, undisturbed, clear ★**tempestuous**

series *n.* sequence, progression, succession, run, string

serious *adj.* grave, earnest, solemn, thoughtful, severe, grim ★**trivial**

serve *v.* attend, assist, aid, oblige, help, officiate, act

service [1] *n.* aid, help, assistance, attendance, employment [2] ceremony, rite *Stuart is studying the marriage rites of the ancient Incas*

set [1] *n.* group, pack, outfit, series [2] *v.* settle, put, place, seat, locate [3] stiffen, congeal, harden [4] *adj.* decided, resolved, determined, fixed

setback *n.* defeat, delay, problem, snag, hold-up ★**advantage**

settle [1] *v.* establish, regulate, fix [2] pay, liquidate, finish [3] populate, colonize [4] live, dwell, reside

several *adj.* various, numerous, sundry, separate

severe *adj.* strict, rigid, unkind, hard, austere, ▷*stern* ★**lenient**

sew *v.* stitch, tack, baste, fasten, seam so SOW

shabby *adj.* torn, ragged, mean, shoddy, tatty, ▷*squalid* ★**neat**

shack *n.* hut, cabin, shanty, shed, hovel

shackle *v. & n.* manacle, handcuff, chain, rope, fetter

shade [1] *n.* shadow, gloom, darkness, dusk [2] blind, awning, screen [3] colour, tint, hue, tone [4] ghost, spirit, wraith *Out of the darkness, a wraith-like figure loomed up before us*

shadow [1] *n.* ▷*shade* [2] *v.* follow, stalk, tail

shady [1] *adj.* shadowy, shaded ★**sunny** [2] crooked, infamous, disreputable ★**honest**

shaft [1] *n.* pillar, column, support [2] hilt, handle, rod [3] mine, pit, well, tunnel

shaggy *adj.* hairy, tousled, unkempt, rough ★**smooth**

shake *v.* flutter, tremble, throb, shudder, ▷*quiver* ★**still**

Ships and Boats

Gondola

Trawler

Kayak

shallow ⟦1⟧ *adj.* not deep ⟦2⟧ trivial, empty, silly, empty-headed **✶profound**

sham *adj.* false, imitation, counterfeit, forged, ▷*bogus* **✶genuine**

shame *n.* & *v.* dishonour, discredit, ▷*disgrace*

shameful *adj.* disgraceful, scandalous, outrageous, ▷*disreputable* **✶honourable**

shape ⟦1⟧ *n.* form, structure, outline, pattern ⟦2⟧ *v.* form, fashion, make, create

share ⟦1⟧ *v.* allot, divide, participate, co-operate ⟦2⟧ *n.* portion, allotment, allowance

sharp ⟦1⟧ *adj.* acute, keen, pointed ⟦2⟧ clear, distinct, clean-cut ⟦3⟧ painful, severe, intense ⟦4⟧ pungent, acrid, acid ⟦5⟧ alert, shrewd, acute, ▷*clever* **✶dull**

shatter *v.* smash, wreck, break, fracture, ruin, ▷*destroy*

shave *v.* shear, crop, slice, shred, graze, trim

Liner

Motorboat

Catamaran

Ferry

115

shear v. fleece, strip, cut, ▷*shave* SHEER

sheath n. scabbard, quiver, holster, holder, case, casing

shed 1 n. hut, barn, lean-to, shanty 2 v. cast off, moult *Our dog is moulting, and leaves white hairs all over the carpet*, spill 3 beam, radiate

sheepish adj. timid, diffident, foolish, embarrassed, shame-faced ★**unabashed**

sheer 1 adj. absolute, simple, pure, unmixed 2 transparent, filmy, thin 3 steep, abrupt, perpendicular *The trail ended at the foot of huge, perpendicular cliffs* SHEAR

shell n. pod, case, husk, hull, shuck, crust

shelter 1 n. roof, sanctuary, safety, home, retreat, cover 2 v. shield, cover, protect, screen ★**expose**

shield n. & v. guard, screen, safeguard, ▷*shelter*

shift 1 v. alter, move, change, displace, remove 2 n. turn, spell, stint

shifty adj. untrustworthy, devious, treacherous, ▷*wily* ★**honest**

shine v. & n. glow, gleam, glitter, sparkle, flash

ship 1 n. boat, barge, craft, vessel 2 v. export, send, transport *(see page 115)*

shirk v. dodge, avoid, shun, evade, slack

shiver v. quaver, quiver, shake, shudder, ▷*tremble*

shock 1 n. blow, jolt, clash, collision 2 scare, start, turn 3 v. stupefy, daze, stun

shocking adj. scandalous, awful, frightful, ▷*horrible* ★**agreeable**

shoot 1 v. fire, discharge, bombard, propel 2 germinate *We grew some beans in a glass jar and watched them germinate*, grow, bud, sprout 3 n. bud, twig, sprout CHUTE

shop 1 n. store, market, emporium 2 v. buy, market, purchase

shore 1 n. beach, coast, strand, seashore, seaside 2 v. prop, support, bolster up, brace

short 1 adj. brief, concise, condensed ★**long** 2 deficient, incomplete, scanty ★**full** 3 sharp, severe, bad-tempered 4 small, puny, squat, diminutive, tiny ★**tall**

shortcoming n. defect, fault, flaw, inadequacy, ▷*weakness*

shorten v. cut, crop, abbreviate, lessen, ▷*diminish* ★**lengthen**

shortened adj. abbreviated, abridged, condensed ★**enlarged**

shortly adj. presently, soon, before long, directly

shout n. & v. cry, scream, roar, shriek, cheer, whoop, bellow

shove v. push, jostle, prod, nudge, move, propel ★**pull**

show 1 v. display, parade, exhibit, flaunt, reveal ★**hide** 2 prove, testify to, demonstrate 3 explain, teach, instruct 4 n. exhibition, display, ceremony

shower 1 v. scatter, spray, sprinkle, rain 2 n. downpour, cloudburst 3 barrage, volley, discharge

shred 1 n. particle, piece, scrap, tatter, fragment 2 v. tear, rip, strip

shrewd adj. profound, deep, discerning, ▷*wise* ★**obtuse**

shriek n. & v. screech, ▷*shout*

shrill adj. treble, high-pitched, screeching, ear-piercing

shrink 1 v. contract, dwindle, shrivel, become smaller 2 flinch, cringe, recoil, withdraw

shrivel v. wither, contract, wrinkle, decrease, pucker, parch, ▷*wilt*

shudder v. shake, quake, tremble, ▷*quiver*

shuffle 1 v. mix, jumble, rearrange 2 hobble, limp

shun v. avoid, elude, ignore, spurn, steer clear of ★**accept**

shut v. fasten, close, secure, slam, bar, latch, lock ★**open**

shut up 1 v. imprison, cage, intern 2 be silent, hold one's tongue

shy 1 adj. bashful, diffident, timid, wary, shrinking ★**bold** 2 v. flinch, quail, recoil

sick 1 adj. ill, poorly, ailing, unwell, feeble 2 weary, fed up, displeased 3 nauseated, vomiting

side 1 n. border, edge, flank, margin, half 2 party, sect, group, team SIGHED

sift v. strain, drain, separate, screen, sieve, riddle

sigh [1] *v.* grieve, lament, moan, complain [2] wheeze, breathe

sight [1] *n.* appearance, spectacle, scene, mirage [2] seeing, perception, visibiity [3] *v.* behold, glimpse, observe CITE SITE

sign [1] *n.* symbol, emblem, mark [2] omen, token [3] signboard, signpost, placard [4] *v.* endorse, autograph, inscribe

signal [1] *n.* beacon *As soon as the ships were sighted, beacons were lit all along the coast*, sign, flag, indicator [2] *adj.* distinguished, impressive, outstanding

significant *adj.* symbolical, meaningful, weighty, ▷*important* ★**unimportant**

signify *v.* denote, indicate, suggest, imply, ▷*mean*

silence *n.* quiet, hush, peace, tranquillity ★**noise**

silent *adj.* hushed, noiseless, soundless, still, mute, ▷*quiet* ★**noisy**

silly *adj.* absurd, senseless, stupid, fatuous, ▷*foolish* ★**wise**

similar *adj.* resembling, alike, harmonious, common, ▷*like* ★**different**

simple [1] *adj.* elementary, plain, uncomplicated, ▷*easy* [2] trusting, open, naïve ★**intricate**

simply *adv.* merely, purely, barely, solely, only

sin [1] *n.* misdeed, wrong, vice, evil, wickedness [2] *v.* err, offend, trespass, stray, do wrong

since [1] *conj.* because, as, for, considering [2] *prep.* subsequently, after

sincere *adj.* true, unaffected, frank, open, truthful, ▷*genuine* ★**insincere**

sing *v.* warble, yodel, trill, croon, chant, carol, hum, chirp

singe *v.* scorch, burn, scald, sear, char

singer *n.* minstrel, songster, vocalist, chorister, crooner

single [1] *adj.* one, only, sole [2] solitary, alone, separate [3] unmarried, celibate *The priests of the Roman Catholic Church are celibate*

singular *adj.* odd, peculiar, curious, surprising, ▷*unusual* ★**ordinary**

sinister *adj.* menacing, threatening, unlucky, disastrous, ▷*evil* ★**harmless**

Singers

Alto
Baritone
Bass
Basso profundo
Chorister
Contrabass
Contralto
Countertenor
Falsetto
Mezzo-soprano
Precentor
Prima donna
Soprano
Tenor
Vocalist

sink [1] *v.* drop, dip, descend, decline, ▷*fall* ★**rise** [2] *n.* basin, drain

sit *v.* perch, seat, squat, roost, rest, settle

site *n.* spot, plot, locality, place, station, post, ▷*situation* CITE SIGHT

situation [1] *n.* position, location, place, site, whereabouts, standpoint [2] predicament, plight, state

size [1] *n.* dimensions, proportions, measurement [2] magnitude, bulk, volume, weight SIGHS

sketch [1] *n.* drawing, picture, cartoon [2] draft, blue-print, outline [3] *v.* draw, portray, depict

skilful *adj.* adroit, able, adept, dexterous, expert, competent, ▷*clever* ★**clumsy**

skill *n.* ability, expertness, knack, facility, ▷*talent*

skim *v.* brush, touch, graze, float, glide

skimp *v.* stint, scrimp, economize, scrape

skin *n.* peel, rind, hide, husk, pelt *The trappers traded animal pelts for food and blankets*

skinny *adj.* thin, lean, scraggy, weedy ★**fat**

skip [1] *v.* jump, hop, dance, caper [2] pass over, miss, disregard, omit

skirmish *n. & v.* scuffle, fight, affray, scrap, combat

skirt [1] *n.* petticoat, kilt, frock [2] border, hem, edge, margin [3] *v.* border, flank, evade, avoid

skulk v. lurk, hide, cower, slink, sneak

slab n. board, stone, boulder, piece, chunk

slack 1 adj. limp, flabby, loose, relaxed ★**tight** 2 lazy, sluggish, ▷idle ★**busy**

slander v. libel, malign, accuse, abuse, ▷defame ★**praise**

slant 1 v. & n. incline, angle, cant, ▷slope

slap v. smack, whack, strike, hit, spank

slash v. & n. cut, slit, gash, hack, rip

slaughter v. slay, butcher, massacre, ▷kill

slave 1 n. bondsman, bondswoman, serf, vassal, drudge, captive 2 v. drudge, toil, labour, grind

slavery n. bondage, enslavement, serfdom, servility, drudgery, captivity ★**freedom**

slay v. murder, massacre, ▷kill SLEIGH

sleek adj. shiny, smooth, glossy, slick

sleep v. & n. snooze, nap, doze, drowse, repose, slumber

slender 1 adj. narrow, thin, fine, slight, ▷slim ★**thick** 2 trivial, inadequate, meagre

slice 1 v. shred, shave, cut, strip, segment 2 n. segment, piece, cut, slab

slick 1 adj. shiny, smooth, ▷sleek 2 glib, suave, plausible

slide v. slip, slither, glide, skim, skate

slight 1 adj. delicate, tender, ▷slender 2 small, little, meagre, trifling, trivial ★**significant** 3 n. & v. snub, insult, disdain

slim adj. fine, slight, ▷slender ★**fat**

slime n. mire, ooze, mud, filth

sling 1 v. hurl, toss, throw 2 n. loop, bandage, strap, support

slink v. prowl, creep, sidle, sneak, ▷skulk

slip 1 v. slide, slither, glide 2 fall, lurch, drop, slip over 3 v. & n. blunder, slip up

slippery 1 adj. smooth, glassy 2 untrustworthy, tricky, ▷shifty ★**trustworthy**

slit v. gash, cut, ▷slash

slogan n. motto, catchword, war cry, saying

slope n. slant, grade, gradient, incline, ascent, descent, rise v. lean, incline, descend, ascend

sloppy 1 adj. careless, slipshod, inattentive, ▷slovenly 2 dowdy, messy, tacky 3 dingy, dirty

slot n. recess, opening, hole, groove

slovenly adj. slipshod, careless, negligent, disorderly, untidy, dowdy

slow 1 adj. inactive, tardy, late, slack, leisurely, ▷sluggish ★**fast** 2 v. slow down, slacken, lose speed, relax ★**accelerate** SLOE

sluggish adj. slothful, lazy, inactive, languid, indolent, ▷idle ★**brisk**

slumber v. snooze, doze, ▷sleep ★**awaken**

sly adj. cunning, tricky, furtive, sneaky, artful, ▷wily ★**frank**

smack v. slap, strike, ▷hit

small 1 adj. minute, tiny, slight, diminutive, ▷little ★**large** 2 trivial, petty, feeble, paltry inferior

smart 1 adj. elegant, neat, spruce, dressy 2 alert, bright, ▷intelligent ★**dull** 3 v. sting, burn, throb ▷ache

smash v. break, hit, destroy, wreck, demolish

smear v. plaster, daub, coat, varnish, cover, spread

smell n. aroma, fragrance, scent, perfume, stink, stench, odour, tang

smile v. grin, simper, smirk, beam, ▷laugh

smoke 1 n. vapour, mist, gas 2 v. fume, reek, whiff, smoulder, vent

smooth 1 adj. level, even, flat, plain, sleek ★**rough** 2 v. flatten, level, press

smother v. choke, throttle, stifle, restrain

smudge n. & v. mark, smear, blur, stain, blight

smug adj. self-satisfied, content, complacent, conceited

smut n. dirt, smudge, blot, spot, smear

snack n. lunch, repast, morsel, bite

snag n. catch, complication, drawback, hitch

snap 1 v. break, crack, snip 2 snarl, growl

snare 1 v. trap, catch, seize, net 2 n. trap, noose, pitfall

snatch v. seize, grab, clutch, grip, take, pluck, grasp

sneak 1 v. slink, prowl, crouch, ▷skulk 2 n. wretch, coward, informer

sneer v. jeer, scoff, gibe, scorn, ridicule, taunt

sniff v. smell, breathe in, inhale, scent

snivel v. weep, cry, blub, sniffle, grizzle

snobbish adj. condescending, snooty, lofty, patronizing, stuck-up

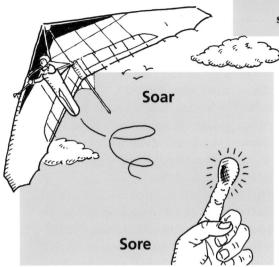

Soar

Sore

snoop *v.* pry, eavesdrop, peep, sneak

snooze *v.* doze, sleep, slumber, ▷*sleep*

snub *v.* slight, slur, spurn, cut, ▷*humiliate*

snug *adj.* cosy, sheltered, secure, safe, restful, ▷*comfortable*

so *adv.* accordingly, thus, therefore, likewise SEW SOW

soak *v.* moisten, wet, douse, saturate, steep

soar *v.* glide, fly, rise, hover, tower SORE

sob *v.* lament, cry, sigh, ▷*weep*

sober *adj.* temperate, abstemious *Uncle Arthur was very abstemious, and never drank anything stronger than ginger beer*, calm, composed, serious, sombre ★**excited**

sociable *adj.* companionable, affable, friendly, genial ★**withdrawn**

social 1 *adj.* neighbourly, civic, public 2 convivial, ▷*sociable*

soft 1 *adj.* pliable, plastic, flexible, supple ★**hard** 2 kind, gentle, mild, ▷*tender* ★**harsh** 3 low, faint, quiet ★**loud**

soften 1 *v.* melt, dissolve, mellow ★**solidify** 2 moderate, diminish, quell

soil 1 *n.* earth, mould, dirt 2 *v.* foul, dirty, sully, taint

sole *adj.* only, single, lone, one SOUL

solemn 1 *adj.* grim, serious, ▷*sombre* 2 impressive, stately, sedate ★**frivolous**

solid 1 *adj.* steady, firm, stable, sturdy 2 dense, compact, hard ★**soft**

solidify *v.* congeal, harden, clot, cake, set ★**soften**

solitary *adj.* alone, lonely, remote, separate, only

solution 1 *n.* blend, mixture, brew, fluid 2 answer, explanation

solve *v.* unravel, untangle, elucidate, ▷*explain* ★**complicate**

sombre *adj.* dark, serious, solemn, grim, gloomy, funereal ★**bright**

some *adj.* any, more or less, about, several SUM

sometimes *adv.* at times, from time to time, occasionally ★**always**

somewhat *adv.* in part, a little, not much

song *n.* air, tune, carol, ballad, ode, ditty *The new pop song was based on an old sailors' ditty*

soon *adv.* presently, shortly, before long

soothe *v.* pacify, appease, mollify, ease, lull, comfort ★**irritate**

sordid *adj.* nasty, miserable, dirty, base, ▷*squalid*

sore 1 *adj.* tender, aching, painful, inflamed 2 annoyed, upset, grieved 3 *n.* ulcer, boil, carbuncle SOAR

sorrow 1 *n.* grief, woe, remorse, anguish ★**joy** 2 *v.* mourn, grieve, lament ★**rejoice**

sorrowful *adj.* sad, disconsolate, mournful, dejected ★**joyful**

sorry 1 *adj.* pained, grieved, hurt, dejected, doleful ★**glad** 2 wretched, mean, poor, shabby ★**delighted**

sort 1 *n.* kind, type, variety, group, class 2 *v.* sift, arrange, catalogue, classify

soul *n.* spirit, substance, mind, vitality, fire, essence SOLE

sound 1 *n.* noise, audibility, din, tone ★ **silence** 2 *v.* blare, blast, blow 3 *adj.* hearty, virile, whole, perfect, ▷*healthy* ★**unfit**

sour 1 *adj.* tart, rancid, bitter, acid ★**sweet** 2 morose, peevish, ▷*harsh* ★**genial**

source *n.* origin, spring, fount, cause, beginning

souvenir *n.* token, memento, keepsake, reminder, relic

sow 1 (as in *how*) *n.* female pig 2 (as in *mow*) *v.* plant, scatter, strew SEW SO

space 1 *n.* extent, expanse, capacity, room, accommodation 2 the universe, the heavens, firmament

spacious *adj.* roomy, extensive, commodious, broad, wide ★**restricted**

span [1] *n.* stretch, reach, extent, length [2] *v.* cross, bridge, link, connect

spare [1] *adj.* extra, reserve, surplus [2] bare, meagre, poor, scanty, ▷*sparse* [3] *v.* afford, preserve, give, allow

sparkle *v.* glitter, glow, gleam, glint, twinkle

sparse *adj.* scanty, thin, ▷*meagre* ★**dense**

spate *n.* flood, flow, deluge, rush, torrent

speak *v.* say, utter, talk, pronounce, lecture, express

spear *n.* pike, javelin, lance

special *adj.* distinct, different, unique, individual, ▷*particular* ★**common**

species *n.* breed, kind, sort, class, family

specific *adj.* definite, exact, precise, ▷*special*

specimen *n.* sample, example, type, model, pattern

speck *n.* dot, speckle, spot, particle

spectacle *n.* sight, scene, exhibition, presentation, ▷*display*

spectacles *n.* glasses, eyeglasses

spectacular *adj.* wonderful, fabulous, surprising, ▷*marvellous*

spectator *n.* onlooker, witness, observer

speech [1] *n.* talk, tongue *The people spoke a strange tongue related to Swahili*, language [2] address, lecture

speed *n.* velocity, rapidity, dispatch, pace, tempo *The tempo of life in the quiet seaside village was much too slow for us*

speedy *adj.* swift, rapid, fleet, quick, lively ▷*fast* ★**slow**

spell [1] *n.* charm, magic, witchcraft [2] period, term, space, time [3] *v.* form words, write out

spend [1] *v.* expend, lay out, lavish, pay, disburse [2] exhaust, use up

spendthrift *n.* wastrel, squanderer, prodigal ★**miser**

sphere [1] *n.* globe, ball, orb, planet [2] realm, orbit, domain, field

spice *n.* seasoning, flavouring, zest, relish, savour

spill *v.* pour, stream, run, overflow, spurt, upset

spin [1] *v.* revolve, rotate, turn, whirl [2] knit, weave, crochet

spine *n.* backbone, needle, quill *The porcupine's body is covered in sharp quills*, ridge

spirit [1] *n.* essence, substance, nature, character [2] soul, air, breath [3] vigour, energy, courage [4] phantom, spectre, ghost

spiritual [1] *adj.* religious, divine, unworldly, holy [2] pure, immaterial

spite [1] *n.* malice, rancour, hostility, hatred [2] *v.* grudge, annoy, offend, injure

spiteful *adj.* vicious, malicious, vindictive, ▷*hateful* ★**kind**

splash *v.* wet, spatter, shower, sprinkle

splendid *adj.* grand, brilliant, magnificent, showy, glorious, ▷*sumptuous* ★**ordinary**

splendour *n.* glory, pageantry, brilliance, ▷*pomp*

split *v.* cleave, sever *Our family quarrelled with our cousins, and severed relationships for years*, crack, snap, splinter

spoil [1] *v.* hurt, injure, harm [2] deface, disfigure, destroy [3] rot, decompose, putrefy, decay

spoiled *adj.* decayed, rotten, broken up, corroded

spontaneous *adj.* natural, impulsive, self-generated, voluntary

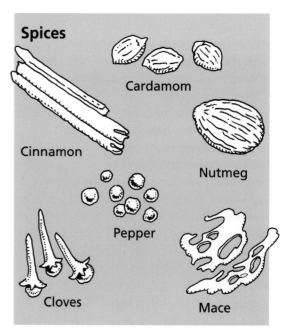

Spices

Cardamom

Cinnamon

Nutmeg

Pepper

Cloves

Mace

spoof [1] *n.* hoax, joke, bluff, prank, satire [2] quip, jest, wisecrack

sport [1] *n.* game, amusement, fun, athletics, recreation [2] *v.* play, frolic, gambol, romp

spot [1] *n.* dot, speck, mark, stain, blemish [2] *v.* espy, notice, recognize, distinguish

spotless *adj.* pure, clean, unstained, faultless, perfect

sprawl *v.* recline, stretch, extend, lie, ▷*lounge*

spray *v.* sprinkle, squirt, splash, shower

spread [1] *v.* scatter, strew, sow, circulate [2] extend, stretch, expand, open

sprightly *adj.* lively, vivacious, cheerful, agile, ▷*brisk* ★**sluggish**

spur *v.* arouse, drive, urge, incite

spurious *adj.* fake, counterfeit, false, ▷*bogus* ★**genuine**

spurn *v.* reject, scorn, disdain, disregard, ▷*snub* ★**respect**

spurt [1] *v.* stream, squirt, emerge, gush [2] hurry, hasten, rush

spy [1] *n.* agent, detective, observer, snooper, scout [2] *v.* see, glimpse, pry, peep, spot

squabble [1] *n. & v.* quarrel, clash, fight, row, ▷*dispute*

squad *n.* group, company, troop, force, band, team

squalid *adj.* foul, dirty, untended, poverty-stricken, ▷*sordid* ★**clean**

squall [1] *n.* blast, gust, blow, tempest [2] *v.* blubber, cry, bawl, howl

squander *v.* misspend, waste, fritter *My brother won a big prize in a lottery, but frittered all the money away in a few years*, lavish

squash [1] *v.* mash, crush, squelch, pound [2] quell, suppress, humiliate

squat [1] *adj.* dumpy, stocky, tubby, plump [2] *v.* crouch, sit, roost, perch

squeal *v.* squawk, squeak, cheep, grunt, cry

squeamish *adj.* fastidious, delicate, finicky, nauseous

squeeze *v.* compress, press, constrict, force, pinch

squirm *v.* wriggle, fidget, flounder, twist, ▷*writhe*

squirt *v.* spray, splash, ▷*spurt*

stab *v. & n.* thrust, cut, jab, puncture, wound

stable [1] *adj.* firm, steady, solid, constant, durable, lasting ★**unstable** [2] *n.* mews, barn, byre

stack [1] *n.* pile, pack, bundle, sheaf, heap [2] *v.* assemble, pile up, amass

staff [1] *n.* stick, cane, pole, rod [2] team, workers, force, personnel

stage [1] *n.* platform, dais, scaffold, podium *The famous conductor stood on the podium and raised his baton*, arena [2] step, degree, position [3] *v.* perform, produce, present, put on

stagger *v.* reel, totter, waver, lurch

stagnant *adj.* motionless, inactive, still, quiet, sluggish

staid *adj.* serious, steady, earnest, sober, demure, ▷*sedate* ★**frivolous** STAYED

stain [1] *n.* blemish, blur, spot, blot [2] disgrace, shame [3] *v.* tarnish, sully, blemish, defile

stair *n.* step, rung, spoke, footrest STARE

stake [1] *n.* stick, stave, paling, spike, pole, ▷*staff* [2] bet, claim, wager, involvement [3] *v.* prop, secure, support STEAK

stale [1] *adj.* musty, old, tasteless, faded [2] common, trite, banal, flat ★**fresh**

stalk [1] *v.* hunt, chase, follow, pursue, shadow [2] swagger, strut, stride, parade

stall [1] *v.* tarry, delay, hedge, obstruct ★**advance** [2] quibble, fence [3] *n.* compartment, booth, stand, bay

stalwart *adj.* rugged, sturdy, stout, lusty, ▷*valiant* ★**weak**

stamina *n.* endurance, vitality, strength, power, energy ★**weakness**

stammer *v.* stutter, falter, hesitate, stumble

stamp [1] *v.* print, imprint, mark, impress *n.* impression, mark, print, brand [2] kind, make, genus, cast [3] seal, postal label, sticker

stand [1] *n.* board, counter, table, platform, ▷*stall* [2] *v.* rest, put, locate, place [3] tolerate, put up with, abide, endure ★**oppose** [4] arise, get up, be erect ★**sit**

standard [1] *adj.* normal, regular, uniform [2] *n.* pattern, criterion, norm [3] flag, banner, ensign

staple *adj.* main, principal, important, leading

stare *v.* gaze, gape, look, peer STAIR

stark *adj.* severe, plain, downright, bare, absolute

start [1] *v.* commence, begin, found, initiate [2] depart, set out, leave [3] startle, jump, wince [4] *n.* beginning, commencement [5] shock, scare, fit

startle *v.* frighten, alarm, scare, surprise, ▷*start*

starve *v.* be hungry, famish, want

state [1] *n.* condition, situation, position [2] country, nation [3] *v.* declare, say, express, utter, ▷*speak*

stately *adj.* imposing, grand, dignified, ▷*magnificent* ★**commonplace**

statement [1] *n.* declaration, utterance, remark, motto [2] bill, account, invoice

station [1] *n.* post, spot, site, position, terminal [2] *v.* park, place, put, establish *We got there early to establish our place in the queue*

stationary *adj.* still, unmoving, standing, fixed ★**mobile** STATIONERY

stationery *n.* paper, envelopes, ink, pens, pencils STATIONARY

statue *n.* carving, bust, figure

staunch *adj.* constant, faithful, true, firm, ▷*loyal* ★**unfaithful**

stay [1] *v.* endure, last, remain, stand, linger [2] check, curb, prevent [3] *n.* halt, wait, ▷*stop*

steady [1] *adj.* firm, fixed, established, constant, ▷*staunch* ★**uncertain** [2] *v.* brace, stabilize, stiffen

steal [1] *v.* thieve, pilfer, filch, ▷*rob* [2] slink, flit, creep, ▷*prowl* STEEL

stealthy *adj.* furtive, sneaky, sly, secret, ▷*underhanded* ★**open**

steep [1] *adj.* sheer, sharp, hilly, precipitous [2] *v.* bathe, soak, souse, submerge

steer *v.* guide, direct, pilot, control

stem [1] *n.* stalk, shoot, stock, trunk [2] *v.* arise from, flow from [3] check, resist, restrain

step [1] *n.* pace, tread, stride, gait [2] action, method, deed [3] *v.* walk, skip, trip, pace STEPPE

sterile [1] *adj.* barren, unfertile, arid [2] sanitary, disinfected

stern [1] *adj.* strict, severe, harsh, grim, ▷*austere* ★**mild** [2] *n.* poop *The name of the ship was displayed in large letters on the poop*, aft end

stew [1] *v.* cook, simmer, boil [2] worry, fuss

stick [1] *n.* stave, pole, rod, cane, staff [2] *v.* adhere, cling, cleave, glue, seal

sticky *adj.* gluey, gummy, adhesive

stick out *v.* project, bulge, extrude, ▷*jut* ★**recede**

stiff [1] *adj.* inflexible, firm, stable, unyielding, ▷*rigid* ★**flexible** [2] formal, stilted, prim, precise ★**yielding**

stifle *v.* suffocate, throttle, gag, muzzle, ▷*smother*

stigma [1] *n.* blot, blur, scar, ▷*blemish* [2] disgrace, dishonour, ▷*shame* ★**credit**

Stationery

Stationary

still [1] *adj.* fixed, stable, static [2] calm, quiet, serene, tranquil, noiseless, hushed, ▷*peaceful* ★**agitated** *v.* quiet, hush, muffle, ▷*calm* ★**agitate**

stimulate *v.* inspire, provoke, arouse, motivate, ▷*excite* ★**discourage**

sting [1] *v.* prick, wound, pain, hurt, injure

stingy (*stin*-jy) *adj.* miserly, tight-fisted, selfish, niggardly, ▷*mean* ★**generous**

stink *v.* smell, whiff, reek

stint [1] *n.* job, task, chore [2] turn, spell, share, quota [3] *v.* limit, stop, scrimp, restrict ★**squander**

stir [1] *v.* move, excite, spur, agitate, ▷*stimulate* [2] whisk, mix, blend [3] waken, arouse ★**calm** [4] *n.* flurry, fuss, uproar

stock [1] *adj.* standard, regular, established, normal [2] *n.* reserve, hoard, supply [3] *v.* provide, supply, equip, hoard

stocky *adj.* chunky, short, stolid, sturdy, ▷*squat* ★**tall**

stodgy *adj.* dull, heavy, tedious, boring

stolid *adj.* stupid, dull, mindless, unintelligent, ▷*stodgy* ★**quick**

stoop *v.* bend, crouch, kneel, bow

stop [1] *v.* cease, desist, end, terminate, halt ★**start** [2] prevent, forestall, avoid [3] arrest, hold, fix [4] *n.* pause, end, cessation *A cessation of hostilities came into force after the peace agreement*

store [1] *v.* put by, reserve, hoard, save ★**use** [2] *n.* stock, supply, reserve [3] market, shop, warehouse

storey *n.* floor, landing, level, flight, deck

storm [1] *n.* tempest, gale, cyclone, hurricane, tornado ★**calm** [2] turmoil, upheaval, attack [3] *v.* rage, rant, fume, attack

story [1] *n.* yarn, tale, narrative, account, anecdote [2] untruth, lie, fib

stout [1] *adj.* sturdy, tough, robust, ▷*strong* ★**weak** [2] fat, corpulent, ▷*plump* ★**thin**

stow *v.* deposit, store, ▷*pack*

straight [1] *adj.* right, undeviating, unswerving, ▷*direct* [2] frank, candid, truthful, ▷*honest* ★**crooked** STRAIT

straightforward *adj.* open, outspoken, reliable, trustworthy ★**devious**

strain [1] *n.* tension, fatigue, exertion, ▷*stress* ★**relaxation** [2] melody, tune, air [3] *v.* struggle, labour, ▷*toil* ★**relax** [4] wrench, injure [5] filter, sift, separate

strait *n.* channel, sound, narrows STRAIGHT

strait-laced *adj.* prim, prudish, strict, puritanical *My family was rather puritanical, and we were not allowed to play any games on Sundays* ★**broad-minded**

strand [1] *n.* coast, beach, shore [2] hair, fibre, tress, lock [3] *v.* desert, maroon, abandon

strange [1] *adj.* unusual, incredible, extraordinary, odd, ▷*curious* ★**commonplace** [2] foreign, alien, remote

stranger *n.* outsider, foreigner, visitor, newcomer, ▷*alien* ★**acquaintance**

strangle *v.* constrict, choke, garrotte, throttle

strap *n.* belt, harness, thong, leash

stray [1] *v.* wander, deviate, depart, rove [2] sin, err, do wrong

streak *n.* stroke, stripe, band, line, bar, strip

stream [1] *n.* current, course, drift, brook, beck, burn [2] *v.* flow, gush, spurt, pour

strength [1] *n.* power, force, might, ▷*energy* [2] boldness, nerve, intensity ★**weakness**

strenuous *adj.* laborious, resolute, determined, ▷*earnest* ★**weak**

stress [1] *n.* tension, force, effort, ▷*strain* [2] accent, emphasis [3] *v.* emphasize, accentuate

stretch *v.* expand, reach, ▷*extend* ★**shorten**

strict [1] *adj.* severe, rigorous, rigid, austere, ▷*stern* ★**lenient** [2] scrupulous, punctilious, accurate, ▷*precise* ★**inaccurate**

stride *n.* & *v.* walk, step, tread, parade, march

strife *n.* *n.* struggle, contest, quarrel, friction, ▷*conflict* ★**peace**

strike [1] *v.* beat, smite, collide, knock, ▷*thump* [2] discover, unearth [3] *n.* assault, thrust, attack [4] walkout, boycott

striking *adj.* eye-catching, wonderful, ▷*extraordinary* ★**commonplace**

strip [1] *v.* take off, peel, skin, shave, remove [2] *n.* ribbon, stroke, streak, line

stripe *n.* streak, band, bar, chevron *Soldiers in the army have chevrons on their sleeves to indicate their rank*, rule, ▷*strip*

strive *v.* endeavour, attempt, aim, compete, ▷*try* ★**yield**

stroke [1] *n.* shock, blow, knock, thump [2] seizure, fit, convulsion [3] *v.* pat, rub, caress, smooth, comfort

stroll *v. & n.* walk, promenade, saunter, tramp, ramble

strong [1] *adj.* powerful, vigorous, hardy, muscular, ▷*robust* [2] solid, secure, fortified ★**weak** [3] potent, hot, spicy, ▷*pungent*

structure [1] *n.* building, edifice, erection [2] construction, organization, composition

struggle [1] *v.* endeavour, labour, battle, wrestle ★**yield** [2] *n.* conflict, battle, ▷*fight* [3] distress, trouble, ▷*effort*

strut [1] *n.* support, mainstay, prop [2] *v.* parade, prance, swagger

stubborn [1] *adj.* dogged, persistent, tenacious [2] pig-headed, perverse, wilful, ▷*obstinate* ★**docile**

stuck-up *adj.* vain, conceited, ▷*snobbish* ★**modest**

Structures

Termite's nest

Atomic

Spider's web

Rope bridge

studious *adj.* scholarly, learned, thoughtful, ▷*diligent* ★**thoughtless**

study [1] *v.* read, peruse, examine, scrutinize, examine, train, ▷*learn* [2] *n.* learning, meditation, thought, contemplation, ▷*research*

stuff [1] *v.* fill, congest, pack, crowd [2] *n.* textile, fabric, material, goods

stumble [1] *v.* stagger, lurch, fall, ▷*trip* [2] stammer, falter, ▷*stutter*

stump [1] *v.* perplex, mystify, confuse, ▷*bewilder* [2] *n.* stub, tip, log, root

stun *v.* knock out, overpower, stupefy, dumbfound, ▷*confound*

stunt *n.* deed, feat, achievement, performance, ▷*exploit*

stupefy *v.* daze, muddle, bewilder, astonish, flabbergast, ▷*shock* ★**revive**

stupendous *adj.* astounding, amazing, overwhelming, ▷*wonderful* ★**ordinary**

stupid *adj.* simple, stolid, dull, senseless, ▷*foolish* ★**clever**

stupidity *n.* inanity, silliness, feebleness, foolishness ★**brilliance**

sturdy *adj.* rugged, stalwart, tough, strapping, ▷*hardy* ★**weak**

stutter *v.* stumble, falter, ▷*stammer*

style [1] *n.* mode, vogue, fashion, way, manner, form [2] *v.* christen, name, call STILE

suave (swahv) *adj.* agreeable, elegant, polite, pleasant, sophisticated *After living in the city for many years, my sister had developed very sophisticated tastes*

subdue *v.* suppress, soften, tame, tone down, ▷*repress*

subject [1] (*sub*-ject) *n.* matter, topic, theme [2] subordinate, dependant [3] *adj.* dependent, subordinate, liable [4] (sub-*ject*) *v.* rule over, subdue, subjugate

submerge *v.* plunge, immerse, sink ★**raise**

submissive *adj.* yielding, servile, meek, ▷*obedient* ★**obstinate**

submit [1] *v.* yield, give in, accede, surrender, hand over, [2] offer, tender, present

subordinate *adj.* junior, minor, subject, dependent, secondary ★**superior**

subscribe *v.* sign, enrol, register, agree, assent

subsequent *adj.* later, following, succeeding, after ★**former**

subside *v.* decline, peter out, decrease, diminish, wane *I used to go mountaineering, but my interest waned after some years,* ▷*abate* ★**rise**

substance [1] *n.* matter, object, stuff, material [2] essence, kernel, meaning, ▷*gist*

substantial [1] *adj.* steady, sturdy, firm, ▷*stable* [2] ample, large, real, solid ★**imaginary**

substitute [1] *n.* alternative, makeshift, stopgap [2] *v.* swap, change, replace, duplicate

subtle (*sutl*) [1] *adj.* shrewd, fine, delicate [2] clever, crafty, perceptive

subtract *v.* take away, withdraw, deduct, remove ★**add**

succeed [1] *v.* flourish, prosper, thrive, triumph ★**fail** [2] follow, inherit, replace ★**precede**

success *n.* prosperity, triumph, victory, achievement ★**failure**

successful *adj.* victorious, prosperous, fortunate, thriving ★**unlucky**

suck *v.* inhale, take in, draw in, imbibe

sudden *adj.* unexpected, abrupt, impulsive, swift, prompt ★**gradual**

suffer [1] *v.* bear, endure, put up with [2] encounter, undergo, ▷*sustain*

sufficient *adj.* adequate, ample, plenty, ▷*enough* ★**deficient**

suffocate *v.* smother, choke, ▷*stifle*

suggest *v.* recommend, advise, submit, hint, intimate

suit [1] *v.* fulfil, gratify, please, suffice, accommodate, befit [2] *n.* costume, ensemble, outfit

suitable *adj.* fitting, appropriate, correct, proper, becoming ★**unsuitable**

suite [1] (*sweet*) *n.* set, series, succession [2] apartment, rooms

sulk *v.* pout, grouch, brood, mope

sulky *adj.* glum, morose, churlish, moody, ▷*sullen* ★**genial**

sullen *adj.* gloomy, heavy, dismal, cheerless, ▷*sulky* ★**cheerful**

sum *n.* amount, total, whole, entirety SOME

summary *n.* synopsis, précis, abstract, summing-up, outline, analysis

summit *n.* peak, pinnacle, top, apex, zenith ★**base**

summon *v.* call, beckon, command, invite, muster ★**dismiss**

sumptuous *adj.* profuse, costly, gorgeous, splendid, ▷*lavish* ★**frugal**

sundry *adj.* different, separate, several, ▷*various*

sunny *adj.* bright, cheerful, light, clear, ▷*radiant* ★**gloomy**

superb *adj.* magnificent, stately, gorgeous, ▷*grand* ★**commonplace**

supercilious *adj.* contemptuous, haughty, arrogant, ▷*snobbish* ★**modest**

superficial *adj.* slight, imperfect, shallow, skin-deep, ▷*trivial* ★**profound**

superfluous *adj.* in excess, inessential, spare, ▷*surplus* ★**essential**

superior [1] *adj.* better, greater, higher, loftier, ▷*excellent* [2] eminent, conspicuous, principal ★**mediocre**

supersede *v.* succeed, replace, displace, suspend, usurp *The president's authority was usurped by her assistant* ★**continue**

supervise *v.* superintend, control, manage, ▷*direct*

supple *adj.* lithe, pliable, flexible, bending

supplement [1] *n.* addition, complement, sequel, postscript [2] *v.* supply, add, fill

supply [1] *v.* provide, furnish, yield, contribute, purvey [2] *n.* hoard, reserve, ▷*stock* ★**retain**

support [1] *v.* uphold, bear, sustain, maintain, help, ▷*favour* ★**oppose** [2] hold up, prop, strut, brace [3] endure, tolerate, suffer [4] *n.* maintenance, upkeep

suppose *v.* assume, presume, believe, imagine, imply, ▷*consider*

suppress *v.* restrain, extinguish, destroy, stop, ▷*quell* ★**incite**

supreme *adj.* dominant, highest, greatest, maximum ★**lowly**

sure [1] *adj.* certain, positive, definite [2] secure, steady, safe [3] permanent, abiding, enduring ★**uncertain**

surface [1] *n.* area, expanse, stretch [2] outside, exterior, covering ★**interior**

surge [1] *v.* swell, rise, heave, rush [2] *n.* ripple, billow, wave SERGE

surly *adj.* morose, cross, testy, touchy, crusty, ▷*sullen* ★**affable**

surmise *v.* guess, speculate, conjecture, suspect, ▷*presume* ★**know**

surpass *v.* eclipse, outdo, outstrip, excel, exceed, ▷*beat*

surplus *n.* excess, remainder, balance, residue ★**shortcoming**

surprise [1] *v.* startle, astonish, amaze, ▷*astound* [2] *n.* amazement, astonishment, ▷*wonder*

surrender *v.* quit, give up, yield, submit, ▷*relinquish*

surround *v.* enclose, encircle, encompass

survey [1] (sur-*vey*) *v.* look at, examine, scrutinize, ▷*study* [2] estimate, measure [3] (*sur*-vey) *n.* assessment, appraisal

survive *v.* live, exist, continue, outlast, abide ★**surrender**

susceptible *adj.* sensitive, impressionable, inclined, capable ★**insensitive**

suspect [1] (sus-*pect*) *v.* disbelieve, doubt, distrust [2] (*sus*-pect) *adj.* unbelievable, questionable

suspend [1] *v.* interrupt, delay, arrest, ▷*stop* ★**continue** [2] swing, dangle, ▷*hang* ★**drop**

suspense *n.* anticipation, waiting, abeyance *The council couldn't decide on a new chairperson, so the matter was left in abeyance*, stoppage, uncertainty, ▷*tension* ★**decision**

suspicious *adj.* incredulous, sceptical, doubtful, suspecting ★**trustful**

sustain [1] *v.* uphold, keep, maintain, provide for [2] suffer, undergo, experience [3] nourish, nurture, feed

swagger [1] *v.* parade, prance, ▷*strut* [2] brag, bluster, ▷*boast*

swallow [1] *v.* absorb, consume, eat, digest, devour, ▷*gulp* [2] *n.* mouthful, gulp [3] bird

swamp [1] *n.* fen, bog, marsh, morass, quagmire [2] *v.* submerge, submerse, overflow, deluge, ▷*drench*

swap *v.* exchange, switch, trade, barter

swarm [1] *n.* throng, horde, shoal, flock, crowd [2] *v.* teem, abound, jam, mass, crowd, cluster

swarthy *adj.* dusky, dark, brown, tawny

sway [1] *v.* swing, rock, totter, lean, incline, ▷*waver* [2] *n.* rule, authority, control, ▷*influence*

swear [1] *v.* promise, warrant, affirm, attest [2] curse, damn, blaspheme

sweat *v.* perspire, ooze, leak, exude, swelter *During that time of the year it was very hot, and we sweltered all day*

sweep *v.* brush, scrub, clean, scour

sweet [1] *adj.* sugary, syrupy, luscious ★**sour** [2] melodic, tuneful, musical, mellow ★**discordant** [3] gentle, tender, mild, lovable ★**unpleasant** [4] fragrant, pure, clean, fresh ★**putrid**

swell *v.* expand, distend, inflate, bulge, ▷*enlarge* ★**contract**

swerve *v.* veer, deviate, skid, skew, lurch, ▷*waver*

swift *adj.* speedy, rapid, quick, ▷*fast* ★**slow**

swill [1] *v.* swig, consume, imbibe, tipple, ▷*gulp* [2] *n.* refuse, waste, garbage

swim *v.* bathe, wade, paddle, float, glide

swindle [1] *n.* trick, fraud, blackmail, racket [2] *v.* hoodwink, deceive, hoax, dupe, ▷*cheat*

swine *n.* pig, boar, sow, porker

swing [1] *v.* hang, suspend, dangle, lurch, reel [2] *n.* tempo, time

switch [1] *v.* change, exchange, alter, substitute, swap [2] *n.* lever, pedal, control, button

swivel *v.* pivot, spin, rotate, revolve, turn

swoop *v.* pounce, descend, stoop, plummet, plunge

sword *n.* rapier, blade, foil, épée, cutlass, sabre, steel SOARED

symbol *n.* character, figure, numeral, letter, sign, token, emblem CYMBAL

sympathetic *adj.* thoughtful, understanding, kind, affectionate ★**indifferent**

system [1] *n.* method, plan, order, scheme, arrangement, routine [2] network, organization: a *motorway system*

T t

table 1 *n.* board, stand, slab, tablet, counter, stall 2 list, catalogue, schedule, index, statement

tablet 1 *n.* pill, capsule, lozenge 2 board, table, pad

tack 1 *n.* drawing-pin, nail, pin, brad 2 aim, direction, set 3 *v.* baste, affix, fasten, join, stitch

tackle 1 *n.* outfit, gear, rig, harness 2 *v.* grasp, halt, intercept, seize 3 deal with *I dealt with the problem of the school fund shortage*, undertake, set about

tact *n.* diplomacy, judgment, skill, discretion TACKED

tactful *adj.* diplomatic, wise, subtle, prudent, ▷*discreet* ★**tactless**

tactics *n.* strategy, campaign, method, procedure

tactless *adj.* inconsiderate, gauche, clumsy, boorish, ▷*inept* ★**tactful**

tag *n.* label, ticket, docket, slip, voucher, sticker

taint *v.* sully, tarnish, infect, stain, contaminate, ▷*defile* ★**purify**

take 1 *v.* grasp, grab, seize, procure 2 receive, accept, obtain 3 carry, convey, lead, conduct 4 interpret, understand

take place *v.* occur, happen, befall *Our parents were concerned about what might befall us when we left school*

tale *n.* story, fable, anecdote, yarn, narrative TAIL

talent *n.* knack, genius, gift, ability, aptitude ★**stupidity**

talk 1 *v.* speak, say, utter, gossip 2 describe, comment on, talk about 3 *n.* speech, chatter, conversation 4 lecture, speech, discourse

tall *adj.* lanky, lofty, big, high, towering ★**short**

tally 1 *v.* count, enumerate, compute 2 agree, conform, coincide ★**disagree**

tame 1 *adj.* domesticated, gentle, mild, docile ★**savage** 2 flat, dull, boring, tedious 3 *v.* train, discipline, domesticate *Our tame European cat was first domesticated by the ancient Egyptians*

Tame

Our tame European cat was first domesticated by the ancient Egyptians.

tamper with *v.* meddle, interfere, damage, tinker

tang *n.* smell, scent, aroma, flavour, savour, taste

tangible *adj.* concrete, solid, substantial, real, material ★**spiritual**

tangle *n. & v.* twist, muddle, jumble, knot

tantalize *v.* tease, taunt, thwart, disappoint ▷*frustrate* ★**satisfy**

tantrum *n.* rage, fit, hysterics, storm

tap 1 *v.* pat, hit, knock, rap, strike 2 *n.* spout, cock, nozzle, faucet, bung

tape *n.* ribbon, filament, braid, strip, riband

taper *v.* dwindle, narrow, contract, decline, wane, narrow ★**widen** TAPIR

tardy *adj.* slow, sluggish, reluctant, slack, ▷*late* ★**prompt**

target *n.* goal, aim, ambition, purpose, butt, end

tariff 1 *n.* tax, rate, toll, duty, payment 2 menu, bill of fare

tarnish *v.* stain, sully *Mark's reputation at school was sullied after he was accused of stealing*, spot, darken, blemish, rust ★**brighten**

tarry *v.* delay, stall, wait, loiter, ▷*linger* ★**hurry**

tart [1] *adj.* acid, sour, sharp, pungent [2] *n.* pie, quiche, pastry, flan

task *n.* job, stint, chore, assignment, undertaking

taste [1] *n.* bite, mouthful, flavour, savour, tang [2] *v.* try, sip, sample, relish

tasteful *adj.* artistic, graceful, elegant, smart, ▷*refined* *****tasteless**

tasteless [1] *adj.* flavourless, insipid [2] gaudy, inelegant, ▷*vulgar* *****tasteful**

tasty *adj.* appetizing, piquant, savoury, ▷*delicious* *****disgusting**

tattle *v.* gossip, tittle-tattle, blab, prattle

taunt *v.* jibe, reproach, rebuke, ridicule, scoff at, ▷*sneer* *****compliment**

taut *adj.* tense, tight, stretched, ▷*rigid* *****relaxed** TAUGHT

tawdry *adj.* flashy, loud, gaudy, showy, ▷*vulgar* *****superior**

tax [1] *n.* levy, duty, impost, tithe, toll [2] *v.* load, oppress, overburden TACKS

teach *v.* instruct, educate, tutor, coach, guide, train, drill

teacher *n.* educator, professor, schoolmaster, schoolmistress, coach, tutor

team *n.* party, group, gang, crew, company TEEM

tear (tare) [1] *v.* rip, rend, tatter, shred [2] dash, bolt, rush, sprint TARE

tearful (teerful) *adj.* weepy, moist, wet, sobbing, sad

tease *v.* annoy, harass, vex, irritate, torment, ▷*tantalize* *****soothe** TEAS TEES

tedious *adj.* wearisome, tiresome, irksome, exhausting, ▷*boring* *****fascinating**

teem *v.* abound, swarm, overflow, increase, be full *****lack** TEAM

tell [1] *v.* disclose, speak, state, talk, utter [2] discern, discover, distinguish

temper [1] *n.* temperament, disposition, nature, humour [2] anger, annoyance, passion [3] *v.* moderate, soften, weaken, restrain

temporary *adj.* short, limited, impermanent, brief *****permanent**

tempt *v.* entice, invite, attract, persuade, ▷*lure* *****deter**

tenacious [1] *adj.* stubborn, firm, obstinate, unwavering *****weak** [2] adhesive, glutinous

tenant *n.* occupant, householder, occupier

tend [1] *v.* take care of, manage, serve, guard *****neglect** [2] affect, lean, incline, verge *****diverge**

tendency *n.* disposition, leaning, inclination, bent *****aversion**

tender [1] *adj.* delicate, soft, ▷*fragile* [2] mild, kind, sympathetic, ▷*gentle* [3] raw, painful, sore [4] *v.* proffer *Charlotte proffered her services as a baby-sitter*, present, volunteer, bid

tense *adj.* tight, strained, taut, nervous, edgy *****relaxed** TENTS

tension *n.* strain, stress, rigidity, suspense, worry *****relaxation**

term [1] *n.* expression, denomination, title, phrase [2] time, season, spell *We stayed in Hong Kong for a spell during our trip to the Far East*, duration [3] *v.* entitle, call, dub

terminate *v.* cease, stop, end, conclude, ▷*finish* *****begin**

terrible *adj.* frightful, terrifying, fearful, dreadful, ▷*horrible* *****superb**

terrify *v.* petrify, shock, appal, alarm, ▷*frighten* *****reassure**

territory *n.* region, area, expanse, dominion, land, ▷*country*

terror *n.* alarm, panic, horror, dismay ▷*fright* *****confidence**

terse *adj.* brief, concise, short, pithy, abrupt, ▷*curt* *****long-winded**

test [1] *n.* trial, check, proof, experiment [2] *v.* try out, check, quiz, analyze

testy *adj.* irritable, bad-tempered, touchy, peevish, ▷*cross* *****genial**

tether *n.* rope, cord, lead, leash, chain

text *n.* contents, reading, passage, clause

thanks *n.* gratitude, credit, appreciation

thaw [1] *v.* melt, fuse, liquefy, soften *****freeze** [2] unbend, relax

theft *n.* robbery, fraud, larceny, plundering

theme *n.* subject, text matter, topic

theory *n.* idea, supposition, concept, hypothesis

therefore *adv.* consequently, hence, accordingly, thus

thick [1] *adj.* dense, solid, bulky, compact [2] stiff, set, congealed [3] viscous, gummy, stodgy ★**thin**

thief *n.* crook, robber, burglar, bandit, pirate

thin [1] *adj.* slender, slim, slight, lean, skinny ★**fat** [2] wafer-like, delicate, filmy [3] watery, dilute, unsubstantial ★**thick**

thing *n.* article, object, something, being, substance

think [1] *v.* ponder, consider, ▷*reflect* [2] conceive, imagine, ▷*fancy* [3] surmise, conclude, ▷*reckon*

thirsty *adj.* parched, dry, craving, burning

thorn *n.* barb, prickle, bramble, thistle

thorough *adj.* outright, absolute, complete, utter, absolute ★**haphazard**

though *conj.* although, even though, notwithstanding, however, yet

thought *n.* reflection, consideration, study, concept, deduction

thoughtful [1] *adj.* pensive, studious, contemplative [2] considerate, kind, heedful, careful ★**thoughtless**

thoughtless *adj.* heedless, careless, rash, neglectul, ▷*indiscreet* ★**thoughtful**

thrash [1] *v.* whip, flog, hit [2] stir, pitch, toss *I couldn't sleep last night: I tossed and turned for hours*

Thrash

I couldn't sleep last night: I tossed and turned for hours.

thread *n.* filament, cotton, twist, yarn, fibre

threadbare [1] *adj.* shabby, ragged, worn [2] commonplace, hackneyed, stale ★**fresh**

threaten *v.* intimidate, bully, blackmail, ▷*menace* ★**reassure**

thrifty *adj.* frugal, careful, economical, saving, sparing ★**wasteful**

thrilling *adj.* exciting, gripping, stimulating

thrive *v.* prosper, flourish, succeed, grow, increase ★**decline**

throb *n.* tick, beat, palpitation *v.* beat, palpitate, vibrate

throng *n.* crowd, horde, mob *v.* pack, crowd, swarm, fill

throttle *v.* choke, smother, ▷*strangle*

through *prep.* by way of, by means of, as a result of

throw *v.* fling, cast, hurl, project, propel, thrust ★**keep** THROE

thrust *v. & n.* push, project, drive, force, prod

thug *n.* hoodlum, bandit, assassin, mugger, ruffian

thump *v. & n.* beat, hit, knock, bang, wallop

thunderstruck *adj.* open-mouthed, amazed, astounded, staggered

thus *adv.* accordingly, so, therefore, consequently

thwart *v.* frustrate, balk, baffle, hinder, obstruct ★**assist**

ticket *n.* label, docket, voucher, card, coupon, token

tickle [1] *v.* caress, stroke, pat, brush [2] titillate, convulse, amuse [3] delight, gratify

tide *n.* stream, current, drift, ebb, flow TIED

tidings *n.* information, intelligence, report, advice, ▷*news*

tidy [1] *adj.* neat, well-kept, spruce, orderly [2] ample, large, substantial

tie [1] *v.* fasten, join, attach, secure, unite, ▷*fasten* [2] *n.* cravat *In the old days, it was common to wear a silk cravat instead of a tie*, necktie [3] bond, connection

tight [1] *adj.* fast, close, compact, tense ★**loose** ▷*taut* [2] mean, tight-fisted, ▷*stingy* ★**generous**

tighten *v.* strain, tauten, constrict, cramp, crush, ▷*squeeze* ★**loosen**

till [1] *prep.* until, up to, as far as [2] *v.* plough, cultivate, tend [3] *n.* cash-drawer, cash-register

tilt *v. & n.* slant, slope, incline, lean, list, tip

time [1] *n.* period, duration, season, age, era, term, span [2] metre, measure, tempo, rhythm THYME

timid *adj.* fearful, afraid, timorous, diffident, modest, ▷*shy* ★**bold**

tinge *v. & n.* colour, tincture, tint, stain, shade

tingle *v.* thrill, throb, tickle, vibrate

tinker *v.* meddle, fiddle *Bill fiddled with the old clock for ages, trying to make it work*, patch up, potter, trifle

tinkle *v.* jingle, jangle, ring, clink

tint *n.* dye, hue, tinge, shade, ▷*colour*

tiny *adj.* wee, puny, diminutive, small, ▷*little* ★**huge**

tip [1] *n.* apex, peak, point, extremity, ▷*top* [2] gratuity, gift, donation, reward [3] information, hint, tip-off [4] *v.* list, lean, tilt, ▷*slope*

tipsy *adj.* inebriated, drunk, drunken

tire *v.* exhaust, bore, fatigue, harass, weaken TYRE

tiresome *adj.* wearisome, tedious, boring, ▷*humdrum* ★**interesting**

titbit *n.* delicacy, morsel, dainty, snack, treat

title [1] *n.* name, denomination, term, style, designation [2] claim, interest *When my father died, I was left an interest in his business*, ownership

toady *v.* fawn, crawl, grovel, crouch, cringe

toast [1] *n.* pledge, compliment, salutation [2] *v.* brown, roast, heat

together *adv.* collectively, jointly, simultaneously, at the same time ★**separately**

toil [1] *v. & n.* struggle, labour, travail, ▷*work* ★**relaxation**

token *n.* memento, keepsake, symbol, omen, ▷*souvenir*

tolerable *adj.* endurable, supportable, bearable, passable ★**unbearable**

tolerant *adj.* forbearing, indulgent, liberal, easy-going, ▷*lenient* ★**intolerant**

tolerate *v.* accept, bear with, put up with, endure, suffer, ▷*allow* ★**resist**

toll [1] *v.* ring, strike, chime, clang [2] *n.* charge, duty, tax, levy

tone [1] *n.* pitch, loudness, noise, note [2] emphasis, accent, inflection [3] temper, manner, attitude [4] colour, cast, hue, shade

too [1] *adv.* also, as well, besides [2] extremely, very, unduly

tool [1] *n.* implement, utensil, machine, agent [2] pawn, puppet, catspaw, stooge TULLE

top [1] *n.* summit, pinnacle, peak [2] lid, cover, stopper, cap [3] upper surface ★**bottom** [4] spinning toy [5] *adj.* highest, best, uppermost *After climbing for four days, we reached the uppermost part of the range*

topic *n.* subject, motif, question, ▷*theme*

topical *adj.* contemporary, popular, up-to-date

topple *v.* collapse, founder, overturn, totter, ▷*fall*

topsy-turvy *adj.* upsidedown, overturned, confused, chaotic

torment [1] *v. & n.* pain, distress, ▷*torture* ★**ease**

torrent *n.* flood, stream, cascade, cataract, waterfall ★**trickle**

torture *v.* agonize, rack, anguish, ▷*torment*

toss *v.* fling, hurl, pitch, cast, project, heave, ▷*throw*

total [1] *n.* aggregate, whole, sum, completion [2] *v.* add, tot up, reckon [3] *adj.* complete, entire

totally *adv.* completely, absolutely, entirely, utterly ★**partially**

touch [1] *v.* feel, finger, fondle, handle, stroke [2] move, affect, concern [3] beat, hit, collide with [4] adjoin *Our house is situated at a spot where three counties adjoin*, meet, border [5] *n.* tinge, hint, suspicion

touchy *adj.* peevish, petulant, snappish, ▷*cross* ★**genial**

tough [1] *adj.* hard, strong, vigorous, rugged, sturdy [2] arduous, difficult [3] *n.* hooligan, bruiser, bully

tour *n.* trip, journey, jaunt, excursion, ride, visit

tournament *n.* contest, championship, competition, ▷*match*

Empress

Thane

Professor

Pharaoh

Ayatollah

Titles

admiral ambassador archbishop
baron baroness brigadier
cardinal chancellor colonel
commodore constable count
countess czar
dame deacon dean don doña
duchess duke
earl emir emperor
general governor graf
infanta
kaiser khan king knight
lady laird lama lieutenant lord
madame maharajah maharini
major mandarin marchioness
margrave marshall mayor mikado
miss mogul monsieur monsignor
pasha pope priest prince
princess provost queen
rabbi regent
senator sẽnor señora señorita
sergeant signor signor signorina
shah sheik shogun sheriff sir sultan
sultana
taoiseach
vicar viceroy viscount viscountess

Rajah

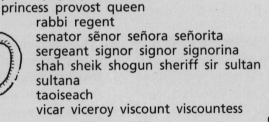

Sheriff

Bishop

Captain

Mister

Samurai

131

Toys

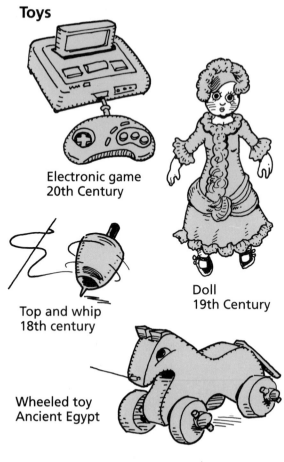

Electronic game
20th Century

Top and whip
18th century

Doll
19th Century

Wheeled toy
Ancient Egypt

tow *v.* haul, drag, tug, haul, heave, ▷*pull* TOE

tower [1] *v.* soar, dominate, surmount [2] *n.* turret, spire, belfry

toy [1] *n.* plaything, doll, game [2] *v.* play, tinker, fiddle, twiddle

trace [1] *v.* trail, track, follow, pursue, discover [2] sketch, draw, copy [3] *n.* trail, track, spoor [4] drop, speck, vestige

track *v.* search out, follow, ▷*trace*

tract [1] *n.* area, space, extent, plot [2] booklet, leaflet, pamphlet TRACKED

trade [1] *v.* barter, exchange, buy, sell, patronize [2] *n.* occupation, work, livelihood, business

tradition *n.* custom, convention, practice

traffic [1] *n.* business, barter, ▷*trade* [2] transportation, vehicles, movement

tragedy *n.* catastrophe, disaster, adversity, ▷*calamity* *comedy

tragic *adj.* disastrous, catastrophic, miserable, wretched, ▷*deplorable* *comic

trail *n.* spoor, track, ▷*trace*

train [1] *v.* teach, educate, instruct, drill, school [2] *n.* chain, procession, series

traitor *n.* rebel, mutineer, renegade, quisling, betrayer

tramp [1] *n.* vagabond, wanderer, vagrant, ▷*beggar* [2] jaunt, stroll, ramble [3] *v.* roam, rove, range, walk, travel

trample *v.* tread, walk on, flatten, ▷*crush*

tranquil *adj.* peaceful, placid, serene, restful, ▷*calm* *restless

transaction *n.* business, performance, dealing, negotiation, proceeding

transfer *v.* move *My sister is being moved to head office after her promotion*, displace, change, ▷*exchange*

transmit *v.* dispatch, forward, relay, ▷*send* *receive

transparent *adj.* clear, lucid, crystal, diaphanous

transport [1] *v.* carry, convey, conduct, transfer, ▷*move* [2] *n.* transportation

trap [1] *v.* ensnare, catch, net [2] *n.* snare, pitfall, noose, decoy, ▷*ambush*

trash *n.* junk, debris, rubble, ▷*rubbish* *treasure

travel [1] *v. & n.* trek, voyage, cruise, ▷*journey*

treacherous *adj.* traitorous, unfaithful, false, deceptive *We mustn't bathe on this beach; the tides and currents are deceptive*, ▷*disloyal* *faithful

tread [1] *v.* step, walk, tramp, march, go [2] stride, gait, walk, step

treason *n.* treachery, betrayal, sedition

treasure [1] *n.* hoard, fortune, riches, wealth [2] *v.* appreciate, esteem, ▷*value*

treat [1] *v.* deal with, handle, manage, serve [2] regale, entertain [3] doctor, attend [4] *n.* banquet, entertainment, fun

treaty *n.* agreement, covenant, alliance

tremble *v.* quake, quaver, shudder, flutter, ▷*shake*

tremendous [1] *adj.* immense, enormous, ▷*huge* [2] terrible, dreadful, awful

tremor *n.* quiver, shake, flutter, ripple, ▷*vibration*

trench *n.* ditch, moat, trough, gully, gutter

trend *n.* tendency, inclination, direction

trendy *adj.* fashionable, stylish, modish

trespass [1] *v.* infringe, overstep, intrude [2] *n.* offence, sin, transgression

trial [1] *n.* endeavour, testing, experiment [2] ordeal, grief, suffering [3] essay, proof [4] hearing, lawsuit

tribe *n.* clan, family, race, group, set

tribute [1] *n.* ovation, compliment, praise [2] dues, toll, tithe, tax

trick [1] *n.* fraud, artifice, wile, cheat, deception [2] jape, prank, frolic [3] juggling, conjuring, stage magic [4] *v.* deceive, defraud

trickle *v.* leak, ooze, seep, drip, drop, dribble

trifle [1] *n.* bauble, plaything, foolishness, nonsense [2] *v.* dabble, idle, play with

trifling *adj.* paltry, petty, worthless, slight, ▷*trivial* ★**important**

trim [1] *v.* prune, clip, shorten, crop [2] ornament, smarten, decorate [3] *adj.* tidy, neat, orderly ★**scruffy**

trinket *n.* bauble, bead, jewel, ornament, toy

trip [1] *n.* journey, excursion, jaunt, ▷*tour* [2] *v.* stumble, fall, slip

tripe *n.* rubbish, trash, nonsense, twaddle *This is a silly story: I never read such twaddle* ★**sense**

trite *adj.* hackneyed, ordinary, corny, ▷*stale* ★**novel**

triumph *n.* victory, success, achievement, ▷*conquest* ★**defeat**

trivial *adj.* trifling, common, unimportant, ordinary, useless, ▷*trite* ★**important**

troop [1] *n.* band, gang, group, pack, team, unit [2] *v.* flock, crowd, swarm TROUPE

trophy *n.* prize, award, cup, souvenir

trot *v.* canter, jog, scamper, scurry

trouble [1] *n.* disturbance, annoyance, calamity, misfortune, ▷*misery* [2] *v.* disturb, annoy, harass, ▷*distress* ★**delight**

true [1] *adj.* accurate, precise, factual, correct ★**inaccurate** [2] faithful, loyal, constant [3] pure, real, ▷*genuine* ★**false**

trunk [1] *n.* body, torso, stem, stalk [2] chest, case, box [3] proboscis *The tapir's proboscis is not as large as the elephant's trunk*, nose, snout

truss *v.* fasten, secure, strap, tie, ▷*bind* ★**untie**

trust [1] *n.* faith, confidence, belief [2] *v.* believe in, credit, depend on ★**doubt** TRUSSED

trustful *adj.* trusting, innocent, naïve, ▷*gullible* ★**cautious**

trustworthy *adj.* dependable, credible, honourable, ▷*reliable* ★**unreliable**

truth [1] *n.* reality, fact, precision, ▷*accuracy* ★**falsehood** [2] integrity, faith, honour, ▷*fidelity* ★**deceit**

truthful *adj.* reliable, frank, open, ▷*honest* ★**false**

try [1] *v.* endeavour, attempt, ▷*strive* [2] examine, try out, ▷*test* ★**abandon** [3] *n.* trial, attempt, effort

trying *adj.* bothersome, annoying, troublesome, ▷*irksome*

tub *n.* basin, bowl, pot, barrel, keg, tun

tube *n.* pipe, spout, duct, hose, shaft

tuck *v.* stow, fold, pack, pleat, hem

tug *v.* drag, tow, haul, heave, ▷*pull* ★**push**

tumble *v.* drop, descend, trip, topple, stumble, ▷*fall*

tumult *n.* noise, rumpus, racket, uproar, disturbance, disorder ★**peace**

tune *n.* melody, harmony, air, strain, ▷*song*

tunnel *n.* subway, shaft, passage, gallery

turn [1] *v.* spin, revolve, whirl, ▷*rotate* [2] bend, curve, ▷*twist* [3] change, alter, ▷*convert* [4] spoil, ▷*sour* [5] *n.* stint, spell, chance [6] rotation, ▷*revolution* TERN

twaddle *n.* balderdash, nonsense, drivel, rigmarole, piffle, ▷*bunkum* ★**sense**

twinge *n.* pain, pang, spasm, gripe, ▷*ache*

twinkle *v.* glitter, gleam, glisten, glimmer, ▷*sparkle*

twist [1] *v.* bend, curve, turn [2] warp, contort, writhe [3] wind, intertwine *The octopus intertwined its legs around the little boat*, encircle

twitch *v.* jerk, jump, jiggle, blink, flutter

type [1] *n.* kind, sort, character, description [2] prototype, model, pattern [3] letter, symbol [4] *v.* typewrite

typical *adj.* characteristic, symbolic, regular, stock, representative ★**abnormal**

tyrant *n.* despot, autocrat, dictator, martinet

U u

ugly *adj.* unsightly, ungainly, frightful, ghastly, hideous, horrid, nasty ★**beautiful**

ultimate *adj.* furthest, most distant, extreme, eventual, ▷*final*

umpire *n.* referee, judge, mediator

unabashed *adj.* brazen, unconcerned, undaunted, ▷*composed* ★**sheepish**

unable *adj.* helpless, incapable, powerless ★**able**

unaccustomed *adj.* inexperienced, unfamiliar, ▷*strange* ★**familiar**

unaffected *adj.* natural, sincere, true, artless, ▷*naïve* ★**impressed**

unafraid *adj.* courageous, dauntless, intrepid, ▷*fearless* ★**afraid**

unanimous *adj.* harmonious, consenting, agreeing, ▷*united*

unassuming *adj.* diffident, reserved, quiet, simple, ▷*modest* ★**forward**

unattached *adj.* single, free, loose, ▷*separate* ★**committed**

unattended *adj.* alone, unwatched, ignored, ▷*abandoned* ★**escorted**

unavoidable *adj.* inevitable, irresistable, certain, ▷*necessary* ★**uncertain**

unaware *adj.* ignorant, unheeding, unknowing, forgetful, ▷*oblivious* ★**aware**

unbalanced 1 *adj.* top-heavy, lop-sided, uneven 2 insane, unhinged *He seems to have become unhinged ever since he lost his job*, crazy, eccentric

unbearable *adj.* unacceptable, intolerable, ▷*outrageous* ★**acceptable**

unbiased *adj.* impartial, fair, just, ▷*neutral* ★**prejudiced**

uncanny *adj.* weird, ghostly, unearthly, creepy, ▷*eerie*

uncertain *adj.* doubtful, vague, chancy, indefinite, ▷*dubious* ★**certain**

uncivilized *adj.* primitive, barbaric, coarse, gross, ▷*vulgar* ★**civilized**

uncomfortable *adj.* awkward, embarrassed, cramped, self-conscious ★**comfortable**

uncommon *adj.* rare, scarce, infrequent, extraordinary, ▷*unusual* ★**common**

unconscious 1 *adj.* ignorant, unheeding, ▷*unaware* 2 insensible, senseless, stunned ★**conscious**

unconventional *adj.* unorthodox, peculiar *I have my own peculiar way of looking at things*, individualistic, ▷*eccentric* ★**conventional**

uncouth *adj.* crude, coarse, clumsy, vulgar, ▷*boorish* ★**polite**

uncover *v.* expose, discover, show, divulge, ▷*reveal* ★**conceal**

under 1 *adv.* underneath, below, beneath 2 *prep.* less than, lower than, subject to

undergo *v.* endure, tolerate, bear, suffer, ▷*sustain*

underground 1 *adj.* secret, concealed, private, concealed 2 *n.* tube, subway, metro

underhand *adj.* stealthy, undercover, deceitful, ▷*sneaky* ★**honest**

underneath *adj.* beneath, under, ▷*below* ★**above**

underrate *v.* undervalue, understate, disparage, belittle ★**exaggerate**

understand *v.* comprehend, appreciate, grasp, sympathize, ▷*realize* ★**misunderstand**

understudy *n.* stand-in, deputy, substitute, reserve

undertake *v.* attempt, commence, contract, embark on *We must choose our equipment carefully before we embark on the expedition*, ▷*tackle*

undesirable *adj.* objectionable, unpleasant, distasteful, ▷*unpleasant* ★**desirable**

undignified *adj.* improper, inelegant, ▷*unseemly* ★**graceful**

undo *v.* unfasten, disentangle, unravel, free, ▷*release* ★**fasten**

undress *v.* disrobe, strip, remove, take off, ▷*divest* ★**dress**

unearthly *adj.* eerie, uncanny, supernatural, ▷*ghostly*

uneasy *adj.* uncomfortable, restive, self-conscious, edgy ★**calm**

unemployed *adj.* unoccupied, redundant, workless

uneven *adj.* irregular, rough, bumpy, lop-sided, unequal *even

unexpected *adj.* abrupt, impulsive, chance, surprising, ▷*sudden* *normal

unfair *adj.* prejudiced, one-sided, partial, unjust *fair

unfaithful *adj.* faithless, untrue, dishonest, ▷*false* *faithful

unfamiliar *adj.* alien, obscure, fantastic, bizarre, ▷*strange* *familiar

unfasten *v.* release, open, unlatch, untie, ▷*undo* *fasten

unfinished *adj.* incomplete, imperfect, lacking, crude *finished

unfit *adj.* unqualified, unsuitable, incapable, unsuited *suitable

unfold *adj.* open, expand, develop, reveal, disclose, unwrap *withhold

unforeseen *adj.* surprising, sudden, accidental, ▷*unexpected* *predictable

unforgettable *adj.* memorable, impressive, noteworthy, exceptional

unfortunate *adj.* deplorable, lamentable, adverse, hapless, ▷*unlucky* *fortunate

unfriendly *adj.* antagonistic, surly, cold, ▷*hostile* *friendly

ungainly *adj.* gawky, awkward, graceless, unwieldly, ▷*clumsy* *graceful

ungrateful *adj.* thankless, selfish, ungracious, ill-mannered *grateful

unhappiness *n.* depression, misery, sadness

unhappy *adj.* miserable, dismal, luckless *Try as he might, the luckless Tom was almost last in the race*, melancholy, ▷*sad* *happy

unhealthy [1] *adj.* unwholesome, harmful [2] sick, ill, diseased *healthy

uniform [1] *n.* regalia, livery *It was a very grand affair, with the footmen in full livery*, costume, dress [2] *adj.* stable, steady, unchanging, level *varied

unimportant *adj.* puny, trivial, insignificant, ▷*petty* *important

unintentional *adj.* inadvertent, involuntary, unwitting, ▷*accidental* *deliberate

union [1] *n.* alliance, association, league [2] agreement, accord, harmony [3] fusion, blend, compound

unique *adj.* original, exceptional, exclusive, single, sole *commonplace

unit *n.* entity, single, one, individual

unite *v.* join, combine, connect, merge, blend, fuse *separate

united *adj.* joined, combined, undivided, ▷*unanimous* *separated

unity *n.* union, harmony, uniformity, agreement *disagreement

universal *adj.* general, all-embracing, entire, worldwide *Our company has been very successful, with its products being sold worldwide*

unjust *adj.* partial, prejudiced, unfair, wrong, ▷*biased* *just

unkempt *adj.* dishevelled, shabby, sloppy, slovenly, ungroomed, ▷*scruffy* *neat

unkind *adj.* inhuman, heartless, brutal, callous, ▷*cruel* *kind

unknown *adj.* hidden, mysterious, undiscovered, dark *familiar

unless *conj.* if not, except when

unlike *adj.* unrelated, dissimilar, distinct, ▷*different* *similar

unlikely *adj.* rare, improbable, doubtful, incredible, unheard of, ▷*dubious* *likely

unlucky *adj.* unfortunate, luckless, ill-fated, unhappy *lucky

Uniform

It was a very grand affair with the footmen in full livery.

unnatural [1] *adj.* artificial, stilted, strained [2] inhuman, cruel, ▷*heartless* ★**natural**

unnecessary *adj.* inessential, excess, superfluous, ▷*needless* ★**necessary**

unoccupied [1] *adj.* uninhabited, empty, deserted, ▷*vacant* [2] idle, spare, ▷*unemployed* ★**occupied**

unpleasant *adj.* disagreeable, displeasing, objectionable, ▷*offensive* ★**pleasant**

unpopular *adj.* obnoxious *I was glad to leave the party, for I had been forced to talk to the most obnoxious people ever*, detested, shunned, rejected, ▷*disliked* ★**popular**

unqualified [1] *adj.* unable, incompetent, inadequate, ▷*unfit* [2] complete, thorough, absolute

unreal *adj.* imaginary, fictional, artificial, false, fanciful ★**real** UNREEL

unreasonable [1] *adj.* extravagant, excessive, extreme ★**moderate** [2] far-fetched, absurd, foolish ★**rational**

unreliable *adj.* untrustworthy, undependable, irresponsible, ▷*fickle* ★**reliable**

unrest [1] *n.* defiance, disquiet, protest, rebellion [2] anxiety, distress, worry ★**calm**

unrestricted *adj.* unrestrained, unlimited, open, free, unhindered ★**limited**

unripe *adj.* green, immature, callow *I was but a callow youth in those days, but I hope I have learned since then!*, unseasoned, unready ★**ripe**

unrivalled *adj.* inimitable, unequalled, matchless, peerless ★**inferior**

unruly *adj.* disorderly, troublesome, restive, ▷*rowdy* ★**orderly**

unseemly *adj.* incorrect, indecent, improper, unbecoming, shocking ★**seemly**

unselfish *adj.* generous, liberal, charitable, hospitable, ▷*kind* ★**selfish**

unstable *adj.* unsteady, shaky, inconstant, fickle, volatile ★**stable**

unsuitable *adj.* improper, unacceptable, unfitting, inconsistent ★**suitable**

untidy *adj.* bedraggled, disorderly, muddled, messy, ▷*slovenly* ★**tidy**

untie *v.* unfasten, unravel, free, release, ▷*undo* ★**tie**

until *prep.* till, as far as, up to

untimely *adj.* inopportune, ill-timed, premature, previous ★**opportune**

unusual *adj.* curious, strange, queer, exceptional, quaint, ▷*odd* ★**normal**

unwilling *adj.* averse, disinclined, grudging, opposed, ▷*reluctant* ★**willing**

upheaval *n.* disturbance, disruption, overthrow, ▷**turmoil**

uphold *v.* sustain, keep up, endorse, ▷*support*

upkeep *n.* maintenance, care, conservation, support, expenses ★**neglect**

upper *adj.* higher, superior, elevated, uppermost ★**lower**

upright [1] *adj.* sheer, steep, perpendicular ★**horizontal** [2] honourable *Sister Mary Josephine was one of the most honourable people I ever met*, ethical, virtuous ★**dishonest**

uproar *n.* hubbub, noise, disorder, tumult, turmoil, ▷*clamour*

upset [1] *v.* bother, perturb, unsettle, annoy [2] overthrow, overturn, topple [3] *adj.* disturbed, confused, worried

upside down [1] *adj.* overturned, upturned [2] chaotic, muddled, jumbled

urge [1] *v.* goad, plead, spur, beseech ★**deter** [2] *n.* encouragement, compulsion, ▷*impulse*

urgent *adj.* important, earnest, intense, vital ★**trivial**

use [1] *v.* employ, practise, apply [2] consume, exhaust, deplete, expend [3] *n.* usage, wear

useful *adj.* valuable, favourable, practical, beneficial ★**useless**

useless *adj.* trashy, paltry, futile *Trying to learn Latin was for me a futile waste of time!*, inefficient, ▷*worthless* ★**useful**

usual *adj.* common, general, habitual, familiar, ▷*normal* ★**exceptional**

utensil *n.* tool, implement, instrument, apparatus, device

utilize *v.* employ, apply, exploit, ▷*use*

utmost *adj.* extreme, supreme, greatest, ultimate, last, distant

utter [1] *adj.* thorough, absolute, complete [2] *v.* declare, pronounce, speak, ▷*say*

utterly *adj.* extremely, completely, entirely, fully, wholly

V v

vacant [1] *adj.* empty, unoccupied, exhausted *occupied* [2] stupid, blank, expressionless, mindless

vacation *n.* holiday, rest, recess, intermission

vagabond *n.* vagrant, tramp, loafer, beggar, rover

vague *adj.* indefinite, imprecise, inexact, uncertain, ▷*obscure* *certain*

vain [1] *adj.* conceited, arrogant, ▷*proud* *modest* [2] fruitless, useless, worthless, ▷*futile* VANE VEIN

valiant *adj.* stout, valorous, worthy, gallant, ▷*brave* *cowardly*

valid *adj.* genuine, authentic, official *No one is allowed into the meeting without an official pass*, proper

valley *n.* gorge, dale, coomb, dell, glen, vale

valour *n.* courage, fortitude, heroism, gallantry, ▷*bravery* *cowardice*

valuable [1] *adj.* costly, precious, priceless, expensive *worthless* [2] meritorious *She was awarded the medal for meritorious service during the war*, righteous, worthy

value [1] *n.* worth, benefit, merit, price [2] *v.* appreciate, esteem, prize, treasure [3] appraise, assess, rate, estimate

van *n.* cart, truck, vehicle, wagon, lorry

vandalize *v.* damage, sabotage, harm, ruin

vanish [1] *v.* disappear, fade, dissolve [2] exit, depart, go *appear*

vanity *n.* pride, conceit, pretension *modesty*

vanquish *v.* conquer, defeat, overpower, subdue, ▷*beat*

vapour *n.* steam, fog, mist, moisture, smoke

variable *adj.* changeable, fickle, unsteady, fitful, wavering *invariable*

varied *adj.* various, diverse *She was a woman of diverse interests*, miscellaneous, mixed, assorted *uniform*

variety [1] *n.* assortment, array, mixture, medley *The singers entertained us with a medley of popular songs* [2] sort, type, kind, class

Vehicles

Ambulance, Automobile, Bicycle, Bulldozer, Bus, Cab, Car, Cart, Charabanc, Chariot, Coach, Fire engine, Gig, Go-cart, Hansom cab, Hearse, Jeep, Limousine, Lorry, Motorbike, Motorcar, Rickshaw, Saloon, Scooter, Stagecoach, Surrey, Tank, Taxicab, Tractor, Tram, Trap, Trishaw, Trolleybus, Truck, Street car, Van, Victoria, Wagon, Wheelchair

various *adj.* mixed, different, many, ▷*varied*

vary *v.* differ, alter, change, diversify, diverge

vase *n.* jug, jar, beaker, ▷*pitcher*

vast *adj.* great, enormous, extensive, huge, wide, ▷*immense* *narrow*

vault [1] *n.* grave, mausoleum, cellar, crypt, dungeon [2] *v.* jump, clear, bound, leap, hurdle

veer *v.* swerve, skid, turn, tack, deviate, change

vehement *adj.* impassioned, fiery, passionate, ardent, eager, zealous, ▷*strong* *indifferent*

vehicle [1] *n.* car, conveyance, carriage, cart [2] agency, means, expedient

veil [1] *n.* cloak, cover, wimple, curtain [2] *v.* hide, conceal, shade, screen *expose* VALE

vein [1] *n.* seam, strain, streak, stripe, thread, course [2] disposition, mood, style, phrasing VAIN VEIN

velocity *n.* rate, pace, tempo, rapidity, impetus *After I won the school prize, I had greater impetus to follow my studies,* ▷*speed*

venerable *adj.* respectable, revered, august, dignified, honoured, ▷*sage*

vengeance *n.* reprisal, retaliation, ▷*revenge* ★**pardon**

venomous ☐1 *adj.* poisonous, toxic, vitriolic ☐2 spiteful, malicious, hostile, ▷*vindictive*

vent ☐1 *v.* discharge, emit, express, let fly, release ☐2 *n.* aperture, duct, opening, outlet

ventilate ☐1 *v.* aerate, cool, fan, blow ☐2 express, debate, discuss, examine

venture ☐1 *n.* enterprise, undertaking, endeavour ☐2 *v.* risk, bet, hazard, ▷*chance*

verbal *adj.* stated, said, expressed, spoken, unwritten ★**written**

verdict *n.* decision, judgment, finding, conclusion, opinion

verge ☐1 *n.* border, brink, edge, boundary ☐2 *v.* incline, tend, border, come close to

verify *v.* confirm, declare, authenticate, corroborate *The witness corroborated the story told by the defendant* ★**discredit**

versatile *adj.* adaptable, variable, adjustable, handy ★**inflexible**

verse *n.* poem, rhyme, stave, canto, jingle, doggerel *Call this stuff poetry? It's just doggerel!*

version *n.* account, form, interpretation, adaptation, type

vertical *adj.* upright, erect, sheer, perpendicular, steep ★**horizontal**

very ☐1 *adv.* extremely, exceedingly, greatly, intensely, absolutely ☐2 *adj.* exact, real, true, actual, genuine

vessel ☐1 *n.* bowl, pot, canister, container, basin, jar ☐2 craft, ship, boat

vestige *n.* remains, remnant, hint, glimmer, residue, trace

veteran ☐1 *n.* old timer, master, old hand, expert ★**novice** ☐2 *adj.* experienced, practised, adept ★**inexperienced**

veto ☐1 *v.* ban, reject, prohibit, stop, forbid ★**approve** ☐2 *n.* embargo *The United Nations placed an embargo on the selling of arms to the two countries,* prohibition, disapproval ★**assent**

vex *v.* annoy, provoke, trouble, irritate, harass, ▷*displease* ★**soothe**

vibrate *v.* shake, quiver, oscillate, fluctuate, ▷*tremble*

vice *n.* evil, failing, fault, *sin* ★**virtue**

vicinity *n.* area, environs, neighbourhood, ▷*surroundings*

vicious *adj.* evil, sinful, malignant, immoral, vile, ▷*wicked* ★**virtuous**

victim *n.* sufferer, scapegoat, martyr, prey, pawn, dupe

victor *n.* winner, conqueror, champion, prize-winner ★**loser**

victory *n.* success, triumph, achievement, ▷*conquest* ★**defeat**

view ☐1 *n.* landscape, sight, panorama, spectacle ☐2 estimation, belief, theory, opinion ☐3 *v.* watch, see, behold, witness

vigilant *adj.* attentive, wary, alert, guarded, ▷*watchful* ★**lax**

vigorous *adj.* forceful, energetic, powerful, dynamic, ▷*active* ★**weak**

vigour *n.* energy, vim, stamina, might, power, ▷*strength* ★**weakness**

vile *adj.* low, wretched, contemptible, miserable, nasty, evil, ▷*despicable* ★**noble**

villain *n.* blackguard, knave *You are but a knave who is out to steal my money!,* sinner, rascal, ▷*rogue* ★**hero**

vim *n.* stamina, zip, strength, ▷*vigour*

vindicate *v.* warrant, sustain, support, defend, establish, ▷*justify* ★**accuse**

vindictive *adj.* vengeful, unforgiving, grudging, spiteful, ▷*malicious* ★**merciful**

violate ☐1 *v.* disobey, oppose, defy, resist, infringe ★**obey** ☐2 abuse, defile, outrage, desecrate

violent *adj.* furious, rabid, rampant, forcible, tempestuous ★**calm**

virile *adj.* manly, masculine, vigorous, vibrant, ▷*strong* ★**weak**

virtually *adj.* almost, as good as, nearly, practically, substantially

virtue *n.* goodness, honesty, chastity, purity, ▷*quality* ★**vice**

virtuous *adj.* chaste, innocent, honourable, moral, ▷*righteous* ★**wicked**

W w

visible *adj.* perceptible, discernible, apparent, exposed, obvious *★invisible*

vision [1] *n.* apparition, spectre, ghost, mirage [2] concept, revelation, foresight

visit [1] *n.* call, sojourn, stay, excursion [2] *v.* call on, drop in, tarry, stay

visitor *n.* caller, guest, tourist

visual *adj.* seeable, observable, visible

vital [1] *adj.* essential, indispensible, ▷*necessary* [2] alive, vibrant, virile, dynamic *Our team won a number of matches after we had been trained by the new dynamic coach*

vitality *n.* stamina, virility, vigour, ▷*strength*

vivacious *adj.* lively, spirited, vital, animated, merry, ▷*sprightly* *★languid*

vivid [1] *adj.* clear, bright, ▷*brilliant* [2] vigorous, strong, lucid *★dull*

vocal *adj.* articulate, eloquent, spoken, strident, vociferous *★quiet*

vocation *n.* occupation, calling, job, mission, career, pursuit

vogue *n.* style, fashion, mode, popularity

voice [1] *n.* speech, articulation, utterance [2] choice, preference, opinion [3] *v.* utter, express, proclaim, pronounce

void [1] *adj.* bare, barren, empty [2] invalid, cancelled, useless [3] *n.* cavity, chasm, space, opening, nothingness

volatile [1] *adj.* lively, changeable, fickle, giddy [2] elusive, fleeting, evaporable

volley *n.* discharge, fusillade, barrage, shower

volume [1] *n.* bulk, capacity, mass, quantity, ▷*amount* [2] book, edition, tome

voluntary *adj.* free-willed, optional, intended, gratuitous *★compulsory*

vomit *v.* spew, disgorge, belch, bring up, be sick, emit

vote *n.* ballot, election, poll, referendum *v.* ballot, poll, choose, elect

vow *v.* promise, swear, assure, vouch, testify *n.* oath, pledge, promise

voyage *n.* journey, cruise, passage, trip

vulgar [1] *adj.* common, coarse, crude, indelicate, rude *★elegant* [2] native, ordinary, common

vulnerable *adj.* unprotected, unguarded, exposed, defenceless, tender *★strong*

wad *n.* bundle, chunk, block, plug

waddle *v.* wobble, totter, shuffle, toddle

wag [1] *v.* waggle, shake, ▷*vibrate* [2] *n.* wit, humorist, joker

wage [1] *n.* fee, pay, salary, remuneration [2] *v.* carry out, fulfil, undertake

wager *v.* gamble, bet, speculate, chance, hazard *n.* pledge, stake, bet

wagon *n.* cart, truck, van, ▷*vehicle*

waif *n.* orphan, stray, foundling *In the old days, children were abandoned in the streets, but some people set up homes for such foundlings*

wail [1] *v.* deplore, weep, grieve, lament, ▷*cry* *★rejoice* [2] *n.* lamentation, weeping, grief

wait [1] *v.* expect, await, bide, stay, stop, ▷*linger* [2] attend, serve WEIGHT

waive *v.* relinquish, disclaim, disown, forego, defer, ▷*renounce* WAVE

wake *v.* awaken, stimulate, excite, ▷*arouse*

wakeful [1] *adj.* restless, awake [2] alert, wary, watchful

walk [1] *v.* advance, march, step, progress, move [2] *n.* stroll, hike, ▷*ramble* *★run* [3] lane, alley, way [4] sphere, field *I started my career in the field of journalism, but my later walk of life was in politics*, career, interest

wallow [1] *v.* flounder, stagger, tumble [2] delight, enjoy, revel

wan *adj.* pale, ashen, feeble, sickly, pallid, ▷*weak* *★robust*

wand *n.* mace, baton, stick, sceptre, rod

wander *v.* stray, meander, roam, stroll, deviate

wane *v.* droop, decline, decrease, lessen, ebb *As the little boat neared the rocks, Fred's courage ebbed away*, sink *★wax* WAIN

wangle *v.* fiddle, contrive, fix, arrange

want [1] *v.* desire, covet, crave, need, require [2] *n.* need, necessity, demand [3] dearth, deficiency, ▷*scarcity* *★plenty*

wanton [1] *adj.* unscrupulous, irresponsible [2] playful, frolicsome, wild [3] dissolute, immoral

war *n.* hostilities, fighting, bloodshed, enmity, strife ★**peace** WORE

ward [1] *n.* pupil, minor, charge [2] apartment, district, quarter WARRED

ward off *v.* prevent, forestall, avoid, stop, ▷*avert*

wardrobe [1] *n.* locker, cupboard, closet [2] outfit, clothes, apparel

warm [1] *adj.* tepid, hot, lukewarm [2] sympathetic, ▷*warmhearted* [3] eager, hot, zealous [4] *v.* heat, bake, cook, prepare

warn *v.* caution, admonish, advise, alert, apprise WORN

warning *n.* caution, admonition, forewarning, alarm, tip

warp *v.* contort, bend, twist, kink, deform ★**straighten**

warrant *v.* guarantee, certify, justify, permit, allow *n.* assurance, permit, licence, authority *She produced documents which showed her authority on the council*

wary *adj.* cautious, alert, careful, heedful, ▷*prudent* ★**rash**

wash *v.* bathe, scrub, rinse, cleanse, wet *n.* washing, cleaning

waste [1] *n.* rubbish, garbage, debris, trash [2] *v.* squander, spend, lavish, fritter [3] wither, decay, shrivel, perish WAIST

wasteful *adj.* lavish, prodigal, spendthrift, ▷*extravagant* ★**economical**

watch [1] *v.* note, observe, guard ★**ignore** [2] inspect, look at, oversee [3] *n.* timepiece [4] guard, sentry, watchman

watchful *adj.* attentive, observant, vigilant, ▷*wary* ★**inattentive**

water *v.* wet, bathe, wash, douse, drench, sprinkle, spray

wave [1] *v.* brandish, flourish, waft, swing [2] *n.* breaker, billow, undulation WAIVE

waver *v.* falter, hesitate, haver, vacillate ★**decide**

wax *v.* increase, rise, grow, expand, enlarge ★**wane**

way [1] *n.* route, road, path, passage, track [2] technique *The company introduced a new technique for making glass*, procedure, method, style WEIGH

wayward *adj.* contrary, perverse, obstinate, ▷*stubborn* ★**docile**

weak [1] *adj.* feeble, frail, puny, helpless, delicate [2] foolish, soft, senseless, stupid [3] thin, watery, insipid [4] fragile, flimsy, tumbledown ★**strong** WEEK

weaken *v.* enfeeble, relax, sag, flag, ▷*languish* ★**strengthen**

weakness *n.* defect, fault, frailty, flaw ★**strength**

wealth *n.* riches, luxury, prosperity, money, opulence ★**poverty**

wealthy *adj.* rich, affluent, prosperous, opulent ★**poor**

wear [1] *v.* dress in, don [2] rub, scrape, waste, consume [3] last, endure, remain WARE

weary [1] *adj.* exhausted, tired, fatigued ★**fresh** [2] *v.* exhaust, tire, bore ★**refresh**

weather *n.* climate, clime, conditions

weave *v.* braid, plait, unite, blend

web *n.* net, tissue, webbing, textile, netting

wed *v.* marry, join, link, splice, tie the knot

wedge [1] *n.* block, chock, lump, chunk [2] *v.* crowd, force, jam, push, thrust, squeeze

wee *adj.* little, small, minute, ▷*tiny* ★**large**

weep *v.* blubber, snivel, sob, whimper *The lost puppy was found at last, whimpering in a corner*, ▷*cry* ★**rejoice**

weigh *v.* balance, estimate, ponder, examine, consider WAY

weight [1] *n.* load, pressure, burden, heaviness [2] importance, onus, significance, gravity WAIT

weighty *adj.* heavy, hefty, ponderous, onerous ★**trivial**

weird *adj.* eerie, supernatural, unearthly, mysterious, ▷*uncanny*

welcome [1] *adj.* pleasing, desirable, ▷*agreeable* [2] *v.* greet, accost, hail, salute [3] *n.* greeting, salutation, acceptance

welfare *n.* well-being, comfort, happiness, benefit, advantage ★**harm**

well [1] *adj.* robust, healthy, hearty, sound ★**ill** [2] *adv.* properly, suitable, adequately, accurately ★**badly** [3] *n.* fountain, spring

well-off *adj.* comfortable, prosperous, ▷*wealthy* ★**poor**

Weather Conditions

Clear weather
blue skies
clear
cloudless
fair
sunny
sunshine

Cold weather
arctic bitter brisk
chilly cold cold snap cool
freezing frost glacial hail
icy nippy sub-zero
hoar frost
freeze ice over

Hot weather
close hot
humid muggy
sultry sweltering
torrid tropical
heat wave
drought

Overcast weather
cloudy
dark
foggy
foul
hazy
misty
murky
overcast
smoggy

Mild weather
balmy calm dry fair mild
temperate warm
thaw

Recurring events
autumn equinox fall solstice
spring summer sundown sunrise
sunset winter winter solstice

Windy weather
blowy blustery breeze draft
flurry gale gusty
swirling turbulent windy

Wet weather
deluge downpour drizzle
rainy inclement
showers sleet slush snowing
soaking mizzle precipitation

---

wet 1 *adj.* moist, damp, watery, drenched 2 drizzling, showery, raining 3 *v.* soak, moisten, dampen

wheedle *v.* coax, cajole, inveigle *We were inveigled into buying some of the local lace,* persuade ★**coerce**

whet 1 *v.* sharpen, hone, strop ★**blunt** 2 excite, stimulate, rouse ★**dampen**

whim *n.* fancy, humour, desire, urge, notion, impulse

whine 1 *v.* howl, wail, whimper, moan 2 complain, grouse, grumble, whinge

whip 1 *v.* flog, lash, thrash, chastise, spank 2 whisk, mix, blend

whirl *v.* twirl, spin, rotate, revolve, whir, ▷*twist*

whisk *v.* beat, brush, hasten, hurry, sweep, ▷*whip*

whisper 1 *n.* murmur, hint, suggestion, breath 2 *v.* breathe, murmur, divulge, buzz, intimate ★**shout**

whistle *n. & v.* cheep, chirp, warble, call

whole 1 *adj.* all, entire, total, intact 2 sound, complete, unbroken ★**part** HOLE

wholesome *adj.* healthful, nutritious, beneficial, sound, good ★**noxious**

wicked *adj.* infamous, corrupt, depraved, unrighteous, sinister, sinful, ▷*evil* ★**virtuous**

wickedness *n.* corruption, depravity, iniquity, sinfulness, villainy, ▷*evil*

wide *adj.* broad, ample, extended, spacious, roomy, extensive, vast ★**narrow**

widespread *adj.* prevalent, far-flung, extensive, sweeping, universal *The use of a universal language would be of great help in the United Nations* ★**limited**

wield 1 *v.* brandish, flourish, manipulate 2 control, command, exert, maintain

wild 1 *adj.* savage, ferocious, fierce, untamed ★**tame** 2 violent, unrestrained, boisterous ★**civilized** 3 careless, mad, reckless ★**sane**

wilderness *n.* desert, jungle, wasteland, wilds, outback

wilful *adj.* temperamental, headstrong, deliberate, ▷*obstinate* ★**docile**

will 1 *n.* resolution, decision, zeal, accord 2 order, wish, command, request, demand 3 legacy, testament 4 *v.* choose, desire, elect

willing *adj.* disposed, zealous, ready, earnest, ▷*agreeable* ★**unwilling**

wilt *v.* wither, waste, sag, dwindle, ▷*ebb*

wily *adj.* cunning, sly, tricky, deceitful, ▷*crafty* ★**sincere**

win *v.* succeed, gain, get, acquire, procure, ▷*triumph* ★**lose**

wince *v.* shrink, quail, flinch *My little sister didn't flinch once when she had her vaccination*, start, ▷*cringe*

wind (as in tinned) *n.* breeze, blast, gust, gale

wind (as in mind) *v.* coil, turn, twist, bend WINED

wink *n. & v.* blink, flutter, flicker, glint

winner *n.* champion, master, ▷*victor*

wipe *v.* clean, brush, mop, remove, swab

wire 1 *n.* cable, telegraph, telegram 2 cable, flex

wisdom *n.* judgment, discretion, tact, thought, reason ★**folly**

wise *adj.* sensible, profound, astute, subtle, discreet, ▷*sage* ★**foolish**

wish 1 *v.* desire, crave, want, hanker for, long for 2 *n.* command, will, desire, liking

wistful 1 *adj.* pensive, musing, wishful 2 forlorn, melancholy, soulful

wit 1 *n.* fun, humour, levity, pleasantry 2 brains, sense, judgment, intelligence ★**stupidity**

witch *n.* enchantress, sorceress, crone, hag

withdraw 1 *v.* retire, retreat, depart, leave, ▷*flee* 2 extract, take out

withdrawn *adj.* unsociable, retiring, reclusive, aloof, solitary ★**sociable**

wither *v.* waste, fade, pine, languish, ▷*shrivel*

withhold *v.* retain, reserve, restrain, hold back, ▷*keep* ★**grant**

within *adj.* inside, interior, inner

withstand *v.* resist, oppose, confront, ▷*defy* ★**support**

witness 1 *n.* spectator, onlooker, bystander *One of the bystanders at the accident came forward to give evidence*, signatory 2 *v.* behold, observe, see, attest

witty *adj.* funny, jocular, waggish, amusing, ▷*comical* ★**dull**

wizard *n.* sorcerer, magician, conjurer

woe *n.* sorrow, sadness, grief, misery, trouble ★**joy**

woman *n.* lady, girl, female, she, wife

wonder 1 *n.* marvel, miracle, rarity, curiosity 2 bewilderment, surprise, amazement, ▷*awe* 3 *v.* speculate, question, marvel, muse

wonderful *adj.* marvellous, fabulous, spectacular, superb, ▷*splendid* ★**commonplace**

woo *v.* make love, court, pursue

wood 1 *n.* timber, planks 2 forest, copse, woodland, grove, thicket WOULD

word 1 *n.* expression, term, utterance 2 pledge, promise 3 tidings, news, information

work 1 *n.* toil, drudgery, labour, grind 2 task, job, stint, chore 3 *v.* operate, function, manipulate, run, drive

world *n.* globe, earth, sphere, planet

Borrowed Words

Modern French
police
rendezvous
liaison
menu

Dutch
boss
brandy
decoy
landscape

Scandinavia
fjord
geyser
lemming
ombudsman
ski

Italian
balcony
cameo
fiasco
influenza

German
blitz
delicatessen
dollar
kindergarten

Chinese
kowtow
sampan
typhoon
wok

Japanese
bonsai

futon

judo
karate
origami

Turkish
coffee
kiosk

Spanish
armada
fiesta
macho
patio
siesta
sombrero

Afrikaans
aardvark

apartheid
boer
trek
veldt

Inuit
anorak
igloo
kayak
parka

Gaelic
blarney
bog
brat
brogue
smithereens

Aztec
avocado
cocoa

tomato

Arabic
admiral
alcohol
algebra
alkali
sherbet
sofa
zero

Aboriginal languages
boomerang
dingo
budgerigar
kangaroo

Persian
bazaar

caravan
divan
paradise
tulip
turban

Hindi
bungalow
chintz
cot
pyjamas
thug
veranda

Native American
chipmunk
moccasin
moose
papoose
wigwam

---

worry [1] *v.* bother, annoy, disturb, ▷*trouble* ★**soothe** [2] vexation, anxiety, concern, fear ★**delight**

worsen *v.* aggravate, decline, deteriorate, degenerate ★**improve**

worship [1] *v.* revere, adore, esteem, honour, praise ★**despise** [2] *n.* adoration, devotion, reverence

worth *n.* value, benefit, merit, calibre *The year's students were of a high calibre* dignity

worthless *adj.* valueless, paltry, trifling, useless, ▷*cheap* ★**valuable**

worthwhile *adj.* valuable, helpful, useful, beneficial ★**useless**

worthy *adj.* upright, admirable, excellent, honest, fine ★**vile**

wound [1] *v.* hurt, injure, gash, pain, distress, ▷*harm* ★**heal** [2] *n.* injury, bruise, harm

wrangle *v. & n.* squabble, fight, row, scrap, ▷*quarrel* ★**accord**

wrap *v.* fold, envelop, enclose, cover, clothe, conceal ★**unfold** RAP

wrath *n.* fury, ire, rage, passion, ▷*anger* ★**pleasure**

wreck [1] *v.* demolish, smash, ruin, destroy, spoil, ravage ★**repair** [2] *n.* derelict, hulk, shipwreck, ruin

wrench *v.* twist, wring, strain, sprain, pull

wrestle *v.* struggle, battle, combat, grapple, tussle, ▷*fight*

wretch *n.* vagabond, blackguard, villain, rogue, ▷*scoundrel*

wretched [1] *adj.* dejected, abject, miserable, ▷*despicable* [2] saddening, pathetic, ▷*pitiful* ★**joyful**

wriggle *v.* twist, writhe, squirm, worm, dodge

wring *v.* choke, squeeze, throttle, strangle, twist RING

wrinkle *n. & v.* crease, pucker, ruffle, rumple, crinkle, furrow

write *v.* inscribe, pen, sign, scrawl, scribble RIGHT RITE WRIGHT

writer [1] *n.* scribe, penman, clerk [2] author, essayist, narrator, playwright, poet, dramatist

writhe *v.* wind, twine, weave, twist, ▷*wriggle*

written *adj.* recorded, set down, documentary, transcribed

wrong [1] *adj.* unjust, unfair, immoral, wicked [2] false, mistaken, erroneous [3] *v.* injure, hurt, abuse [4] *n.* offence, atrocity, iniquity, sin, injustice ★**right**

wry *adj.* crooked, askew, awry, aslant, twisted, distorted ★**straight** RYE

Y y

yank *v.* draw, pull, snatch, ▷*jerk*

yap 1 *v.* bark, yelp 2 prattle, jaw, blather, gossip

yard 1 *n.* courtyard, court, garden, quadrangle 2 three feet

yarn 1 *n.* story, account, tale, narrative 2 thread, wool, linen, twist

yawn *v.* gape, open

yearly 1 *adj.* annual, perennial, per annum *We shall pay a salary of £10,000 per annum* 2 *adv.* every year, annually

yearn *v.* ache, crave, desire, pine, hunger for ★**dislike**

yell *v.* shriek, squawk, whoop, screech, shout, ▷*bellow* ★**whisper**

yield 1 *v.* produce, provide, furnish, supply 2 surrender, give in, submit ★**withstand** 3 abdicate, resign, renounce 4 *n.* crop, harvest, product, output

yielding 1 *adj.* obedient, submissive, unresisting ★**stubborn** 2 plastic, malleable, flexible ★**solid**

yoke 1 *v.* join, couple, link, harness 2 *n.*chain, bondage *The children of Israel moved out of bondage in the land of Egypt*, enslavement YOLK

yokel *n.* bumpkin, rustic, boor, peasant

young *adj.* youthful, tender, juvenile, junior, little ★**old**

youngster *n.* child, youth, boy, lad, adolescent

youth 1 *n.* adolescence, prime, salad days ★**age** 2 lad, boy, ▷*youngster*

youthful *adj.* boyish, girlish, young, spry, juvenile, lively ★**aged**

yule *n.* Christmas

Z z

zany *adj.* crazy, daft, droll, goofy, eccentric, ▷*funny* ★**serious**

zeal *n.* devotion, eagerness, enthusiasm, keenness, ardour ★**apathy**

zealous *adj.* devoted, fervent *Dave was a fervent supporter of the local football team*, fanatical, earnest, ▷*eager* ★**apathetic**

zenith *n.* climax, height, apex, peak

zero *n.* nothing, nought, nil, nullity, aught

zest 1 *n.* relish, gusto, appetite, keenness 2 flavour, piquancy, taste 3 rind, peel

zone *n.* area, district, region, tract, sector

zoom *v.* flash, fly, shoot, streak, hurtle, whizz